GORILLA

TANGO

From Businessman to Convicted Felon and Surviving the US Prison System

Warren Stelman

FOURTH QUARTER PRESS
Montreal, Quebec, Canada

Gorilla Tango
From Businessman to Convicted Felon
and Surviving the US Prison System
by Warren Stelman

Copyright © Warren Stelman 2018

ISBN 978-1-9994504-2-7

Published by Fourth Quarter Press

Fourth Quarter Press
Montreal, Quebec, Canada

Contents

Chapter 1

Federal Correctional Institution
Allenwood, 2017

I'M A CANADIAN IN A US prison. I robbed old people and got caught.

Now I live with murderers, drug lords, bank robbers, mobsters, gang members, arsonists, pimps, pedophiles and a sprinkling of white collar criminals like myself. The white-collar guys received too much time to be in one of the Federal prison camps because they need less than ten years remaining on their sentence to qualify. Once they're under ten and as long as they've stayed out of trouble, they'll get transferred to a camp and a better life with more freedom. As for me, I'm a security risk because I'm a foreigner. I'll never see a camp. I'm also a criminal mastermind if you believe the newspapers.

It's six thirty in the morning, and they've just called the "ten-minute move" over the PA system. The "move" allows inmates to go from place to place on the compound before they lock it down again. I'm heading up to the rec yard for my morning workout. I won't need ten minutes to get there, which is good, because half the time they only leave it open for five. If I'm caught on the compound after the "move" closes, I'll get a "shot"—a disciplinary incident report or extra work detail cleaning goose shit off the sidewalks, even if it is their fault for closing the move early.

When I first got here, the ten-minute move reminded me of period breaks in high school when you had a few minutes to get to your next class. But this isn't high school, not even close. This is prison. In here, it's not the principal they'll send you to see; it's the compound Lieutenant who's ready to break your balls.

I've been doing this for more than four years now, and I have eleven months left to the door. When my sentence is over, I'll probably be taken to some shit hole county jail to await transfer back to Canada. From there, they'll either put me on a plane or drive me to the closest Canadian border crossing. We're in Pennsylvania about a four-hour drive from the border and eight hours from Montreal the city I'm from. I think they'll take option two to save money.

They won't tell me which in advance because that would be a security risk. I try and imagine how or why. It's amusing thinking about someone trying to attack the van transporting me to break me out of my last forty-five minutes of Federal custody. I guess dealing with felons they have to consider everything.

With eleven months to go, if they opened the front gate, gave me 100 thousand dollars in cash and a ten-day head start, I wouldn't even consider leaving. Nor would I have on day one. The last thing I need is another five years for an escape charge.

For those same security reasons, I won't be allowed to call my family to give them a heads-up either. The good news is it will be the last brush with the US justice system I will have to bear before I get my life back. No matter how I explain it, no one will ever really understand. It's just one of those things that can't be understood unless you have the misfortune of living it. I hope you never do.

Anyway, I'm still here so it's best not to think outside these walls. All that does is slow down your time. It's hard not to think about the future, but I need to stay in the present. That's how you do time.

The present is my work out "car" has the weight bar for one hour until the next move at seven thirty. In prison, an exercise group is called a "car." There are four of us, myself, Mark Murdock a big marijuana dealer who worked with a Mexican cartel supplying the tri-state area for years until he got caught. They gave him twenty-five years and he's halfway in. The second man is Igor, a Russian gangster from New York. Like me, he's Jewish. This is his second Fed bid, and he's two in on a nine-year sentence. He's a huge guy, very strong. He works out like an animal and I wouldn't want to be the guy who pisses him off. We're getting pretty close and I know he's got my back. The last man in our car is a crazy half Irish, half Puerto Rican who goes by the name Ghost. He did nine in a pen in California before transferring to a medium in Kentucky for four more. He got here about eight months ago, and he's got two more years to the door. He's really institutionalized, so we're trying to get him to lighten up. He's always ready to fight for any little thing he perceives as disrespectful. Oh yeah, respect. A really big deal in prison, but I'll get to that.

Our car pays four fish a week for the bar. Ready-to-eat mackerel filets in packages that don't require refrigeration are sold at commissary for one dollar. They are the compound currency. Anything you buy or sell gets settled with fish. Guys gamble for fish, clean cells, shoes and wash dishes for fish. They buy dope or hooch with fish. Some buy sex for fish and a lot of chomos (child molesters) get extorted or robbed for fish. That's the way the prison economy works. A locker full of fish makes you prison rich. It also makes you a target, so anytime I have a lot of fish, I store it with someone else, for you guessed it, a few fish.

We pay the four fish to the guy who runs the weight pile in the mornings. It's not an official job, it's his hustle. There are 1300 inmates here and only eight weight bars so he makes sure the bar is available for us in the time slot we arranged. That's how he makes his money. If someone's using our bar, he deals with it. We pay him; we get the bar, period. In the afternoon and evenings, someone else handles the pile. The guards are here to maintain order, but make no mistake about it, the inmates run this place.

Everyone has a hustle in prison, a way to make money. The money you earn from your official prison job isn't enough to make a phone call home. I'm an in-unit orderly. I clean the quiet room, a small room used for reading and studying. The job takes less than five minutes to do, and I'm paid two dollars a month by the government. I pay one of the Mexicans five fish a month to do my job and I earn my money through more viable endeavors.

I don't ask my children for money. They work too hard for it, and I'm ashamed of what I did to end up here and how my actions impacted them. Oh yes, I should mention that my wife was also convicted and sentenced to four years in Federal prison for the same crime. She's been home for fourteen months now and doing well, but she had a very difficult time. I won't tell her story because I think she has to be the one to do that.

Lana and I have been married for twenty-eight years, and we have four grown children. I'm fifty-seven, but I'm probably in better shape than the average twenty-five-year old because all we do in here is work out.

The way I see it, once you're over the initial shock of what's happened to you and where you are, the situation is tougher on the family than it is on you. If I didn't earn any money I'd still get three meals a day, a bed to sleep in, and the opportunity to take care of my health. They have to survive in the real world with all the pressure of paying bills and meeting deadlines plus spend their days worrying about me.

It amazes me when guys complain their families aren't sending them any money, or when I hear them on the phone yelling at their wives or baby mamas for not putting money "on their books." An hour later they're gambling or buying dope.

So rather than rely on my family for money I always make sure to have a lucrative hustle. I'm in food distribution right now. I have three *kids* who work in the kitchen and mule out food almost every day. Stitch and Raz are from upstate New York and Jigz is from somewhere in Maine. They're all here on drug cases. I know because I checked their paperwork. By paperwork I mean all the legal documents related to your case, including plea agreement, sentencing transcripts, the judgment and commitment listing your charges, sentence and fines and your pre-sentence report, which is prepared by the probation office. They didn't tell on anyone, and they aren't *chomos* so that makes them "good." In prison, baseline due diligence is checking paperwork before you do anything with anyone. I only deal with people who I know are good. The guards know who the snitches are, and they always work them to find out who's doing what. Oh yeah, I'm also good. When I got here, people wanted to vet me, so I showed them my paperwork. News spreads fast on the pound, and once it was confirmed that I was good, everyone knew. The guards know why we're here and how we handled our cases, and the stand-up guys actually get greater respect from them.

Back to the kids. Now that the Feds have terminated their drug selling careers, they work in the prison kitchen and steal food for a living. They've been supplying me for about four months, but I'm already developing some new "connects" because Stitch and Raz are getting hot. One of the guards who I know well said that kitchen staff told him to give the kids an extra look when they're leaving. That means a body search and possibly a strip search. If he's working the same shift as the kids, there won't be a problem. He doesn't care because they throw out so much food after every meal anyway. Other guards will shake them down more often so it's just a matter of time before they get caught and sent to the hole.

The hole is the SHU or Special Housing Unit. It's in a separate building on the compound designated for punishment and protective custody. You're locked down in a ten by ten cell twenty-three hours a day. You get one hour of exercise time in a tiny fenced in area. You get a shower every third day. They feed you through a slot in the door. I've been there.

I'm pretty sure they're stand up kids, and they'll keep their mouths shut if they get jammed up, but you never know. For a lot of guys, it's easier to "tell" and get transferred to another prison for their protection, than do SHU time. If they give me up to Special Investigation Service or SIS, they'll come for me too, and they can leave me in the hole for up to three months under investigation. After three months, they have to release me, but once I walk through the doors to the housing block they can take me away again under another trumped-up charge for investigation. It happens all the time.

In the meantime, I take everything the kids steal by guaranteeing them money every week regardless of their production. So, on bad weeks, they get paid, and on really good weeks, I might top them off a bit. I pay two dollars for whole cooked chickens and two dollars for a bag of sliced meats.

Food sells here like crack. I have an exclusive clientele who buy everything for double. On an average week, I make about 100 dollars, big money in prison. Because I have no bad habits; no drugs, no drink,

9

and I don't gamble, it's more than I can spend. I get paid in fish, and whatever I need, I buy for fish. The prison commissary sells food and other items we need to live. Each unit goes once a week, and each inmate can spend up to their monthly limit of 360 dollars. Limiting criminals doesn't work though, and there are ways around it. I know a few, so I always have more than I need. I also make sure to have extra to sell at a profit if someone else needs something and the commissary's out of stock.

Back to my hustle. I never actually touch the food. I have the kids deliver it to someone who re-packs it and hands it off to another guy who works at the yard. He delivers it to my customers. I have a standing arrangement with the New York Italians who buy everything I have. They can buy chicken from the Mexicans or the Puerto Ricans for a dollar less, but they like the reliability I offer. They even invite me to sit with them at their table in the chow hall, and sometimes I do, but I like to keep my distance. They kill their friends.

I also have another guy who works "veggie prep." He mules out onions and peppers every day, which I take for a dollar and sell for two.

I plan to get out of the business in the next few months. I'm going to lay off most of it to the Albanians and keep the rest for my personal use. We already discussed it and agreed on terms. Just to be clear, I'm not a gangster. I'm a businessman. I keep my word, and I tell the truth. Everyone understands anything can happen at any time because we can't control the environment we're in. If you talk and act straight up, you won't have any problems. When you start bullshitting or trying to beat people for money, you will find yourself in a world of hurt.

You're probably wondering how I got here. It's a crazy story that's for sure. Let me take you back to the beginning.

Chapter 2

Santo Domingo, Dominican Republic, August, 2012

-APURATE, MANUEL! TENGO QUE ir al banco antes de irnos para el aeropuerto.

Hurry, Manuel! I need to go to the bank before we leave for the airport.

-Okay, Jefe. ¿Están listos Lana y Andie?

Okay, Boss. Are Lana and Andie ready?

-Están esperando abajo con el equipaje.

They're waiting downstairs with the luggage.

Manuel and I are leaving my apartment. I live in a high-rise luxury condominium building in Sanchen Naco, an upscale neighborhood in what is often referred to as the "golden mile" of Santo Domingo, the capital of the Dominican Republic, an island country in the Caribbean.

We're rushing to pick up my wife, Lana, and our youngest daughter, Andie, who just turned sixteen a few months ago. They live ten minutes from here in Evaristo Morales, another upscale neighborhood.

It's the first week of August, and, in a few hours, our flight leaves for Montreal. Our fourteen-year-old son, Jace, is attending summer camp after spending two weeks with his older sisters and grandparents. He starts school in late August, so we have to pick him up and bring him back with us. Andie and Jace go to the American School of Santo Domingo, a private English school.

11

Lana and I have been separated for the past four years. It happened when we were still in Montreal. We came down here to make money and tried living together, but it didn't work. The wounds from my infidelity were too fresh. On top of that, I had a terrible drinking problem that developed over a ten-year period, which complicated everything. I was just too far gone and too blind to see it. That was in 2008.

I quit drinking two and a half years ago with the help of Alcoholics Anonymous. I hit rock bottom, apparently a prerequisite for the program to work. I was just sick and tired of being dependent on alcohol and dealing with the terrible things that come with it. Life has since improved, and Lana and I are moving in together. That's another reason for the trip: to tell Stephanie and Paige our older daughters, in person.

Stephanie or *Roo*, the nickname I gave her when she was little, is twenty-one. Paige is nineteen. We can't wait to see them. The last time was over the Christmas holidays when we rented a beach front house in Punta Cana, a two-and-a-half-hour drive from where we live.

They flew down with my parents and we all spent two wonderful weeks together.

The last reason for this trip home is my thirty-seventh high school reunion. There were reunions before, but I never went. Because of Facebook, people from everywhere are reconnecting and suddenly I'm in touch with old high school friends that I forgot existed. It looks like there will be a huge turnout, so I'm excited to go and meet everyone after so many years. I just turned fifty-three, which is still hard to believe, because it feels like yesterday I was walking down the hallways of Chomedey Polyvalent High.

Manuel is our driver and security person, and he's been with us for two years. He's former military, and his primary responsibility is to drive Andie and Jace to and from school and anywhere else they want to go. We don't anticipate trouble, but you never know, so he's armed. The kids speak fluent Spanish, and they're very familiar with the city and culture, but they don't go anywhere without him; same for Lana. If she wants to get her hair done, go shopping, or meet friends for a drink, Manuel takes her. To Dominicans, white-skinned foreigners are rich, so it's better to be safe than sorry. We're not rich, but we're doing very well. Everything is relative, and just owning a new car and living in a nice apartment makes us Oligarch rich to the average Dominican.

This is a third world country after all, and the majority of the ten million people who live here are very poor. The average monthly salary is about 10 000 pesos or 250 US dollars.

The government does a pretty good job of educating its people, and the literacy rate is quite high. The problem is underemployment, which translates to very low wages. Someone graduating college with a bachelor degree, lucky enough to land an entry-level job as a bank teller with one of the country's big banks, only earns about 300 dollars a month. A policeman's salary is about 200 dollars a month, a situation that leads to massive corruption. In a country where the only way out of poverty is to become a major league baseball player, a politico (politician), one of the lucky few who can become a successful entrepreneur, or a narco (drug dealer) a propina (tip) or soborno (bribe) can go a long way.

Don't get me wrong, there are a lot of very rich people in this country, and there's a burgeoning middle class. The golden mile is street after street of luxurious condominium towers with new ones popping up every day. Foreign money is pouring into the country at unprecedented rates. There are world-class shopping malls and office towers. There are well known American businesses and brands, major hotel and real estate projects and a brand new underground metro system. New roadway and highway infrastructure is bringing economic growth to areas of the island that were too difficult to reach when we first came here. The country is changing rapidly and Santo Domingo is at the pinnacle offering everything you can get in any major North American city, including great entertainment, fine dining, amazing shopping, art and culture. With some money you can live very nicely here. We love it.

After Manuel drives the kids to school, he spends the day in our office running errands or helping with anything that needs doing. At two thirty, he picks the kids up and brings them home. At five, he goes to our other office to pick up the daily receipts from the small finance company we started so he can deposit them in the bank.

The business has been growing and the deposits have become substantial. I warn Manuel not to get complacent. He instinctively knows to take a different route and go to a different bank branch every day, but he still has to be alert. The possibility of getting robbed while making his run is very real.

As for me, I don't have my own driver. I don't want one. Instead, I carry a handgun on my hip at the small of my back, which is obvious to anyone really looking. Seeing a weapon deters most. They don't expect this from a *gringo* and immediately assume I must be someone important because a tourist, or visiting businessman, would never carry a weapon. I also keep a Glock in the glove box, just in case. My Spanish is good; I worked hard in my first two years here to learn the language. If someone hears me speak, they assume I know the score.

Santo Domingo isn't the vacation destinations that the country's famous for. It's the big city. I've met foreigners who've been robbed, usually because of their own stupidity and naivety. Just the other day, I stopped a young American couple who were riding rented bicycles on a busy downtown street, wearing expensive back packs, jewelry and holding iPhones. I told them to go back to their hotel and change. I understand why they think it's safe. The city seems civilized. They see familiar things and police presence everywhere, not realizing that the police may be the first to rob them.

Anyway, Manuel's helping me today so he's driving, and I'm in the passenger seat. We're pulling out of the underground garage in my Kia Sportage; low key is my policy. We stop at the electronic gate waiting for the doorman to open it. Instead, he signals to us, so Manuel lowers the window.

-Dime, hermanito.

Talk to me, bro, Manuel says.

-Por favor espere un minuto...quiero hablar con Usted.

Wait a minute please. I want to speak to you.

He enters the garage and approaches the car on Manuel's side, leans on the window frame and says to me;

-jefe, ¿hablaste con el hombre que trabaja de noche?

Boss, did you speak to the guy who works nights?

- ¿No, por qué?

No, why?

-Porque ayer, vinieron dos hombres buscandolo. Ellos querian entrar al apartemento suyo, pero yo no lo deje entrar. Uno dijo que era policía y el otro era fiscal.

Because yesterday two men were looking for you. They wanted to go to your apartment, but I didn't let them in. One of them said he was police and the other a prosecutor.

- ¿Policía? ¿Fiscal? ¿Estás seguro? No tengo ningún problema con nadie. ¿Por qué me estan buscando? ¿Te dijeron?

Police? Prosecutor? Are you sure? I don't have a problem with anyone. Why would they be looking for me? Did they tell you?

-Yo les pregunte, pero no quisieron decir nada. Se fueron despues.

I asked them but they wouldn't say. They left after.

-Okay, gracias por la información. Si ves algo raro, dejame saber inmediatamente.

Okay, thanks for the information. If you see anything strange, let me know immediately.

I hand him 500 pesos, knowing he'll pay extra special attention. What the hell is this about? Police? Prosecutor?

My first thought is someone is looking to rob me. Manuel and I discuss it and agree it's possible. I know someone who was stopped by police while driving his car downtown. They made him drive to his house and then robbed him. It's very disconcerting, and I'll need to deal with it when I get back.

There's another possibility. Our lending business makes small collateralized loans to working people who aren't able to, or don't want to borrow from the banks. We offer much better rates than our established competition, so we ended up with all of their customers. I know this upset them, and I always worried about potential fall-out. Can it be they're trying to do something about it? Two people pretending to be authority is easy to pull off here. Anything's possible, especially when you're taking food off someone's table. It's worrisome, for sure.

Chapter 3

Las Americas Airport

I'M TEMPORARILY BLINDED BY the tropical sun as we exit the garage. Eleven in the morning and already eighty-six degrees. I'm grateful for the weather, even more grateful for air conditioning. We head down Abraham Lincoln, a major boulevard. Traffic is heavy but moving steadily.

At the next intersection we hit a line of cars waiting for the light to change. Facing us across the street is a mega Nacional Supermarket that covers two city blocks. I glance around at the contrasts. Mercedes Benz, BMW, an old beat up Nissan Sentra, a late model Range Rover, a Honda Accord, a new Audi, a wagon hitched to a donkey over flowing with plantain. Behind him, a brand-new Ferrari.

One lane over is a carro publico that drives up and down the boulevard transporting people like a bus service. Its interior, packed with bodies. Arms and even a couple of heads spew out its windows for lack of space. Motorcycles, some burning black smoke, revving their engines waiting for the light to change. Others weave between waiting cars, moving to the front. There's a family on a 125cc motorcycle two lanes over; father in front, mother in back, sandwiching their three small children between them.

Another motorcycle approaches with two Policia Nacional dressed in standard grey uniform and black military boots. The one in back has a rifle strewn across his lap. They pay us no mind.

A squeegee kid approaches and is about to splash my windshield with water from a plastic bottle. He draws the squeegee like a gunslinger when Manuel hits the wipers to warn him off. The kid curses, so Manuel flings his arms in the air with a "what are you gonna do about it" look. Kid's on to the next one, hurling water across the windshield before its driver can make a choice.

Street vendors hawk pre-paid phone cards, battery chargers, fresh fruit, cold drinks, steering wheel covers, clothing, toys and even puppies. A woman begging with new born in arms. She may have rented the baby for her performance; desperation will do that. Honking seems mandatory. Everyone does it, though it's sometimes hard to decipher the reason. Sound systems from the backs of cars and SUVs blare reggaetón music so loud that the bass makes you nauseous if you're too close.

At the next corner the Bomba has a line of cars waiting for gas. They still serve you here. People flow in and out of its convenience store, some with cold cervezas in hand, already. Drinking is acceptable almost anywhere any time.

At night, liquor stores morph into gathering spots and quasi night clubs, selling drinks by the glass. People hang out in front drinking, talking and dancing. Car sound systems provide the entertainment. Beautiful girls in short skirts, low cut tops and high heels everywhere; enough to drive a man crazy.

The Policia Nacional are there too, appearing to keep order and protect the public. But really, they're earning a stipend from the liquor store to keep the flow of business unimpeded. They help direct the parking of cars and get a piece of the propina paid to street parkers who use public parking spots as their own inventory. Just try and park there without paying them....

This city is a modern-day Wild West. Its vibrancy is infectious and its spirit exhilarating. There are socio-economic problems for sure, but the progress is unstoppable and inevitable. Man, I love it here. It makes me feel alive in a way I haven't felt for many years.

We make our way to Lana's building and as we pull up, she and Andic are waiting inside the parking lot behind the electronic security gate.

"What took you so long? We've been down here for thirty minutes," Lana says half aggravated, and looking nervous.

"I told you to wait upstairs. We tried to get here as fast as we could, but there was traffic. We have plenty of time, stop worrying."

"I know, but I want to get there and eat something before the flight."

-Manuel, los equipajes por favor.

Manuel, the luggage please.

-Los tengo, jefe.

I got it, Boss.

-Dime Andie. ¿Cómo estás querida? ¿Estás emocionado de ir a Montreal?

Talk to me, Andie. How are you, my dear? Excited to go to Montreal? Manuel asks Andie.

-Ya sabes, quiero ver a mis hermanas, abuelos y amigas. Los extraño muchísimo.

You know, I want to see my sisters, my grandparents and my friends. I miss them so much, she answers.

-No olvides a tu hermano Jace.

Don't forget your brother Jace, Manuel adds.

-No lo extraño!

I don't miss him!

-Andie, No digas eso. Estoy seguro de que él te extraña.

Andie don't say that. I'm sure he misses you, Manuel says.

- ¿Crees? Entonces, ¿cómo es que él nunca me escribe?

You think? Then how come he never writes me? Andie asks.

"Andie, you know how camp is. He has no time to write letters. Besides, even if he did, you wouldn't get it until next year with the Dominican mail," I tell her.

"He can email me! I email him all the time! He never answers!"

"Well, there is that, but you know boys are different from girls with that stuff, Andie." I say.

"Whatever," she answers.

An hour later, we're pulling into Las Americas International Airport, a forty-minute drive from the city and the biggest of the six international airports in the country. Manuel pulls up to the departure area and speaks to a Policia who's there to manage traffic flow. He tells him he's going to leave the car parked in front for ten minutes.

18

The Policia says he can't, so Manuel slips him 100 pesos, and he lets him.

We make our way to the Delta desk. We're flying to Montreal with a connection in Miami, a flight we take a few times a year. After we're checked in, I tell Manuel he can leave. Then, Lana, Andie and I head through the security check point.

The Dominican Government charges a departure tax to anyone who's stayed in the country for more than three months if they don't reside here. They collect it at Customs. We don't pay the tax because we're residents. Lana and the kids have their permanent residence. I have my temporary residence, but I'm expecting my permanent status any day. They processed their paperwork a couple of months before I did and used a different lawyer.

When we get to the Customs window we hand her our tickets, residence cards and our cedulas (Dominican identity cards) to the woman Customs official. She's a bit surprised we're not tourists and begins typing at her computer terminal. A few minutes later she lifts her head, looks at me and says:

"Señor, Usted no puede viajar."

Sir, you can't travel.

- ¿Qué? ¿No puedo viajar? ¿Por qué? Qué significa eso?

What? I can't travel...what does that mean?

-No puedes salir del país. No puedes viajar. No sé por qué.

You can't leave the country. You can't travel. I don't know why.

Lana and I look at each other not understanding what's going on. I explain to the woman that I need to take this flight and whatever the problem, it must be related to the processing of my permanent residence. I know the process is currently undergoing drastic changes. I tell her I'll deal with it when I return and I place twenty dollars on the counter. She looks at me and says:

-Señor, no sé cuál es el problema, pero es seguro que no puedes viajar. Lo siento.

Sir, I don't know what the problem is, but for sure you can't travel. I'm sorry.

Shit, she's serious. She has to be if she's not taking the money. Worse, this means it's bigger than her. What the hell is going on? I realize I won't be getting on the flight.

"Lana, you and Andie go ahead. I'll find out what this is about. It's got to be because of my residence. You know they introduced all kinds of new rules and procedures. Maybe you can't leave the country during the process. I'll call Victor and straighten it out. I'll take another flight tomorrow. What a drag! I have to pay for another flight, unbelievable!"

"Are you sure? You don't want us to go with you tomorrow?" Lana asks.

"No, that's crazy. We'll lose all the money we spent on the tickets. No, you guys go, and I'll see you tomorrow."

The Customs official hands us back all our documents, and Andie and Lana head to the gate.

I call Manuel and tell him to turn around to pick me up. My bag was already checked at the Delta desk, so I go back to retrieve it. I still have my carry on and laptop with me.

Fifteen minutes later Manuel shows up as I wait for my bag. After another thirty minutes there's still no sign of my bag and I'm beginning to feel extremely uncomfortable. Something, I don't know what, but something, isn't right.

- ¡Manuel! ¡Vamonos!
Manuel! Let's go!

Chapter 4

Serious Trouble

"VICTOR, IT'S WARREN. HOW are you?"

"Very well, Warren, and you?"

"Not so good. Victor, I was leaving to go to Montreal with Lana and Andie at Las Americas, and Dominican Customs told me I can't travel. They didn't say why. Whatever it was, she saw it on her computer. Can this be related to my permanent residence?"

"Wouldn't let you travel? I have no idea what that's about. I don't think it's related, but I'll verify. They're changing the entire process. I think I've mentioned that. It's much more complicated, so anything's possible. Give me a couple of hours, and I'll check with my contact at immigration. I'll call you back as soon as I know something."

"Okay Victor, I'm waiting. I have to get to Montreal ASAP."

"Okay, I'll call you back."

Three hours later Manuel and I are in my apartment. I've been dialing Lana's phone incessantly. I have a bad feeling, and it's getting worse with every unanswered ring. I can't stop thinking about what my doorman told me, and it makes me think about what we'd done. We have a dirty little secret. Holy fuck! Could that be it? Please no!

They should have been in Miami by now. What the hell is going on?

My phone rings and I look at the caller ID....Victor. "Yeah, Victor."

"Warren, I spoke to the person handling your residence file at immigration. They didn't do anything to keep you from leaving the country. They have no idea what it's about. He did ask if you have any legal problems. Do you?"

"What do you mean, legal problems? You're my lawyer Victor. You know I have no problems. I mean, none that I'm aware of. How can I know?"

"It's just that he intimated that it sounds like some kind of detainer order. He said the police usually impose them."

"The police? Victor, this morning when I was leaving my building, my doorman said two men were looking for me yesterday. One of them said he was police and the other a fiscal. Do you think it's related?"

"Shit. I don't know. Warren, my uncle's a retired police General. He still has a lot of influence. I'm going to call him and ask if he can check if something's going on. If there's a problem, he'll find out for sure. Let me work on it. I'll call you back."

"Okay, I'm waiting. Please hurry," I say and hang up.

I'm feeling sicker by the moment. Why won't Lana answer her phone?

An hour later Andie answers. She's completely distraught and crying. She can hardly speak.

"Andie, calm down, honey, please. I can't understand what you're saying. Take a second. Take a few deep breaths."

She's sobbing uncontrollably and sounds like she's having trouble breathing. A couple of minutes later she regains some composure and says:

"Daddy, the FBI arrested Mommy."

"What? What did you say Andie?" Blood rushes to my head and butterflies fill my stomach.

"Daddy, three FBI agents met us when we got off the plane. They told Mommy she's under arrest. They left me here all alone. I'm so scared. What do I do? What's going to happen to Mom? Why was she arrested Daddy? What did she do wrong?"

My worst fears are confirmed. They fucking got us! Oh My God!

"Andie, listen to me. This is very important. Do you have money on you?"

"Yes. I have the money Mom gave me to hold. She wanted me to hold it because she had to keep opening her purse, and she didn't want anyone to see it. Daddy, I'm scared. The FBI lady told me I won't see my mother for a very long time. She was such a bitch. She was so mean. I asked her how I was going to get home and she said, "You're sixteen. You'll figure it out." Daddy what do I do? Mommy was scared. I'm worried about her."

"Sweety, listen to me. I need you to listen very carefully. We'll straighten this out. I don't know what it's about (I lied). The only thing that matters right now is that you're safe. Is your phone charged?"

"It's Mom's phone. I was holding hers, and she had mine. They took mine."

"Okay, is the phone charged?" I ask again.

"Yes, it's on half."

"Do you have a charger with you?"

"Yes. I have one in my purse."

"Okay, good. Make sure it's charged at all times. Don't close it for any reason, do you hear?"

"Yes, Okay."

"Now I want you to go to the Delta desk and ask for a supervisor. Tell them you're a minor, and you were left alone in the airport. You can tell them what happened. Tell them you need to get home to Montreal. I'll contact Delta on this end. Do you understand?"

"Yes, but what about Mom? We have to help her, Daddy. She was crying. She was so scared. What do we do?"

"I don't know, honey, but I will soon. You just worry about you, and let me worry about Mom, okay? Will you do that for me, Andie?"

Here I was trying to calm Andie down, but I was freaking out myself. We're so fucked. Our lives are ruined. We've shamed our children, our parents, ourselves. What will happen? How will I explain this to my family? What will people think? Are we going to jail? Why did they separate us? Was it premeditated? Are they coming for me too? What will happen to Lana? She must be terrified. Holy Fuck! I need to help her. How? Just calm down. You need to remain calm for Andie and your other three kids right now. Pull yourself together.

"Andie, please do what I said. I'll have Stephanie call you soon. Go to Delta and if you need anyone call me or Stephanie right away, okay?"

"Okay, Dad. Daddy, please help Mom, please!"

"I will, Andie. I promise."

I spend the next few hours talking to Stephanie and Paige. I tell them everything. I also tell them somehow it would be okay, but they know better. Paige is falling apart and Stephanie is trying hard to keep it together. We've already put these kids through so much with all the fighting and the separation, and now this. Nothing is okay.

I Google "criminal lawyers Miami" and a few names come up. I call four of them and hire the first one who gets back to me, over the telephone. He checks Lana's status while I wait on the phone and tells me she's being held at the Federal Detention Center in Miami. A preliminary hearing is scheduled two days from now. He'll see her first thing in the morning. All I have to do is send him a ten-thousand-dollar retainer. I impress upon him that he has to make sure she knows I'm doing everything I can to help her. He agrees to include the human comfort in the price. I asked if he knew whether I'm in trouble too, but he said the indictment is sealed so he can't say, but I should assume the worst.

Now everything makes sense. I understand why the police came looking for me. They weren't trying to rob me. They probably wanted to arrest me. Shit! I better get out of here before they come back. I need time to figure out what to do. They could be back any minute.

Then it dawns on me. Why didn't they let me fly to Miami like Lana and Andie did, and arrest me on US soil? Maybe I'm not in trouble. Maybe they aren't going to arrest me. It doesn't make sense on the surface. If they wanted me, all they had to do was let me fly with them. Wait a minute, how did they even know we were flying to Montreal today? Someone told them, that's how. Someone close to us gave us up. I need to really think this through. I can't trust anyone. Fuck!

I grab a few things and tell Manuel to drive to the Hilton on the Malecon, a strip of hotels by the ocean. It's a huge hotel so I'll blend in easily. I tell him to park the truck a few blocks away on a side street.

At the front desk I ask to speak with the manager. When she comes out, I explain I'm here on business and all my documents along with my credit cards were stolen in the airport, I've already reported it to the police, and I have an appointment with the Canadian Embassy tomorrow afternoon to arrange temporary documentation. Luckily, I keep my cash separate from my credit cards. She's very sympathetic and offers to assist me in any way she can. I pay for three nights in advance and give her a twenty-dollar tip for her help.

When I get to the room, I drop my bags on the floor and fall on the bed. My head is splitting and the back of my neck is throbbing from the tension. I try breathing deeply to ease the discomfort, but it doesn't work. What the fuck am I going to do?

I think about the people who knew we were going to Montreal. There's Manuel, of course, and Maria, Lana's housekeeper. Then I remember. I met with Frederico, a business associate, twice last week. I wanted him to invest money in our loan business because a new opportunity had presented itself. I first met him through Roland. He used to cash checks for Roland and later for us. He owns a very established business selling construction supplies. I bet he's the one. They must have followed the money back to him. It has to be. Damn!

When we met he was asking me a lot of questions about Roland. Where is he? Have I seen him? Do I talk to him? I told him I haven't had contact with him in almost two years, and last I knew, he was living in Punta Cana.

Then I asked him to give me an answer on the investment opportunity when I got back from my trip to Montreal. I told him we were all going home to visit. It's him! It's got to be! They must have traced the checks back to him so he's cooperating with them.

Chapter 5

Reckoning

CALM DOWN...THINK...THINK....

I've been in stressful situations before in my life, many of which were out of my control, but never before have I felt so completely overwhelmed. It's like watching everything happen to someone else; surreal, unbelievable. I can't reconcile how I perceive my own character with what I did and with what's happening.

I never broke the law before or did anything that could get me arrested. Exaggerating expenses or understating earnings for tax purposes was the extent of my misdeeds. I figure I didn't do what any businessman didn't do. I thought of myself as an honest, hard-working provider. Until I did what I did, of course.

I started in business at a young age and worked very hard. In 1998 I was thirty-nine and after a string of successful businesses I sold an internet start-up and did quite well. I wasn't set for life, but I was in good shape. I had a lot of money in the bank, several properties and my children had college funds. We also had a nice retirement savings plan.

Then later that same year with my own money and outside investors I started a new business, an internet driven, digital signage company that had large screens in the food courts of every major Canadian shopping mall, broadcasting real time content and advertising.

The business was known in media circles internationally. In 2002, I signed a revenue deal with Bell Globe Media, Canada's largest media company. They owned the largest national TV network, the biggest newspaper in the country and many other media properties. They wanted to expand their offerings through convergence with other platforms. We were perfect for them. They would pay us to supply video and graphic content to our screens nationally and use their sales force of hundreds to sell advertising.

Just before the deal closed, I was contacted by their mergers and acquisitions department and told they would only close the deal if they could buy an interest in our company. Chaching!

After intense negotiations, we agreed to sell them a 17 percent stake at an attractive valuation. They also had the right to buy a majority interest after five years. This was going to be my biggest win yet and easily propel me to real wealth and, if I chose, early retirement.

But things weren't as rosy as they seemed. I was having mounting problems in my personal life as a result of some very bad choices. I was unfaithful to my wife and was involved in an on-and-off affair that lasted close to ten years. Lana found out about it, and it hurt her badly. We argued continuously and our kids were subjected to this insanity. She gave me chance after chance, but the more we fought, the more I looked for distractions. Lana was a loving and dedicated wife and mother who didn't deserve what I was doing.

There was also my increasing dependence on alcohol. I never drank before, but I was traveling a lot and entertaining media buyers all the time, so I began drinking wine with dinner frequently. After a while wine with dinner turned into wine to sleep, and then wine to anything. One day someone ordered vodka and I discovered how little I needed to feel good. It became my preferred beverage, accelerating my down fall. My judgment became clouded and my performance affected. I didn't recognize the extent.

Financial pressure in my personal life was also taking a toll. In 2000, the Dot Com bubble left me with a significant market loss and since launching the business I was supporting my family on a salary that didn't cover my nut. I was subsidizing the difference and depleting my savings.

Still, I managed to pull off a miracle. I looked South to the US market and closed a partnership deal with Clear Channel Outdoor, one of the largest billboard companies in the world. We formed a new entity of which our company owned 49 percent and began rolling out to food courts in American malls. With the Bell Globe Media deals in the works, the company's future was looking very optimistic. All roads were pointing to a successful outcome. I was all in.

These deals were critical because we were burning cash. Even though revenue was growing at a steady clip year over year, we still weren't breaking even. Investors were impatient. To complicate matters, there was terrible in-fighting between some of them from other unrelated interests they had together. It spilled over into our business and created a poisonous, dysfunctional environment. I was spending way too much time trying to manage these distractions.

As the pressure mounted there was a constant threat of closure from key investors which was exacting a toll on me. No amount of pressure was going to produce sales any faster. The process of educating and attracting new business was slow but steady. We were digital pioneers, and we had to almost single-handedly change the long-term mindset and buying habits of advertisers at a time when most global advertising agencies still didn't understand the internet or alternative digital mediums. The Bell Globe Media purchase was going to fix everything.

Then disaster struck. A new CEO took over the parent company of Bell Globe Media and his new directive was to divest their "convergent" relationships. Everyone we were working with was let go. The revenue deal had already been signed and executed, and we were just waiting on their board to rubber-stamp the equity purchase agreement.

In support of the new CEO's strategy, they killed the purchase in the last minute and left us in the lynch. Even though we had the revenue from the first deal, without the legitimate "buy in" of the parent company, the sales distribution never materialized, and we struggled to make the company profitable as quickly as investors expected.

At the end of 2006 my principal investor withdrew support with little notice, leaving me no choice but to find a buyer for the company for pennies on the dollar. My equity vanished just like that, and my savings were gone. I was in debt for the first time in my life, jobless, and the event I had been waiting for and counting on, vanished.

I stepped up the drinking, feeling the victim and drowning in self-pity. I had never really failed at anything before in my life, and I didn't understand why it happened or what I needed to do to rebound. Truth is, even if I did, the booze wasn't going to let me. I was a broken mess.

We were forced to sell our properties, which by now were remortgaged, and the pressure on our fragile marriage was too much. Lana and I separated. The hardest part for me was dealing with the fall from grace. I'd always been successful. I was able to send my kids to private schools, summer camps and give them nice things. Suddenly, I couldn't give them anything. I was a failure. Had I not been so poisoned by alcohol, I might have coped better.

Lana moved across town with Andie and Jace and took a job as a manger in a retail store. She was struggling to make ends meet on her salary. I landed a consulting contract with a high-tech start-up but it was short lived because of my drinking. I thought I could hide it, but I couldn't. Then I got a job in business development for a new product, which I hated, mostly because I hated myself and where I was in life.

About a year later, the incessant fighting between Lana and I calmed down. One day she called me and told me she wanted to take the younger ones to live with her in Santo Domingo in the Dominican Republic. Apparently, someone we knew from our old neighborhood, a guy named Roland Ross offered her a job selling time sharing on the telephone. He had moved there several years earlier and assured her she would make a lot of money. I was livid. I told her she wasn't leaving the country with my children.

One afternoon, she came to see me to try and convince me to let them go and suggested I go as well. She said there's nothing in Montreal for us and maybe a fresh start was what we needed. I was so unhappy and so miserable and felt like such a failure, I decided I had nothing to lose. I rented Stephanie and Paige an apartment in downtown Montreal so they could live together, and off we went.

Turns out there was no time-sharing. He was scamming people and telling them they won a sweepstakes. It was a scam I knew existed and never imagined I would do such a thing. Yet here we were in a foreign country with no resources and nothing to go back to. I felt desperate to make money so I rationalized that I would do it just until I got back on my feet. Many people experience financial hardship, and they don't resort to stealing money. Twisted by alcohol, filthy, misguided greed and scared to death of where my life was heading, I did it anyway.

At this point, to escape reality I was drinking vodka at eight o'clock in the morning. I couldn't even do a good job scamming people. I spent days at a time in my apartment not going to work. Just me and a bottle. The fighting between Lana and me got worse, of course. How could it not? We lived apart because we couldn't even live as roommates.

One day I finally had enough. I was hurting my kids. They told me they weren't going to speak to me if I didn't stop drinking. It was also clear that if I didn't, I would die. I was forty pounds overweight, very unhealthy, and I was slowly destroying myself and the people I loved most. Plus, booze had gotten me into several dangerous situations in Santo Domingo, like the time we were in a hotel and I punched a man from England in the face for hitting on my daughter Paige who was only sixteen. The police were called, and in my drunken state, I was belligerent and uncooperative. I was lucky no one killed me.

I knew if I wanted to keep my kids in my life I had to quit. I knew if I wanted a chance at any type of decent life or happiness I had to quit. I was ready. Scared to death but ready.

I gathered all my strength and conviction and returned to Montreal to get sober. I quit drinking and Stephanie and Paige were with me every step of the way. So were my parents. It was the hardest thing I've ever done. I puked for two weeks straight from withdrawal, but I dragged myself to three AA meetings a day. It worked.

When I returned to Santo Domingo, I found a meeting in English and went three times a week. I never drank again.

Once sober, I started looking for business opportunities that would get me away from scamming people which I continued doing. I met a businessman and together we bought and sold products wholesale. Eventually, I had enough money to launch a lending business. Without the alcohol I was becoming more like my old self again and everything started to turn around. I was living modestly and the business started growing. Everything was back on track.

Too little, too late. It seems our scam just caught up with us.

Chapter 6

Hilton Hotel Santo Domingo

I LIFT MYSELF OFF the bed and look at the mini bar and think why not? Just one little shot to relax. Oh yeah, that's why not. Your family needs you!

Any self-pity I'm fostering evaporates quickly, and I focus my energy on navigating this shit storm. I'm pretty rational as things go, so I accept reality and think:

Do what you have to for Lana and the kids before you face the music.

I start a to-do list. A few minutes later, a knock on the door. I get up, nervous, and look through the peep hole. Oh good, Manuel....

I let him in.

"You alright?" I ask.

"Yeah, Boss. I'm okay."

"You parked on a side street, not too close, right?" I ask.

"Like you told me."

"You want something to drink? There's water, juice and soft drinks in the mini bar. Have something."

"Thanks, Boss. I'll take water."

"Okay, Manuel, listen. We're in some serious trouble. That's why Lana was arrested in Miami, and they probably want me too. I doubt you're in any type of trouble, but if you're worried and you don't want to help me, I understand. Once I know exactly what's going on, I'll decide if I want to turn myself in. Before that, I need to take care of some things. Are you okay with that?"

"Yes, Boss, whatever you need. You guys are like family. I love you guys," he says.

"We feel the same about you, Manuel, thank you."

"I know, Boss."

"Manuel, I need to ask you something. Did you tell anyone that we were going to Montreal?"

"Tell anyone? Who? What do you mean?"

"I mean anyone. Did you tell anyone?"

"I told my wife last night. I told her I had two weeks off, so I will drive the taxi. I told her you guys were going to Montreal. Besides her, I never said anything to anyone. Why, Boss? Did I do something wrong?

"No, no, Manuel. You didn't do anything wrong. It just seems like they knew we were going home to Montreal. Never mind. Forget it."

"Okay, Boss."

"Okay, listen...this is important. You have a lot to do. I'm going to wait here for you. I can't risk going outside unnecessarily. First, take a taxi to two different cell phone stores and buy six cheap burner phones. Make sure they're small independent stores. Then buy twenty thousand pesos in phone cards on the street. Don't buy them in the stores. You got that?"

"Yeah, no problem. I know where to go."

"Good. After that, use one of the burners to call Maria on her cell phone. She's still at Lana's apartment. Tell her to take the dogs for a walk and meet you two blocks away. Tell her she's not going back to the apartment so she should take her purse, the extra set of apartment keys, and the keys to Lana's car."

"Okay, Boss."

"Take the keys from her and explain there's a problem and that she has to take Duke and Leyla home with her. She'll need to take care of the dogs until we can figure out what's happening. Give her thirty thousand pesos and tell her Andie or I will call her as soon as possible. Oh, and Manuel, trash the phone immediately. Destroy it after you speak to her and give her one of the new phones. Make sure you have the phone number and tell her to always keep it turned on and charged."

"Okay, Boss. Should I tell her Lana was arrested?"

"Yeah, she has to know the truth. Manuel, try and make sure no one's following or watching either of you."

He nods his head. "Boss, what about Andie? Is she okay?"

"She's safe. I doubt she's okay, but she's safe. We're getting her home as fast as possible."

"What about you, Boss? Are you okay?"

"I'll be okay. Just go and get that done fast. I can't call anyone until I get a new phone. Don't use your phone to call me either. Only call if it's urgent, and use a burner."

"Okay, Boss, I'll be back as soon as I can, but rush hour is starting."

"I know, Manuel. One last thing. After Maria leaves, if you're sure no one's watching, go up to the apartment. In Lana's bedroom in the cupboard is a safe with money and important documents. I wrote down the combination with instructions on how to open it. Dump everything into a bag and bring it to me. Manuel, if you feel like someone's watching the apartment don't go up."

"Okay, Boss, do you need anything from your apartment?"

"No! Don't go there! I think we got lucky once already. I have everything I need for now. We'll worry about my apartment later. Just go and come back quickly."

We go over everything one more time, and he assures me he knows exactly what he has to do. I give him enough money for everything, and he says:

"Okay, Boss, I'll see you soon," and walks out the door.

I need to speak to Stephanie and Paige, but I can't use my phone. I'll wait until Manuel gets back. I consider for a few seconds that it may have been Manuel that told the police we're going back to Montreal, but I don't believe that. If Manuel was working with them, they would have me already.

It's too risky to go to my apartment, but I can't avoid the banks. I need money. I won't go to my regular branches where the staff know me. I'll go to other branches. They may be monitoring our accounts, so if it seems like it's taking too long or doesn't feel right, I'll get out fast. On the other hand, this is a foreign country, so I assume the FBI probably can't operate as easily as they do in the US. Maybe there's some wiggle room. I guess I'll know soon enough.

I try to find some perspective. I understand life as I knew it is over. These are unfamiliar waters, so I don't know what to expect. There's no point worrying what people will say or trying to find some magical way out of this. There is no way out. We knew better. A lot of people will be shocked. They'll say we deserve what we're getting, and they're right. We did this for quick money and now we're in a world of trouble. I think about the people we stole from and how we hurt them. What a shameful thing. Yeah, we deserve what we're getting. Unfortunately our children and parents don't.

Chapter 7

My God

MANUEL COMES BACK a couple of hours later, and I tell him to go home and get some rest. We agree to meet downstairs in the lobby at seven thirty in the morning. I spend the next few hours talking with Stephanie, Paige, Jace and my parents. It is the worst few hours of my life.

I do my best to provide comfort and stability, but the shock, betrayal and utter disappointment in their voices is all I feel. What example have I set in their eyes? What kind of father am I? What kind of son? What sort of comfort can I possibly provide?

My biggest concern is Andie. They assure me she is safe and will fly home in the morning. They will be at the airport to pick her up, and they will all go to my parent's house and stay together.

I want to sleep, but I can't. I want to close my eyes and wake up to a new day where this is just a bad dream. I want to know Lana is okay. Most of all, I want my children to love and respect me like they always have, even when I was at my worst with alcohol.

It is the first of many times over the next few years that I pledge to make them proud of me again. I can never erase what I did, but I will work hard to redeem myself, to be a good person, a good son, husband and father.

I know right now that I am at the beginning of a difficult journey, and I am afraid of what is coming and what we will all be subjected to, and then a prayer enters my mind. It's a prayer that stays with me throughout this harrowing experience, a prayer that scorches a permanent place in my psyche, a prayer that helps me survive.

Please God,

Let this be the extent of my punishment. We will recover from the trauma, the humiliation, the disgrace. Just don't let anything happen to anyone in my family. Don't let anyone fall sick, get hurt or worse. Do with me what you want, just don't let anything happen to them. They are innocent.

I think of some people I've come across in my years in business. People who made a lot of money but left a trail of blood and destruction in their path with every dollar. Some of them have loved ones that suffer from illness or disease. Some, tragically, lost a child or an innocent. I don't know how this works, and I don't pretend to understand, but I am prepared right here and now to be punished in any way God sees fit as long my family is kept safe. Let me be the one to suffer. They are already suffering more than they deserve.

Alone in the hotel room I feel the presence of God. I was never religious, and I'm still not, but what will happen to me in the course of the years to come, increases my spirituality and my connection to a Higher Power. I am about to embark on a very difficult journey. One that will subject me to some bad things. It will get easier over time, but the prayer always stays with me. It's still here, even now.

Chapter 8

The Plan

THE NEXT MORNING MANUEL and I meet in the lobby and had a quick bite before heading out. I've already spoken to Stephanie and Paige several times. I told them if they didn't hear from me for an extended period, assume the worst; I've been arrested. Beyond that, I will be okay and will call as soon as I am able to.

I'm nervous to stay in the same hotel for more than one night so I speak to the manager and tell her my plans have changed. She is quite accommodating and refunds the two extra nights.

Manuel and I spend the next few hours running to different bank branches where I make withdrawals without any problems. My concern that they might be monitoring my bank accounts seems to be an over-reaction.

I continue to speak to Stephanie and Paige throughout the day and by mid-afternoon they go to pick Andie up at the airport and return to my parent's house. Andie is home safe, which is a tremendous relief. We are all in survival mode.

Lana is able to call home and speak to the kids and she tells them the guards confiscated her Crohn's medication and refuse to give it to her. She is getting sick and needs her meds. I call the lawyer who says he is already aware; he went to see her earlier that morning. At her preliminary hearing he will ask the judge to order the Bureau of Prisons to administer the medication.

He said she will plead not guilty to the charges. After that, she will be transferred to the Southern District of New York, the Second

Circuit, and be incarcerated at Metropolitan Correction Center in Manhattan. We make plans to speak again after the hearing.

Later that afternoon, I go to see Victor. He has spoken to his uncle, the retired Police General, who told him he hasn't found anything in the system pertaining to me. Still, it doesn't make sense. Why didn't they let me travel? What difference would it have made if I was there when they arrested Lana? And why just Lana? Why separate us? Something doesn't add up.

Then I think, maybe this was just a Dominican bureaucratic fuck up. Maybe Lana wasn't supposed to leave the country either. I have to believe if they wanted me, they would have had me by now. Maybe they aren't going to arrest me after all. Wishful thinking.

It's evening when we leave Victor's office, and I have Manuel drive me to the old city, the Colonial Zone. When they refer to Santo Domingo as the oldest city in the Western Hemisphere, they are actually referring to the old city. In recent years, it's been undergoing rapid gentrification and a huge boost in tourism. New boutique hotels have opened and that's what I am looking for. I don't want to risk staying in one of the larger hotels in the city.

Once I find a place, Manuel parks a few blocks away in a parking garage, and I give him taxi money. He will come back at seven the next morning. I check in using my passport, which I know can be fatal, but it's already close to nine, and I will be gone first thing in the morning.

Besides, putting things in perspective, I realize this isn't television, and there isn't some CIA-like operations center coordinating a massive man-hunt for me using satellite technology and electronic surveillance. I already know they aren't monitoring my bank accounts. I am on an island after all. They know that, and if they want me, they'll get me, eventually.

I knew I'll have a better chance of mitigating any problems if I am not in custody. Crossing the border to Haiti comes to mind. I know I can pay someone to get across and, from there, I can make my way to another country where I can deal with things on my terms. But do I really want to be a fugitive? I won't be able to speak to my family or operate normally. Plus, it will cost a lot of money. I doubt I have enough.

I realize I'm not thinking straight. It has been a long night and day. I need sleep. I call the kids and tell them I love them. I promise to call first thing in the morning. Those poor kids. What have we done? They are supposed to be going about their normal lives, instead they're huddled around a telephone, their worlds crashing down, waiting on their idiot father to call and praying their mother is okay.

The next morning, I'm nervous to go into the banks. I'm convinced everyone in line is an undercover cop. I'm trying hard to appear normal, but I'm sweating profusely. In reality, no one is giving me a second glance and everyone is sweating.

It is the height of summer in the Caribbean, and it is ninety degrees outside. Everything goes smoothly.

Over the next few hours I meet with Victor to give him money and instruct him to send it to my family. I also give Victor extra to provide for me in the event I'm arrested.

Victor has the original contracts and loan agreements for our lending business, but I don't think he has all the documentation pertaining to other business I was doing that could prove the money we have was earned legally. I want him to have everything. The originals are in our office so we drive there, and I wait in the truck while Manuel goes in to get the files. A few minutes later he comes back and tells me that the office has been ransacked. It's empty. There is nothing left; no files, no office equipment not even furniture. I can't believe it. I ask Manuel to go and speak with our neighbor across the hall. It turns out the police were there yesterday afternoon, and they loaded everything into pick-up trucks and left.

I need those records. Without them I won't be able to prove money we have was earned through our business. I have a back-up of everything on a memory stick, but it's in my apartment. I know it isn't the smartest idea, but I decide to get it. I'm worried they may have been to my apartment also, so we will be careful.

We park down the street and watch the building and surroundings for close to an hour. From what we can see nothing looks out of the ordinary. We circle around the block and pass in front several times and park down the street. I ask Manuel to go and check it out. Ten minutes later he's back and reports everything normal.

The doorman tells him no one has been there, and he hasn't seen anyone or anything suspicious. We park in front of the building and go up. The plan is to get in and out fast.

Chapter 9

Busted

I FEEL A WAVE of relief when I open the door to the apartment and find everything as I left it. No one has been there. I go straight to my bedroom cupboard where I keep important documents and valuables and take the memory stick. We leave immediately.

As I get into the passenger seat I place the memory stick in my pocket. Just then my phone rings. It's Victor. He has news from his uncle, and he wants me to come back to his office right away. I'm sitting in an awkward position, and my gun is digging into the small of my back, so I put it on my lap while I finish the call.

Manuel has already made the turn on to John F. Kennedy Avenue and is slowing down at the first traffic light when, suddenly, out of nowhere, a black SUV cuts in front of us and stops dead, blocking our path.

"Manuel!"

-¿Qué maldita vaina! Manuel says as he turns the steering wheel hard to the left and tries to go around.

What the fuck?

Within seconds four more vehicles surround us, their doors already open with men jumping out, guns drawn. They yell:

- ¡Policía! ¡Levanten las manos!

Police! Put your hands up!

-jefe, Cuidado, ¡no se mueva!

Boss, Careful, don't move! Manuel says to me.

I look at him and see he's scared. We raise our hands, but all I can think about is the Browning 380 on my lap. Don't touch it. They'll kill me if they think I'm going for a gun.

The windows are only open a crack on my side, so Manuel yells loudly:

- ¡Tranquilo! ¡Tranquilo! Cálmensen, amigos! ¡Tranquilo!

Easy! Easy! Calm down, my friends! Easy!

They look like they want a reason to shoot. I'm freaking out. My arms are raised, and I don't want to say I have a gun on my lap for fear they'll misunderstand and take it as a threat. So, I yell:

- ¡No disparen! ¡No disparen! ¡Estamos obedeciendo! ¡Oyes! ¡Estamos obedeciendo! ¡No disparen!

Don't shoot! Don't shoot! We're obeying! You hear! We're obeying! Do not shoot!

One of them approaches the front windshield on the passenger side, but I'm not sure if he can hear or understand what I'm saying through the window and the noise of passing traffic from the overpass above.

Manuel says to me in a quiet voice:

-No se mueva jefe! ¡No se mueva!

Don't move, Boss! Don't move!

He doesn't need to tell me. I instantly think back to a night I was leaving a casino in a well-known downtown hotel, where I saw the aftermath of a police operation in the parking lot. Three car thieves were lying dead on the ground. I don't think they were armed.

-Oye, no me estoy moviendo, ¡pero tengo una pistola arriba de mis piernas! No voy a tocarla!

"Listen, I'm not moving, but I have a gun on my lap! I'm not going to touch it!" I tell him as I gesture with my chin towards my lap.

He looks through the front windshield at my lap and sees the gun.

-¡Mantenga sus manos arriba!

Keep your hands up!

I keep my hands raised, afraid to move a muscle. I have no doubt if I move he'll blow my head off. Another one approaches the driver's side and shouts at Manuel:

- ¡Abra las puertas!

Unlock the doors!

Manuel releases the locks, and they pull both doors open.

- ¡No se muevan! ¡No se muevan!

Don't move! Don't move!

The cop reaches inside and takes the gun off my lap. Then he grabs me by the arm and begins to pull me out of the car. The same thing is happening to Manuel. Another cop grabs my other arm, and they throw me to the ground and tell me to lie still. The other cops are standing over me, guns pointed at my head. Seconds later, they have my hands behind my back and place handcuffs on my wrists. Then they lift me off the ground violently and ask me if there are any more weapons in the car. I tell them there's a gun in the glove box. They've already disarmed Manuel.

I want to deflate the situation so I say:

-No somos peligrosos. Solo tenemos las armas para la protección. Tenemos licencias para las armas. No haremos nada. Estamos cumpliendo.

We aren't dangerous. We only have the guns for protection. We have permits for the weapons. We won't do anything. We are complying.

It must have some effect because their demeanor changes from aggressive to calmer vigilance. Two of them jump into the front of my truck while two place me in the back and close the doors. Then they do something unexpected. The one in the passenger seat turns around and removes my handcuffs and tells me if I try to run he'll shoot me.

"What's in your pockets?" the one in the passenger seat asks.

"My wallet, passport, a memory stick, and some money."

"Empty them!" he orders.

I take my wallet, passport, and the memory stick out and hand them to him.

"What are you going to do with that? I need my passport, and there's only credit cards and my Cedula in my wallet. And I need that memory stick."

"Don't worry. We'll take good care of this."

"The money?" he asks.

"What about it? It's my money. You can't have it."

"Señor, give me the money I will put it in an envelope. It will remain with your property. You can give it to me, or I can take it from you. Which one do you prefer?"

I take the money out of my pocket.

"Count it, so we know how much there is!"

"It's about ten thousand dollars," I say.

"Count it to be sure," he tells me.

He watches as I count. "There's 9840 dollars."

"Count it again."

I recount the money. He takes a manila envelope from his briefcase and writes my name and the amount on it. He places the money in the envelope and seals it. Then he places my wallet, passport, and the memory stick in another envelope and seals that one.

I start to believe they may be entering my things into evidence and aren't going to rob me.

I say again: "I need my things. You can't take them from me. I need them."

"Don't worry, Señor. They're safe with us. We're taking you to our office. Someone is waiting to see you."

He signals to one of the other cars to go ahead of us and another takes our rear. The lead car puts a siren on its roof, and seconds later, we're moving through parting traffic.

We arrive at a large complex, and I'm hustled out of my truck and into a court yard. They handcuff me again. I ask the cop what they're doing with my vehicle and he answers:

"Don't worry, Señor. It's safe with us."

Two of them take positions to the right and left of me, hold my arms and begin to escort me into the building. I hear another vehicle pull up as we walk, so I look back to see two cops get out and open the backdoor to remove Manuel. They are escorting him into the building also. They seem to want us separated.

We walk up three flights of stairs and down a long corridor to a door with a sign on it that reads: Interpol.

Interpol? What the...?

We walk inside, and I see a large work space with about ten desks; people working. I notice one man who looks incredibly familiar. The cops escorting me tell me to sit down and wait as they disappear through a door.

I keep looking at the familiar guy and suddenly it comes to me. He was sitting next to me at the barber shop only days before. He must be able to tell by my expression that I figured it out because he smiles, gives me a nod and puckers his lips pointing them in my direction: a Dominican trait.

Minutes later, the one cop returns, removes my handcuffs and tells me to walk ahead of him through the door he went into earlier. There's another short corridor, and we walk to another office.

We go in. There are three men waiting for me. One of them looks Dominican, but the other two seem like Americans. That's when I realize I know one of the Americans also. He was playing at my golf club on the weekend. He was in a group in front of me, and they were playing incredibly slowly. We crossed them at the greens on almost every hole. Unbelievable!

The Dominican says:

"Señor, my name is General Francesco-Javier Gomez, and I am the head of the International Police in Dominican Republic. These two gentlemen are special agents Conroy and Wendell. They are with the FBI. Jou have been arrested under a warrant and extradition request filed by the United States Government. Jou have the right to an attorney. Do jou want one?"

"Sir, why am I here? I've done nothing wrong," I say mostly because I don't know what else to say."

"Señor eStelman. I will ask jou again, do jou want an attorney? Is jour right."

"No. Not at this moment."

"Okay, gentlemens. Jou need me, I'm in my office," he says as he gets up to leave the room.

Conroy is the older and bigger of the two. Wendell is the one who was at the golf course.

Conroy looks at me and says:

"Mr. Stelman, you know why you're here. We have your wife. She'll be going to New York where she's being prosecuted for conspiracy to commit wire fraud through telemarketing and money laundering. The same thing is happening to you. We know everything. What we want from you is three things. If we get your cooperation with these three things, we will tell the United States Attorney you helped us, and it will be better for you. If you don't, then it will be very bad for you."

I just look at them.

Thirty seconds pass, and he continues:

"The first thing we want is for you to tell us where we can find Roland Ross. The second thing we want are the people who sold you the leads. The third thing we want is for you to consent to your extradition. It means you will be taken in front of the Supreme Court of the Dominican Republic for a hearing, where you will tell three Supreme Court judges that you are agreeing to be extradited and you have chosen to do so of your own volition and you were not coerced, or threatened, by anyone. Mr. Stelman, we don't like you. Understand, you are going to the United States no matter what you do. However, if you make it easy, we will tell the US Attorney you were cooperative. That may help you."

"I would like an attorney, please."

"You just said you didn't want one."

"No, I said I didn't want one for the moment. Now I do."

"Well, we'll let the Dominicans know, but in the meantime, we want to know if you are going to help us."

"I certainly want to cooperate in any way I can, but I will not say anything until I speak to a lawyer."

"You'll get a lawyer, we just don't know when. Where's Ross?"

"Sir. I want a lawyer please."

"Like I said, we'll tell the Dominicans you want a lawyer. Are you going to help us?"

I look at Wendell and say: "You're a very slow golfer."

"I don't play that often. You play four days a week. You can afford it with all that money you stole."

I say nothing.

Conroy continues:

"We've been watching you for a year now. You're going to prison. How long you go for, is up to you. Don't be an idiot. You have a chance right here, right now, to help yourself. Don't blow your only chance. Your kids are going to miss their parents. Do the smart thing here, Mr. Stelman."

"I would like an attorney please."

And that's how it went for the next three hours. I wouldn't cooperate, and they kept promising me a lawyer. When it became clear I wasn't going to give them what they wanted, Conroy said:

"Mr. Stelman, you had your chance. We'll tell the Dominicans you want to call a lawyer and I suppose they'll get around to letting you do that. In the meantime, you'll be staying in their jail. It won't be pleasant. If you decide to change your mind, tell the Dominicans, and if it's not too late, we can meet again."

They both get up to leave, and Wendell opens the door. I'm sitting and watching them go when Conroy turns and says:

"Oh, and Mr. Stelman, it's been my experience people from our part of the world don't last too long in Dominican jails. It's not like that nice building in Naco you live in. Usually they beg to help us after twenty-four hours. Good luck and have a nice night."

Chapter 10

The Dungeon

AFTER THE HEAVIES FROM the FBI leave, I'm cuffed by the Dominican police and brought back into the main office. Manuel is sitting cuffed in a chair.

They tell him to stand up, and they escort us out of the Interpol offices and back the way we came. We cross the court yard to another building that looks to be in its original state; probably nineteen thirties. It's poorly lit and the plaster walls and ceilings are chipped and cracked. It's so hot it feels like we stepped into an oven. There's a pungent humid odor in the air, and I see water stains all around us. There's black mold growing on the walls and floors.

We pass through a small corridor and down a dark narrow staircase. I'm afraid I'll trip and fall because I feel chunks of stair broken under my feet. I hear Dominican bachata music playing as we descend. At the bottom we turn left into an open area that has a dingy jail cell on its back wall. It's like a Hollywood set for a dungeon scene in a horror movie, only it's real.

The ceilings are low, maybe six feet, with a light bulb in the center that doesn't do the job. The cell is no more than twenty by twenty with one wooden bench against the side wall. I see another prisoner inside sleeping naked on the floor. I hope he's sleeping.

Outside the cell a guard is sitting at a desk on a wooden chair, eating rice and beans and listening to the radio. He's wearing the standard issue Policia Nacional uniform, and he looks as tough as his sun-beaten skin. I notice a black baton lying on top of the desk next to a small fan that's pointed at his face.

The heat is overwhelming. If the building upstairs is an oven down here it's an inferno. My clothes are already damp and sweat's dripping from my brow. I can't imagine staying in this hell hole ten minutes, let alone the twenty-four hours Conroy gave me. Those fuckers know their business.

The guard stands up and salutes one of our escorts referring to him as Commander. Then he takes a ring of keys from the desk drawer and opens the cell, while the other cop removes our handcuffs. The naked guy sits up as we're ushered inside. One of his eyes is swollen shut, and his face is black and blue. He has some nasty welts on his head and green and purple bruises all over his body.

Manuel whispers not to talk in front of him. I understand. He thinks he may be an informant for the police, so I nod. The guard locks the cell door behind us, and the commander tells him to follow him. They disappear around the corner, and I can hear them talking but not what they're saying.

I look around and feel sick. There's garbage from food wrappings and God knows what else on the filth-covered floor. Towards the back is a black barrel filled with dirty putrid water; a small pail floating on top. The smell of human excrement and urine is over powering, and I gag. Manuel looks like he's about to puke. He lifts his T-shirt to cover his nose.

At the back wall, the concrete floor has a two-foot, ten-inch deep feces covered hole, which I realize is the source of the smell and what must be the toilet. There's no water in the hole and from what I can see there probably never is. I just figured out what the pale is for. The floor reeks of old crusty food and spilled drinks. Insects crawl on sticky surfaces. I see a window at the top of the wall near the ceiling that's been enclosed with red brick from the outside, robbing us of any chance to get day light or breathe circulated air. It's stifling.

Even the bench is sticky, and I see mouse, or maybe they're rat droppings, underneath it. I promise myself I won't sit. I'll stand all night if I have to. A failed short-term strategy.

The guard is back and Manuel asks him for something to clean the bench with. He tells him he doesn't have anything. I say "you must have toilet paper at least" and he says he doesn't. Shit, that means…

Our cell mate strikes up a conversation. Manuel asks him how long he's been here and what happened to him. He says three days. The police arrested him because they thought he robbed the wife of an important politician. They beat him badly. He doesn't know when he'll get out. No one will tell him, and he doesn't have any family. He's hungry. He has no money for food. Do we have any? Can we buy him something to eat? The last time he ate was a day and a half ago when another prisoner shared his food with him. Manuel says he'll try and get him something to eat tomorrow. I wave Manuel into the corner with me and whisper to him:

"Manuel, why are they keeping you here? Are they charging you with something?"

"No, Jefe. They brought me here because I asked them to. I told them I've been working for you for two years and you are good people. I told them how much you help my family. They said you haven't broken any laws in this country, but they had to arrest you because the Gringos were applying a lot of pressure. The Gringos don't want you to see anyone, so the only way was for them to put me in here with you."

"Jefe, what happened when you went inside the other office?"

I told him everything that happened with the FBI and then I said:

"Manuel, if you're not in any trouble you don't have to stay here."

"No, Jefe, the guard will let me out when I'm ready. That's what the commander was talking to him about. I know the Commander's wife's brother. He served with me in the military."

"Wow, okay, that's lucky. Maybe I have a better chance than they wanted to give me. Manuel, you need to call Victor and tell him where I am and what's going on. He has to come and get me out of here."

"Okay, Jefe. I'll call him early in the morning and tell him."

"Then call Andie and tell her I'm okay. Don't tell her where I am, just say they have me, and I'm safe. I'll call as soon as I can."

"Okay."

"Manuel, I'm going to pay you three months of salary in advance. Victor will give it to you. I know you're worried about your job right now even if you're not saying it. I need you to be available to help me, and I can't have you worried about money. This way you'll have plenty of time to find work or go back to driving the taxi. I don't know how this will end up, but you need to assume I won't be around."

"Thank you, Jefe. I appreciate it. You know I need to support my family. Thank you. I'll help you. Jefe, I'll bring you food tomorrow."

"You don't think they'll feed me?"

"No Jefe. There's no food here. If someone doesn't bring food, you won't eat. That's why he was asking us for food. I'll bring extra, so if someone is hungry you'll have something to give them. If not, they will try and take yours. Don't trust anyone in here. I'll try to come every day if they let me. If I can't, pay the guard, and he will buy you food. You don't have to pay a lot, just buy him food or give him 150 pesos. You'll need money. I'll tell Victor to bring you money or he can give it to me, and I'll bring it to you.

"Manuel, I don't expect to be here so long. I better not be. I can't live like this."

"The Gringos will make it very hard on purpose. They want you to do what they ask. They know you will suffer in here. Maybe you need to do what they ask, Jefe. Bad things can happen in here."

"Manuel, I don't know. Let's see what happens tomorrow. Manuel, I have a favor to ask. Can you give me your shirt? You have an under shirt. I need it to try and get comfortable. Talk to the guard about getting us some stuff to clean this shit hole. I'll get my roommate to help. Also, ask him to give us clean water to wash the place down."

"Okay, Jefe, I'll try but he may not do anything unless you pay him."

"Just try, Manuel. Tell him I'll pay him. And Manuel, bring toilet paper. If they don't let me use a bathroom it looks like that may be the only way, as I point to the hole in the ground."

Okay, Jefe. I will, don't worry. I'm going now. Jefe, don't trust anyone in here. It's not safe. You're a foreigner to them. It's only him right now but there could be others."

"Manuel, I'll be okay. Just make sure Victor comes quickly. Once I see him, I'll be able to get out of here, I'm sure."

"I hope so, Jefe. I'm not so sure though. These Gringos have a lot of power and influence. But I hope so."

"Jefe, I'll bring a cell phone and put it in the bag with the food. I'll pay the guard, and he will let you have it. Don't let anyone see it, and don't use it when anyone's around. This is a holding jail so people will come and go. If someone sees it they will try and take it from you or they'll want to use it. Hide it. You won't have a way to charge it, so only use it in an emergency to call me."

"It sounds like more trouble than it's worth. Just tell the guard to let me use his. I'll pay him."

"Okay, maybe you're right. I'll talk to him. I don't know if he'll do it though. Anyway, I'll see you tomorrow in the afternoon. Maybe Victor will have you out of here by then and I won't have to come. I hope so," he smiles.

"I hope so. Okay, Manuel, go home to your family. Have a good night."

- ¡Guardia! ¡Abra la puerta por favor!

Guard! Open the door please!

My plan to stand up all night doesn't last long. Five minutes after Manuel leaves, I need to rest. The tension and stress are starting to release and coupled with the heat and bad air flow, I am getting sleepy.

My jeans are damp and heavy on my body so I take them off and roll them up with my T-shirt and place them on the bench as a pillow. I lay Manuel's T-shirt on the bench and lie down. I am miserably uncomfortable so I put my shoes under my clothes to prop up my head. Better. I look over at my roommate who is already asleep on the ground, his clothes spread out under him. I think to myself, the only difference between us is I'm wearing underwear. Otherwise I might be naked too.

I start to drift off, but I hear something scurrying around, and it freaks me out. I imagine a rat biting me so I sit up quickly and call out to my roommate.

-Amigo, ¿qué es ese sonido que escucho? ¿Son ratas?

Friend, tell me what is that sound I hear? Is it rats?

-Sí, americano, pero no te preocupes. No te molestaran.

Yes, American, but don't worry. They won't bother you.

- ¿Estás seguro?

Are you sure?

-Claro americano. Seguro. No hay problema. Duermes bien americano.

Yes, I'm sure. There's no problem. Sleep good, American.

I lie back down and hope he's right. He thinks I'm American. I wonder if that's good or bad in here. I scratch at my ankles. Damn bugs. Please God, get me out of here! Fuck that Conroy!

Chapter 11

The Colonel

IT'S NOT REALLY SLEEP. I'm not sure what it is. I'm aware of the guard standing up, sitting down, adjusting his radio, eating. The scurrying sound becomes background noise and my cellmate's snoring, a symphony. It's like some form of mild trance. Discomfort, soreness, occasional pain, move, adjust, switch sides, reshape the clothes under my head, reposition the shoes, scratch my leg, another bite, my back, my stomach, sit up, lie back down, the heat. Somehow, I drift off into some state of semi-consciousness, and maybe, just maybe, my mind rests enough to help me face tomorrow.

Someone's at the cell door. I sit up and rub my eyes. I'm drenched. My body aches from this fucken bench. The stench is worse now. Flies buzz around the hole in the ground. Roommate's still asleep. Amazing.

"Señor Stelman. Buenos Dias. I am Colonel Ramon Sanchez of Interpol. I'm in charge of your case. I'm going to take you out of here so that you can use the bathroom and get something to eat in our office. Get dressed please, Señor."

There is a God. I'm so happy.

"Colonel, what time is it?"

"It's almost nine o'clock, Señor Stelman."

"Shit, already? Colonel, I'm waiting for my lawyer. Have you heard from him? His name is Victor Perez."

"No, Señor, I don't think so. Maybe someone else, but they would have mentioned it."

"That's strange, I expected him by now. Can I call him?"

"Señor Stelman. I cannot let you use my cell phone. I am sorry."

"A regular phone then, in your office?"

"We will see."

"But Colonel, I have the right to speak to my lawyer. I'm sure calling my lawyer isn't a problem. I mean, aren't I entitled to a phone call? Isn't that how it works?"

"Yes, yes, of course. You will be allowed to speak with your lawyer. Let's take you first to the bathroom, so you can wash and use the toilet.

"Thank you, Colonel. I appreciate it."

We cross the court yard and go back into the building I was in yesterday. We climb the stairs to the fourth floor and walk down a corridor that overlooks a ground floor lobby. Half-way down is a common bathroom.

"Señor Stelman. Please, take as long as you need. I will be right outside the door. I didn't use the handcuffs, but it is required."

"I really appreciate that, Colonel. You won't have any problems with me."

"I have no doubt, Señor Stelman."

There are four toilet stalls, so I choose the last. Since leaving the cell, I haven't felt the need, but I'm trying hard to go because I don't know when I'll get another chance. I hear the outside door opening.

"Señor Stelman, is everything okay, Señor?"

"Yes, Colonel, just trying to use the toilet."

"Okay because we should go."

"Colonel, I just sat down. You told me to take as much time as I need. I need more time, please."

"Yes, yes, of course. Take more time."

"Thank you, Colonel."

I go back to the task at hand, but I'm not having much luck. The thought of having to go on the floor in that filthy cell in all the shit is stressing me out so much that I just can't right now. Damn! The door again.

"Señor Stelman. Are you ready, Señor?"

"Colonel, I'm not. Please give me time."

"Yes, but there is no more time Señor. We need to go now, please.

"Shit! Is this guy serious? "Colonel, I can't seem to go right now, but I know I will need to. Will I be able to come back after?"

"I'm not sure, Señor Stelman. It depends. You can't go now?"

"That's what I said, Colonel. I guess it's because of the pressure. You know how these things can be."

"Yes, yes, of course. We will try, Señor."

"Okay, Colonel. Just give me three more minutes to wash up. I'm very dirty."

"Yes, of course. Please hurry."

Damn, this guy's unbelievable. He says yes to everything but then doesn't let me do anything. I hope he keeps his word about coming back later.

There's three sinks with a soap dispenser above each one fastened to the wall. They're all empty. Shit! I call out to Sanchez who is just on the other side of the door.

"Colonel, there's no soap in the dispensers. Is it possible to get soap?"

"No soap? That's strange. I will ask someone after. For now, you wash with water, si?"

"Yes, Colonel. No choice. Water's better than nothing. Maybe later when I come back I can get soap."

"Yes, yes, of course."

"Okay, Colonel, just give me a few more minutes please."

"Of course, Señor."

I take my T-shirt off and splash water on my neck, chest and shoulders. It's not cold, but it feels nice and refreshing. I begin to rinse my face and head when he walks back in and says:

"Señor Stelman, we need to go right now. You are taking too long, Señor."

"Okay, okay, Colonel, thirty seconds more, please!"

"I am sorry, Señor. We need to go now."

He stands behind me as I splash water on my head and face. I'm getting annoyed, but then I think, I better keep my mouth shut. I can't wait for Victor to get me the fuck out of here.

Five minutes later we're at Interpol and entering the Colonel's office. There's an outer area with two desks pushed together and some filing cabinets along the wall. Two cops are sitting at the desks watching a soap opera on a wall mounted television. The Colonel tells them in Spanish to let me sit at one desk and watch television with them. The he tells me he'll be back. The office is air-conditioned. I'm so happy to be here instead of that filthy cell.

When the show finishes, one of the cops asks if I'm hungry, and I say very. He leaves and twenty minutes later he's back with two grilled cheese sandwiches, which I devour. I ask when I'll be able to make my phone call, and they tell me I need to speak to the Colonel about that. I ask them to get the Colonel, but they say he's very busy and will come when he can. I'm frustrated.

It's two o'clock, and I still haven't seen the Colonel. I tell one of the cops that I must see the Colonel immediately. He tells me I need to wait. At three o'clock I demand to see him so I watch as he goes down the hallway, knocks on his door and enters his office. A few minutes later the cop is back and says the Colonel is coming soon.

An hour later the Colonel appears and asks me to come into his office.

"Señor Stelman, they gave you something to eat, yes?"

"Yes, Colonel Sanchez, thank you. Colonel, I want to call my lawyer now. The entire day is passed, and I haven't had a chance to call him."

"Ah, but they didn't tell you?"

"Tell me? What? Who?"

"I am sorry. I thought they informed you. Your lawyer called, and he will be coming tomorrow morning. He couldn't come today. I am sorry. I thought they told you."

"What do you mean he couldn't come? That's not acceptable, Colonel. Please let me call him."

"There is no need. He will be here tomorrow."

"Colonel, I have been asking for a lawyer since last night. I am not familiar with the law, but I assume you're obligated to let me see a lawyer."

"Yes, of course. The Dominican Republic is a democratic country with the rule of law."

"That's what I mean. I should have seen my lawyer by now."

"Yes, Señor Stelman, but it is he who couldn't come today. That is not our fault."

"I understand, Colonel, but I was hoping to get released today. I don't want to spend another night here in your jail."

"Señor Stelman, may I speak openly?"

"Yes, Colonel, please do."

"You should agree to be extradited. You will not beat the Americans. We see it all the time. You will not be successful fighting them. It will be much easier on you to go to New York and deal with your problem."

"Colonel, I don't know my rights. I need information. That's why I need to see my lawyer."

"I understand, Señor Stelman, and you will see him tomorrow. The problem is we have no choice but to keep you in jail until this issue of your extradition is resolved. It can take a long time if you don't agree. The jails here are not good, Señor. As you already know, you don't want to be in jail here."

"Colonel, it sounds like you're threatening me."

"No, no, Señor. On the contrary, I'm trying to help you. Once you agree to the extradition order, the Americans will bring you to New York. Until you do, we have to keep you here. We have nothing against you, Señor. You did nothing wrong in our country, but the Americans, they want you very much, and they usually get what they want. You will spend time, money, and your life will be very hard. In the end, you will be extradited. I am just giving you my advice based on my experience."

"My lawyer will get me released from here when I see him."

"No, Señor Stelman. No, he won't. He will not be able to."

Señor Stelman, in a couple of hours I will leave for the day, and I will walk you back to the jail. I am busy with an important matter so I cannot spend any more time with you right now. If you need to use the bathroom I will ask one of my men to take you just before we go back. In the meantime, enjoy the comfort of our office. We are trying to make you comfortable."

"Colonel, one last thing, please. The man who works for me, Manuel, did he come today to visit me? Do you know?"

"Yes, he did, Señor. We told him you could not have visitors today. He said he will try to come tomorrow."

"Colonel, please. Let me see him tomorrow. He's in touch with my children. They are very worried.

"We will see tomorrow, Señor."

"Colonel, will I spend time here tomorrow?"

"We would love to have you, Señor Stelman."

Chapter 12

The Musician

IT IS ALMOST SEVEN when Sanchez comes out and tells me he will escort me back himself. I am dreading it. I ask to use the bathroom one more time. As we walk across the court yard to the fifteenth century dungeon, I complain about the deplorable conditions.

He agrees, then says the government doesn't have the money to spend on such problems. He's very sympathetic though and explains it's the reason he let me spend the day in the office, and furthermore, why I should consent to be extradited. He says, once I sign, they'll house me in a large prison under much better conditions until the Americans pick me up. I find it hard to believe any prison in this country could provide good conditions, but I'll take better.

As we walk down the stairway to hell, I hear voices, lots of voices. I turn the corner at the bottom of the stairs and can't believe my eyes. The guard and two policemen are herding at least twenty men into the holding cell.

Are they fucken serious?

If conditions were inhumane before, they're down-right dangerous now. It's barely big enough for three people and with me and the guy from last night, it's packed like a puppy mill on 60 Minutes. There isn't enough space on the floor for everyone to sleep. Then there's the hygiene issue; only one bathroom.

The one consolation, my friend from last night is picking up the garbage and cleaning the shit in and around the hole in the ground with a small shovel, a broom and a bucket the guard gave him. He's

61

already dumped the barrel of filthy water down a drain next to the stairs and refilled it with cleaner water from a hose that runs from a faucet above the drain. What immediately comes to mind is why wasn't this done sooner? Maybe there's a by-law regarding the ratio of people allowed in a confined area relative to the quantity of piss and shit and filth per square foot of space, before the area has to be cleaned.

I stop dead in my tracks and say to Sanchez: "I'm not going in there."

"I'm afraid there is no choice, Señor Stelman."

"Colonel, I had a heart attack last year and I won't be able to breathe in there. There are far too many people for such a small space, and it's too hot. Please, find me an alternative."

That heart attack happened after playing thirty-six holes of golf for three straight days on two hours of sleep each night. On the last day, I was having pain in my left shoulder and arm and feeling a bit off. The pain was probably from the thousands of swings at a golf ball and the "bit off," dehydration from the tropical sun. Nevertheless, I got scared and talked myself into a frenzy. I went to the hospital where they were convinced I was having a heart attack because my heart rate was forty-five beats per minute. I told them it's always like that, but they insisted on doing an angioplasty a procedure where a small tube is passed through the groin area up to the coronary arteries to remove any plaque that may be causing a blockage.

They couldn't find a problem, but I guess, to save face, the doctor labeled it a heart attack. I'm sure it wasn't, but the story has its usefulness right now.

"There is no alternative, Señor Stelman. You must go in."

"I'm not."

"I don't want to ask the guard to force you. There is no choice, Señor. I will come and get you again tomorrow. It's not so bad."

"Not so bad? It's worse than bad. It's inhumane, Colonel."

"I am sorry, Señor Stelman."

"What will I do if I have trouble breathing? I was having problems last night, and there were only two of us."

"I will tell the guard to let you out of the cell for a few minutes and walk you outside for fresh air. But do not abuse this, because he will only do it once or twice, Señor. I must leave; you need to go in."

"Colonel, please find another place to put me."

"Okay, Señor Stelman, I will."

"Thank you."

"I mean tomorrow. I will try tomorrow."

No choice. I have to endure one more night of hell in this filthy stinking over-crowded rat hole. Shit!

"Colonel, please tell the guard to let me out if I don't feel good."

"Of course, Señor Stelman."

I'm the last one in so everyone's looking. The heat is intolerable. I once read a magazine article about prison conditions in El Salvador. There were pictures of men stuffed into large cages on the prison grounds. This isn't quite as bad, but it's not that far off. A quick count tells me there are twenty-three of us in this stinking sewer.

Actually, the stench isn't as awful as it was last night, but with so many men in here, how long will that last? There are just too many of us for one hole in the ground. The dungeon administrators should really consider breaking a bit more of the floor to expand the toilet facilities; at least two holes, bring this place up to code. I hope the situation is temporary and that some, or most of these guys, get released soon. I don't see how everyone can stay in here for an extended period of time.

Everyone's miserable and soaked in sweat. Most have their shirts off. Two guys are dousing themselves with the water from the barrel. Some are sitting on the floor, others standing because there's no place. The bench is already taken, and obviously I won't be sleeping on it tonight. Last night I was cursing the bench, now it looks like a Sealy Postherpetic King Size bed. Does the word grateful come to mind?

There are two separate groups in here. One is a band of musicians from Santiago who were on their way to play at one of the big hotels in the city, dressed in their stage clothes, when the police stopped them for a traffic violation and found some unregistered fire arms in their van. I suppose they didn't have enough money to pay off the police, so they brought them here. They'll either find a way or spend some time in the dungeon.

The other, is a street gang from a very rough barrio in the city. Their leader is a short sinewy-muscled, tattooed kid of about twenty years old. If you look up "tough" in the dictionary you'll see his picture. His friends aren't much different. These are very hardened kids from a very bad place, where conditions are dismal.

One of them is of particular concern. At about five eight, and 180 pounds, he's a bigger version of his boss. Scars on his forehead, cheek, head and chest, look like old knife wounds, and he's missing some front teeth. He's loud, and he's looking to make trouble for someone, so I'm trying to avoid eye contact with him. The last thing I need is to get the shit beat out of me by him and his friends. I'd have no chance.

My friend from last night asks:

"Americano, where did they take you?"

"Interpol."

"Interpol?"

"Yes, they arrested me for the Americans, the FBI. They want to extradite me to New York." I notice most of the guys are listening.

"Interpol. FBI. You're a narco. A jefe."

"I'm not a narco. I'm here for laundering money." I don't need to explain the whole thing. Money laundering will suffice. He'll understand money laundering.

"Money laundering. You're a narco, I know," he says like a true expert.

It dawns on me, if they think I'm a "narco boss" it may benefit me in my quest for survival. Dominicans have this respect that borders on fear for authority and power. Maybe it's ingrained because of their history. Authoritarian regimes ruled the island for the majority of its existence, so the people have this almost submissive demeanor when confronted with power. They also romanticize the narco life. I decide to exploit this for self-preservation.

"Amigo, what's your name?"

"Roberto," he answers.

"Okay, Roberto, I'm not a jefe, understand? Now don't talk about it anymore, is that clear?

My denial and unwillingness to discuss it convinces him even more and he answers:

"Okay, Jefe. Okay, I'm sorry."

I move towards the wall and two of the musicians make enough room for me to sit on the floor. Seems my newly acquired urban legend is already paying dividends. I decide to carve out this prime piece of real estate for the night. I'll sleep right here next to the wall. This way I'll only have someone on one side of me.

On the other side of the cell, the trouble-maker is terrorizing a new-found victim. He's standing over one of the musicians, a kid of about nineteen, who's sitting on the floor hugging his knees and rocking back and forth. I think autism, but it's probably just fear.

The barrio bully wants the Jordans the kid's wearing. They're probably knock-offs, but it doesn't matter to the bully, because he likes them, real or not. He tells the kid to give them to him in one minute, or he'll take them. The kid is just staring at the floor, rocking.

I look around at the other musicians wondering if anyone will try and stop this but no one does. They're out-numbered and out-classed. They're all scared, I can see it. It confirms how dangerous the situation is. The other barrio kids are laughing and egging the bully on. They think it's hilarious. I feel bad for this kid, and I want to stop it, but I'm afraid I'll end up with a problem I can't handle.

I look at the guard hoping he'll tell him to knock it off, but he doesn't seem to give a shit. I know he sees what's going on, but he chooses to ignore it and do nothing.

Barrio bully starts counting down and his gang joins in.

Diez...nueve...ocho...

The kid is rocking faster now, and he looks very distressed. I look to the guard again expecting him to do something, but the prick just turns up his radio. What the fuck?

...siete...seis...cinco...cuatro...

I'm not sure if anything's really going to happen, but if something does I don't want to get trampled so I stand up and stay against the wall.

...tres...dos...uno.

- ¡Se acabó el tiempo!

"Times up!" The bully announces as he bends down to pull the shoes off the kid's feet.

The kid resists, but the bully grabs one foot and pulls hard. He falls onto his back and continues the struggle.

Then it happens. Barrio bully cocks his fist in the air, and with all his strength and weight, punches the kid violently in the head above his ear. The kid crumbles to the ground unconscious. The bully doesn't care because he hits him again, then again.

The barrio kids are laughing. What entertainment. The musicians are petrified, and I'm staring in disbelief.

Roberto steps in between the bully and the kid and tells him to stop, but his work isn't done and his friends are in a feeding frenzy. He pushes Roberto out of the way, pulls the kids shoes off and raises them in the air triumphantly. Then he sits down, removes his own shoes and puts on his prize.

I'm watching the kid hoping he's not hurt too badly when I see him move. I assume he's coming to but then realize something's wrong. His movements are sharp, staccato-like, and I realize he's convulsing. Shit he's having a seizure!

Enough! I move quickly and notice a pool of blood on the floor. It's leaking out of his mouth, and I'm not sure if it's from the punches he took, or if he's biting his tongue. I try to turn him on his side but his body is too rigid so I ask his band mates for help.

Two of his friends join in, and we manage to get him on his side. We're struggling to keep him there because the convulsions are getting stronger and more frantic. I've seen this sort of thing several times before, and I remember a doctor friend of mine telling me seizures appear more dramatic than they actually are. Still, this kid needs medical attention.

-¡Guardia! ¡El necesita un doctor! ¡Algo está mal con él!

Guard! He needs a doctor! Something's wrong with him!

He's ten yards away, watching through the bars, and the fucker won't even get up out of his chair. I'm looking at him and screaming, but he won't do a thing. It doesn't make any sense. How can a human being watch someone suffer and do absolutely nothing? What the fuck is wrong with this guy?

-¡Guardia! ¡Necesita ayuda! ¡Está en problemas! ¡Por favor! ¡Ayudalo!

Guard! He needs help! He's in trouble! Please! Help him!

He just looks at me emotionless. Meanwhile barrio bully is laughing at me, but I ignore him and continue pleading with the guard for help. I'm getting angry, and I'm shouting at the top of my lungs. The musicians take up the cause and start yelling also.

Then I feel the convulsions slowing. The seizure's over. I stand up and move to the bars and tell the guard he better call someone or he'll have a problem. I don't know what the fuck I'm talking about, but I'm trying anything at this point. Then one of the musicians who was helping me keep him on his side says:

- ¡Americano, no está respirando!

American, he's not breathing!

- ¿Qué?

What? I ask.

- ¡No está respirando! ¡No puedo sentirlo respirar!

He's not breathing. I can't feel him breathe.

-¡Busca un pulso!

Check for a pulse! I say.

- ¡No sé cómo!

I don't know how, he tells me.

Another one of the musicians moves towards him and places two fingers on his neck and then without saying a word begins to administer CPR.

I turn back to the guard and scream:

-¡Hijo de puta! ¡Consigue ayuda ahora! ¡Se está muriendo! ¡No está respirando! ¿Qué sucede contigo? ¡Solo es un chico! ¡Ayudalo! ¿Me escuchas? ¡Ayudalo! ¡Llamá a alguien!

You son of a bitch! Get help now! He's dying! He's not breathing! What's wrong with you? He's only a kid! Help him! Do you hear me? Help him! Call someone!

Even the barrio toughs are quiet now. The bully tries to make light of what's happening, but his boss tells him to shut his mouth. I look towards him and give him a nod. He nods back.

The guard stands up and moves closer to the cell. It's been more than a minute, and the kid on the floor is still not breathing.

A few minutes later the musician administering CPR gives up and falls back to the floor exhausted.

-No sirve de nada. No está respirando. Él está muerto.

It's no use. I can't get him to breathe. He's dead.

Dead? Why? For what? He's a fucken teenager for God's sake. He wasn't bothering anyone. He was just trying to earn a few pesos playing his music, and he ends up dead in this stinking dirty shit hole.

The guard walks over to the cell door and tells me to step back as he opens the door. He yells at the barrio gang to carry the kid outside the cell and place him on the floor. Two of them take him by the arms and drag his lifeless body outside like a piece of garbage.

The guard orders them back into the cell, locks the door and calls someone on his cell phone.

"Now? Now you're calling for help? Fucken bastard! Rot in hell!" I scream in English. He has no clue what I said.

I'm so disgusted with what just happened and so sapped of energy that I just crumble to the floor in my spot on the wall. There's nothing to say. Such disregard for human life. I'm mortified.

Fifteen minutes later I'm staring at the kid's lifeless body lying on the floor. The rational part of me knows he's dead, but I keep hoping he'll cough and start breathing. I think for the first time about how bad a situation I'm in. If something were to happen to me…if I got sick or hurt no one would help. Conroy was right. I need to get out of here!

A big man appears at the bottom of the staircase dressed in a black uniform, and he looks down at the body. It's been more than an hour now. The guard jumps to his feet and addresses him as Commander. Finally, I think to myself. But he's no different than the guard. He just leans against the wall looking at the kid. He doesn't give a shit. I can see it on his face.

I don't say a word. I've got nothing left. The feeling of helplessness is overwhelming. The whole thing is just so senseless. I look at the bully and think; you killed him for no reason you motherfucker. I hope he gets charged with murder. I hope the commander finds out what happened and does something about it.

But deep down I know better. Nothing will happen. He was just a poor kid and nobody gives a shit. The guard was complicit for doing nothing so this won't see the light of day. The truth will never come out. I also know that if I say or do anything it will turn out very badly for me. The musicians won't do anything either for fear of the police.

The commander leaves a few minutes later but not before warning he doesn't want any more trouble. Thirty minutes later three men come and carry the body away.

Chapter 13

Lawyer

"MR. STELMAN, MY NAME is Lise Chalifoux. I'm from the Canadian embassy, and I'm here to make sure you're okay. Are you being treated well?"

We're in the Interpol offices. I was brought here at nine this morning after my night of continued hell. My clothes are smelly, dirty and damp, and I really need a shower. I didn't sleep at all. I tried, but one of the musicians was practically on top of me and with the mixture of heat, stench and the hard-concrete floor, there was no way to get comfortable enough. The only consolation, the sheer number of us kept the rats from visiting. I hope Sanchez keeps his word and puts me somewhere else tonight, if I'm still here.

"I guess so, other than the horrific jail they have me in; the conditions are appalling. I would like to call my family though. Can you help me with that? I haven't spoken to them since I was arrested, and they must be beside themselves with worry. Also, I haven't been able to see my lawyer. I don't know if this is intentional or not, but I need to see him."

"Mr. Stelman, unfortunately we don't have a lot of sway with the police or how they do things, and we can't intervene in your case or anything related. I will ask that you get a phone call. If you give me the information I can call your family and tell them I saw you and that you are okay. Other than that, there isn't much more we can do. I am here to verify that you are being treated humanely; that no one is hurting you and you have access to medical care if you need it. I have an

70

information booklet of consular services for citizens arrested abroad. It details what services we provide and what we don't. I urge you to read it so that you understand our role."

"I see. I am concerned with my legal rights though, Miss Chalifoux. I know I'm entitled to a lawyer, and I feel like they're trying to delay or keep it from happening. Surely you can help with that!"

"Actually, we are limited there as well. If you provide me with your lawyer's number, I can try and call him for you, but we don't get involved in legal representation in any way. I'll speak to the officer in charge to request that you see your lawyer immediately, but that's all I can do."

"Well, then, please do that. I'll give you his name and number. The police told me he called and said he would be here this morning, but I would like you to call anyway to be sure."

She jots down the information.

"Miss Chalifoux, one more thing if I may. When I was arrested the police confiscated everything I had on me including my passport, wallet, an important memory stick, and money that was for my children. They also took my vehicle and everything in it. I need the money, and I definitely need my passport. Can you help with this?"

"The FBI has your property, and they will keep it. As for the money and anything else, we don't get involved. I'm sorry. You'll need to speak with your lawyer."

"As I said, I've been trying to speak with my lawyer."

"You are in a foreign country Mr. Stelman. You are subject to the laws and judicial process of the Dominican Government. We can't do very much. I know you've lived here for a few years, you're a resident, and you speak Spanish. That is more than most. We will try to visit you at least twice a year if you remain incarcerated here, but Mr. Stelman, try not to stay. If you go to the United States and get convicted and sentenced to prison time, you can apply for the treaty transfer to Canada to serve your time closer to home."

She must be friends with Conroy. It's like she's lobbying for him.

"Okay, Miss Chalifoux, I thank you for your advice but I'd like to start by seeing my lawyer. You'll call him when you leave here?"

"As soon as I get back to the office, Mr. Stelman. I'll call your family as well."

"Thank you, I appreciate it."

After Chalifoux leaves I am allowed to use the bathroom, am given something to eat, and I drink two cups of strong black coffee. My head was pounding, but ten minutes after drinking the coffee, I feel better.

I am sitting in the office watching television when one of the cops tells me Victor called and said he would definitely be coming to see me today. Definitely this morning, just became definitely today.

At one o'clock Sanchez, charming and hospitable, comes to ask how I am doing. If the Interpol thing doesn't pan out I'm sure he'll make an excellent hotel manager in Punta Cana. I ask if I can speak to him privately, so he brings me into his office.

"Señor Stelman. How can I help you?"

"Colonel Sanchez, when your men arrested me they took my passport, wallet, a memory stick and cash. I would like to give the money and the memory stick to my lawyer. I withdrew the money from my bank account that morning. Can I get it? They put it in a manila envelope and wrote my name on it. You must have it."

"Money? I don't recall seeing any money. Are you sure?"

"Am I sure? Of course, I'm sure. They made me count it two times before they took it."

"Please wait outside for a few minutes while I check your claim with the arresting officers, Señor Stelman."

"Okay, but Colonel, it's not a claim, it's a fact. That's what happened."

"Let me investigate," he says with a sympathetic smile.

Ten minutes later, I'm in front of Sanchez.

"Señor, there is no record of any money or a memory stick."

"That's not possible, Colonel. I had it, they took it. Can I see the arresting officers? The ones who drove me here?"

"Unfortunately, they aren't available. They are working in another part of the country this week."

"I see. Colonel, what about my vehicle? Did that also disappear?"

"Oh no! In fact, it is outside. I have been driving it. It drives very nice. I didn't want anyone else to drive it, and if it is here on the Policia Nacional compound, someone would. I know the Americans want to seize it as part of your case so I doubt you will get it back."

This guy is amazing. He's basically telling me they stole my money, and he's using my truck. Then I remember the office.

"Colonel, where is everything that was taken from my office? I went there, and the neighbor told me the police took everything."

"I am not sure, Señor. I will check with the officers when they get back from their assignment."

He's giving me the Dominican fuck you. It's the old "the government doesn't pay us enough so we take what we can" routine. There's no point arguing. I have zero leverage. Maybe Victor will have more luck, but I doubt it.

"Colonel, I'd like to…".

His telephone rings, so he excuses himself to answer. A minute later he says:

"Señor Stelman, good news. Your lawyer just arrived. He is being escorted here, and I will give you a room to meet with him privately. He will only be able to stay for one hour. I trust that will be enough time," smiling like a dear friend.

"I hope so, Colonel. I hope so."

He shows me to a small room with a table and three chairs. This must be where they normally interrogate suspects because there isn't even a scrap of paper in here.

I wait nervously for almost fifteen minutes, and then the door opens.

"Victor, where have you been? Why didn't you come yesterday or this morning like you promised?"

"I would have come yesterday, but they said I couldn't. When I came this morning, they told me to come back this afternoon. I've been trying to see you since they brought you here. Are you okay?" He takes a seat across from me.

"No, I'm not okay. This place is a nightmare. They have me in this horrific cell. Last night there were more than twenty of us in there. It's fucken filthy. You need to get me out of here."

"Warren, I don't have good news on that front. Your case is complicated. If it was Dominican charges it would be different, but the United States had you arrested. Nobody will help. Nobody can, I'm sorry. I can't get you out. They're insisting you're a flight risk."

"Victor, they kept me from leaving the island before. I won't run anywhere. I'll put up a bond. They have my passport. I can't stay here in these conditions. Go see a judge, and get me out of here!"

"I've already spoken to a judge I know well. My uncle called a high ranking General in the Policia and another judge who is a good friend of his. It's the Americans. I'm sorry, Warren."

"Damn it! Victor, there's got to be a way!"

"I don't know one."

"Come on, Victor. Pay someone if you have to, but get me out of here! This place is terrible. They let me stay in the office for most of the day, but they put me in the cell at night. How long before they stop letting me stay in the office? I'll die in here. Find another judge! Talk to your uncle again!"

"He can't do anything! He tried! No one will take a chance because of the Americans. Warren, we've known each other for three years. We go out with our wives. Our kids are friends. You've always been a good client. I can take your money and tell you some bullshit, but I won't do that. I wish I could, but I can't get you bail! I could barely get in to see you!"

"I can't believe this! Fuck!"

"But…they want to extradite you. You can fight it."

"How? Explain."

"Warren, did you do what they are saying you did?"

"Yes Victor. I did."

He looks at me and says:

"I want to be up front. It's very hard to fight the Gringos. I had two other cases like this, and in the end, I lost both. They have money, power and influence. I can definitely drag it out for a long time, but it will be expensive for you. And I don't even mean my legal fees. That's not the problem. It's living in prison that will cost you a lot of money while we fight the case. On the other hand, it does give you leverage to deal with the charges from here. You may be able to negotiate a better plea agreement. One of my clients negotiated a five-year plea deal when they originally wanted to give him fifteen years."

"Plea agreement. So, the FBI knows that. That's why they're pushing so hard and why they've got me in this shit hole jail. They know if I fight, it can take a long time."

"Yes, they know that."

"But in the end, they'll win."

"That's been my experience. If you were Dominican you might have a better chance but a foreigner, I really doubt it.

"What do you mean by expensive to live in prison?"

"Look, they can't keep you here in the Policia Nacional jails. They're doing it now to scare you and pressure you into agreeing to be extradited. Once they know you are going to fight, they will have to move you to a prison. The Americans know the conditions here are untenable, and they don't want to risk exposing themselves to human rights violations. Of course, they can get away with it for a while by blaming it on the Dominican authorities. If you decide to fight and they try to keep you here, I will get a judge to order your transfer."

"Okay…" I'm listening attentively.

"But the prisons in this country are very bad. They are also dangerous, especially for a foreigner. If you want to live well and safely, you will have to pay for everything; your cell, your bed, food, everything. If you can't pay, they'll put you in general population. That, you don't want. Believe me!"

"Maybe I'm better off just facing the music and agreeing to extradition. They have Lana. I can't stay here while she's there alone. If I fight them, they can go harder on her. Also, I have some money, but not enough to last in a protracted fight against the United States of America."

"It will be expensive," he reiterates.

"Warren, there's something else. The Money Laundering Department came to my office with a fiscal. They had an order to seize all the documentation and files for the lending company. I had no choice. I had to give them everything. They're also freezing your bank accounts."

"What do you mean? What bank accounts?"

"Your business accounts and your personal accounts. Everything."

"How can they do that? The lending company is a legitimate operating company. It has nothing to do with any crime. In my personal accounts I can prove the money is not the proceeds of a crime."

"The Americans are trying to freeze all your money."

"Well, we're not going to let them. I want you to fight these seizures. Right away. If I have no money, I can't fight extradition, I can't hire a US lawyer, and I can't live in prison. I need my money!"

"Okay, that we can do. There's a good chance the courts will not support the freezing of your accounts providing we have proof the money isn't the proceeds of a crime."

"I had the proof when they arrested me. It was on a memory stick. They took it from me and said they were depositing it into evidence but now they claim they don't have it. A lot of the deposits to my personal accounts were from business I did with Carlos Ruiz. You vetted the paper work for those transactions. It's all legal. Tell me you have copies of those. Please!"

"I have copies of most of it, yes. The deposits we can get from the banks if we need them. Don't worry about that."

"Victor, when they arrested me they also took ten thousand dollars in cash, and now they deny taking it. I have no money. Can I count on you to bring me money when I need it?"

"Of course, that's why you gave me money to hold. I will ask my uncle to see if we can find out who stole your money, but you may not want to piss these guys off."

"C'mon Victor! You mean I should just let them steal it! Are you serious?"

"Look, I doubt you'll get it back, and you'll just make it worse for yourself by trying to bring attention to it. You know how things work here."

"In the meantime, I brought you money. Here's sixty thousand pesos plus Manuel has another twenty thousand to give you. Do not let anyone know or see that you have it."

"Of course not, Victor, thank you."

76

Just then the door opens and a policeman says:

-Caballeros, la hora ha terminado, la visita ha terminado.

Gentlemen the hour is up, the visit is over.

Victor gets up to leave, and I am sick to my stomach. "Victor there's so much more to discuss. What about calling my family? I need to speak with them, and they won't let me call."

"I spoke to your daughter. She knows where you are. Manuel told her. I'll call and tell her I saw you."

"Oh, okay, good. I pictured them sick with worry not knowing where I was. What about Manuel? He was supposed to come yesterday. I don't think they're letting him in."

"Maybe. Listen, I'll be back tomorrow, and I'll speak to the General in charge of Interpol to let you call you family. I will—"

-Señor, tiene que irse ahora.

Sir, you have to leave now, the cop tells Victor.

-Si, sí, me voy.

Yes, I'm leaving.

"Warren, we'll speak tomorrow."

"Are you sure? Victor, will they let you visit tomorrow?"

"I hope so."

Chapter 14

Upgrade

HE KEPT HIS WORD. We're standing in the basement of a different building on the police compound. This one's more modern, late seventeenth century. Sanchez is speaking with the guard and telling him to take good care of me.

On the walk over here, I got to use the bathroom again, and this time there was no pressure, so I'm happy, considering. I even had time to rinse my stinking T-shirt in the sink. I put it back on wet. The things we take for granted.

I convinced Sanchez to let me use his cell phone to call my children tomorrow. He's not supposed to, and he could get into trouble, but he'll do it anyway, as long as no one knows. I don't know whether it's true or not, but I do think he likes me and feels bad.

Slightly different setup down here. The guard is sitting at a desk outside a jail cell that has a solid steel door so I can't see what's behind it. I want to view the room before I commit, but I doubt this establishment has that policy. This place should be nicer though, because instead of listening to an old transistor radio, the guard's watching a twenty-inch black and white television like the one I got for my bar mitzvah in nineteen seventy-two. He's smiling and appears friendlier than my last guard. I hope so. It may just be a show for Sanchez's sake.

"Colonel, this place is better, right?"

"It is, yes."

"There's a toilet and running water of sorts?"

"Yes, something like that. It is better and actually the best you will get here, Señor Stelman."

I look at him skeptically, and he adds:

"I hope you have a better night tonight. I have to go now. I will see you tomorrow."

"For sure?"

"Señor?" he asks.

"I'll see you tomorrow for sure? I'll be in your office for the day again, right?"

"Yes, of course. Unless something unexpected comes up."

"Is that likely?"

"Not likely, but possible. Please, Señor Stelman, relax. I'm sure I'll see you tomorrow."

"Colonel, my lawyer is coming again tomorrow. I need to meet with him so I can decide what to do. You will let him in, I hope."

"Yes, I don't think that will be a problem."

"Colonel, one last thing please. I know my driver Manuel tried to see me, and he wasn't allowed in. I'm sure he'll come back. Please let him in also."

"I will try, Señor Stelman. But now I must go."

"Okay Colonel."

He has me eating out of his hands. I'm programmed like a Pavlovian dog. The only thing that gets me through the night is the promise that they'll take me out tomorrow. What will I do once they stop coming for me? I already know the answer: beg to be extradited. They know it too. Maybe I'm giving them too much credit for this systematic "breaking of the mind," but I'm sure that's what they're doing. If they don't come for me tomorrow or the day after, I'll be ripe for the taking.

After Sanchez leaves, the guard gives me a smile. Lucky me. He opens the cell door, but not all the way, because the door hinges won't allow it. He motions me inside, and I'm immediately struck by the size of this dungeon. It's three times bigger than my last dungeon with a three/quarter wall at the back that divides the space; a model of open concept architecture. I see someone get up off the floor and walk towards me.

-Gringo, ¿que lo que?

Gringo, what's happening?

-Nada, tranquilo, amigo.

Nothing much, all quiet, my friend, I answer.

-Ah, hablas español.

Ah, you speak Spanish.

-Si.

Yes.

-Soy El Lobo Gringo. Necesitas algo, habla conmigo. El Lobo puede ayudarte con todo.

I'm the Wolf Gringo. If you need anything you talk to me. The Wolf can help with everything.

-Gracias Lobo, pero estaré bien.

Thank you, Wolf, but I'll be fine.

-De acuerdo, Gringo, pero házmelo saber si necesitas algo.

Okay Gringo, but let me know if you do need something.

- ¿De dónde eres Gringo? ¿Eres americano?

Where are you from Gringo? You're American?

He's assuming I'm a naive American and wants to take advantage of it. They think every foreigner is American, so I just stick with it. He thinks I have money, and if he can be of use to me, I'll pay. I don't need his help, but I also want to be careful how I tell him. I've seen foreigners in this country deal with street hustlers and vendors in rude, condescending ways countless times, and it almost always ends up in an ugly escalation, putting the foreigner at risk. If and when the police show up, the foreigner is relieved, but quickly finds out it only made the situation worse. The police always take the vendor's side and then want more money for their help.

If they were sensitive to the fact that the vendor's just trying to feed his family and treated him respectfully, there would be no problem. There are no social programs here; no welfare, Medicaid, and very limited social security. People do whatever it takes to earn a peso. If it's selling trinkets on the beach or offering to be a quasi-concierge to help you with what you need, in a country so dependent on tourism, everyone knows twenty-dollars is an afterthought to most foreigners, but the equivalent of three days' work for a Dominican. You can say no, but do it with respect.

-Si Lobo, soy americano. Aprecio tu amabilidad y tu oferta para ayudarme. Si necesito algo, hablaré contigo. Vivi en Santo Domingo por mucho tiempo y tengo mi residencia, así sé cómo funcionan las cosas, pero gracias.

Yes, Wolf, I'm American. I appreciate your kindness and offer to help me. If I need anything I'll talk to you. I've lived in Santo Domingo for a long time, and I have my residence, so I know how things work, but thank you.

- ¿Está bien, americano, pero puedes ayudarme con cien pesos?

Okay, americano, but can you help me with 100 pesos?

-Lo siento Lobo, pero la policía se llevó todo el dinero que tenía. No tengo nada.

I'm sorry, Wolf, but the police took all the money I had. I have nothing.

I actually want to give him the 100 pesos, but I can't let anyone know I have money on me because they'll all want some, or worse, try to take it. Unlike me, these guys aren't being fed by Interpol every day. If they don't have someone bringing them food, they don't eat. With money the guard will buy them food for a fee.

The money is in the front pocket of my jeans. If I take them off, I better keep them close. Lying about not having any money won't go over well either.

-Entiendo. Esta bien Gringo.

I understand, it's okay Gringo.

My feet hurt from my hot leather shoes. I want to sit, but there's no bench. I count seven men lying on the floor, some sleeping, some resting. The one consistent thing with these dungeons is the climate control settings. Just like the last one, it's set at hot and miserable. Everyone's undressed and wearing only their underwear, two are naked.

The ceilings are high and one concrete wall has an opening with bars for a window. A brick enclosure set back ten inches on the outside, covers the opening, but offers the only source of natural light and a whiff of air. Still, it's an upgrade. Sanchez really pulled out all the stops.

Brown paper bags, Styrofoam containers and plastic water bottles litter the floor next to some of the men, suggesting they just ate or may be saving their left overs. Either way the ants are happy.

The unpleasant smell of urine is strong, albeit nowhere as bad as my last abode, but the smell is coming from the back where I surmise the toilet facilities are located. I'm curious, so I go back to take a look, and I'm shocked by what I see.

A black pipe about ten inches in diameter rises three feet from the concrete floor. Perched on it, with two feet negotiating its edges, is a nude Haitian man in a squatting position. For a few seconds I don't understand what I'm looking at, but then I realize he's taking a shit, down the pipe. Did Sanchez say better? Maybe for a Cirque de Soleil contortionist. I apologize for disturbing him, but he doesn't seem to care. I ask where one would take a piss, and he points to the floor at the back wall. At least there's a small drain on the floor where he pointed. So, this is the urinal. Unbelievable!

I look for a water source and notice a small one-inch pipe protruding from the side wall six inches off the floor. I don't see any way to turn it on so I ask El Lobo. He says they only turn the water on every morning at six. It makes me think they should outfit this dungeon with a plastic barrel, like the last one.

The sun is setting quickly, and we're losing light. I look around and decide on a place to camp for the night. I take off my wet t-shirt and realize rinsing it was a waste of time because it's the only thing I have to separate me from the dirty concrete floor. I remove my jeans and shoes and make my bed for the night.

Twenty minutes later it's pitch black. I can't see two feet in front of me, and I don't understand why they haven't turned on the light. I ask anyone what time it is, and seconds later I see the illumination from a digital watch. A voice answers, eight fifty.

The darkness is making me uncomfortable.

-Oye Lobo. ¿Cómo podemos obtener algo de luz aquí?

How can we get some light in here?

-No hay, Gringo.

There isn't any, Gringo.

- ¿Cómo es que no hay?

What do you mean, there isn't any?

From somewhere to my left a voice says:

-La bombilla se quema y no la cambiarán. Llevo aquí seis meses y siempre ha sido así. Vivimos en la oscuridad.

The bulb's burned out, and they won't change it. I've been here six months, and it's always been like this. We live in the dark.

-Eso es ridículo. ¿Por qué no la cambian?

That's ridiculous, why won't they change it?

-No sé.

I don't know.

I'm pretty sure the guy talking is the pipe squatter. I ask why he's been here so long, and he says he had a fight with a Dominican on a construction site. He just got paid for two weeks of work; one thousand pesos or twenty-five US dollars. A Dominican worker tried to take his money so the Haitian pushed him, and he fell backwards and hit his head on a sharp piece of rebar. The Dominican died. The Haitian was arrested and brought here.

Surprise, he's here illegally like a million other Haitians in this country and has no money for a lawyer. He has no idea when, if ever, he will get in front of a judge. Six months. I can't imagine living like this for six days. I ask him how he eats, and he tells me other prisoners share their food with him. Some days though, he doesn't eat. He's always hungry.

During the night the cell door opens several times to admit new detainees. Light from the guard's work area fills the cell momentarily allowing me to see until the door shuts. There are steady sounds of men getting up and making their way to the back to relieve themselves. I don't have to go and don't know how I would find my way in the dark if I did. A couple of guys are sleeping soundly if their loud snoring is any indication. I'm miserable. My back, hips and shoulders are killing from the hard floor. It's impossible to get comfortable. I turn from side to side every few minutes. I'm dripping with sweat and getting eaten by insects.

Somehow the night passes. I see the outline of bodies so it must be getting light out. Our population almost doubled overnight to thirteen. Guys are heading to the back and I assume it's for the water call. I sit up and stay where I am hoping with daylight Sanchez will come and rescue me.

A few minutes later, I hear angry voices. There's an argument over the water spittle. Apparently, one guy is taking too long. El Lobo didn't mention they only keep it on for fifteen minutes. I learn this by listening to the argument. Some guy has already used too much time, and he still won't let anyone else get water.

Curious like a passing motorist at an accident scene, I head to the back, jeans in-hand, to see what's happening. El Lobo is in the middle of the scrum and several men are arguing with a guy called Gordito, which translates roughly as little fat man. Gordito is claiming he hasn't washed in two days because they shut the water before his turn. Today he's using as much as he needs.

The others don't agree with his position, and they're all shouting at him to move. While Gordito is crouched down washing himself with the murky water coming out of the pipe by filling an empty water bottle and spilling it on his head, another big Dominican takes his shoe and hits Gordito across the back of his neck. He falls over and Big Man takes his place at the spittle. Gordito recovers quickly and jumps on Big Man's back locking his legs around his stomach. Big Man stands up fast and tries to throw him off like a rodeo bull. Gordito tightens his grip and starts punching Big Man in the face with both fists while straddling his back. Big Man is frustrated and, in what seems like a last act of desperation, screams and runs backward into the wall full force, practically crushing Gordito. It's like a circus clown act, only it's not. I've seen enough and walk back to my place on the floor. Rats in a cage.

Chapter 15

Visitor

IT'S EIGHT THIRTY IN the morning, and I'm at my spot on the floor trying to fall asleep. The fight between Big Man and Gordito didn't last long. Besides, Gordito realized all was lost when, after the fight ended, three other guys clamored around the spittle trying to get theirs. He can't fight everyone.

My frustration is amplified by the boredom, anxiety and miserable conditions. If I could just sleep, time would pass and Sanchez will get here. Based on the past two days, I know it won't be for a few more hours.

It's light now, and the morning sun is making it even warmer. I can hear some sort of duty call outside. A marching band is playing the National Anthem, and commanding officers are making announcements over loud speakers. El Lobo tells me there are hundreds of police outside in formation, listening to their daily duty assignments before they hit the streets. This repeats again at four in the afternoon.

Thirty minutes earlier, the guard pushed a water filled bucket, broom, shovel, garbage can and some Clorox into the cell. I learn the Haitian cleans twice a week for a bowl of rice each time. It's cleaning day, and the potent smell of Clorox is like *mana* from heaven. Apparently, I'm not the only one who can't straddle the pipe, so guys use the drain.

The guard has already delivered food brought by families for some of the men. I've been offered something to eat four times, and

I'm amazed how they'll share with perfect strangers. I've never been in jail before, but I doubt people would be so generous in America.

I'm hungry, but I'll wait to eat in the Interpol office. Then I think, if they don't come for me, I won't eat. Maybe I should have accepted something. Four days ago, I couldn't decide between a succulent rib steak at "Le Bistro" or lobster at "Don Pepe." Either costs far more than the average Dominican will spend on food for a month. Now I'm hoping I'll get to eat at some point today. My head is starting to pound again. I need caffeine.

At nine fifteen I'm surprised to hear the cell door open and the guard call me outside. I have a visitor, he says. I doubt it's Sanchez this early. I jump to my feet and put on my damp, dirty jeans and T-shirt. I walk outside and see Manuel, plastic bag in one hand and a paper cup with take-out coffee in the other. He knows how much I like my coffee in the morning, and he didn't forget. I am so fucking happy.

"Manuel, thanks for coming. They let you in."

"Yes, Jefe. Today they let me in. I brought you food. My wife cooked for you last night. There's chicken, rice and beans. She hopes you like it. She made extra so you can share with the others. The coffee is cold. I'm sorry."

"That's fine, Manuel," I say as I lift the lid and drink the whole thing.

"Jefe, I don't think you can depend on me coming every day. I don't think they will let me."

"I understand, Manuel. Please thank your wife for me."

"I will, Jefe. Are you okay? It's not good here."

"It's better than the cell we were in, Manuel," I say with a smile. He looks at me concerned.

"I'm okay, Manuel. I just need to get out of here. I'm going to see Victor later, and I'll decide what to do. The Americans want to extradite me to New York, and I'm inclined to go. I can't leave Lana there alone. If I agree, the Colonel from Interpol told me they'll move me to Najayo prison. Do you know it?"

"Si, Jefe. It's in San Cristobal. It's a big prison but not so good. I've visited people there. But, Jefe, it's better than this."

"That's what I'm hoping. I don't think I'll be able to get bail, and if I don't agree to extradition, they'll make it as hard on me as they can. Right now, they take me out every day and let me stay in the office where we were. They also buy me food. I'm sure that will stop if I try to fight extradition."

"Jefe, you can't stay here. You'll get sick in this place. It would be hard for me, and I'm from a poor barrio."

"I know. Victor told me you spoke with Andie. How is she? How are my other kids? Do you know?"

"Yes, Jefe, I spoke with her a few times. She's okay. They are all together with your parents. They're worried, but they're okay."

"Manuel, when you leave here, call her and tell her I may call today. If I can, I'll call my parent's house. I don't know what time exactly but probably later in the afternoon. If I can't call, they shouldn't worry, I'm safe. Tell them you saw me, and I'm okay."

"Okay, I will call her. Jefe, I have some money for you, but I don't want the guard to see. It's in my hand. I'll slip it to you when he isn't looking. Jefe, if you go to Najayo, you'll need more. It isn't enough."

"I know. Victor will give me what I need. Thank you."

"Jefe, the guard said I can only stay a few minutes, so we need to do this fast."

"Okay, he's watching right now, so just wait."

A minute later, the guard's phone rings. Manuel slips me the money, and I stuff it into the back pocket of my jeans. When he's finished his call, he tells Manuel he has to leave. Manuel promises me he'll stay in touch with Andie and will keep trying to visit me. Maybe it was something in his voice, or the way he said it, but I knew right then, that I probably wouldn't see him again.

After Manuel leaves, the guard asks to look inside the plastic bag. I tell him it's just food. He checks anyway. Then he tells me he has to search me.

- ¿Por qué? ¿Por qué necesitas revisarme?

Why? Why do you have to search me?

-Necesito verificar que no tienes un arma.

I need to be sure you have no weapon.

- ¿Arma? No tengo ninguna arma.

Weapon? I don't have a weapon.

-Necesito verificar. Es un procedimiento estándar, americano.

I need to verify. It's standard procedure, American.

Fuck! He'll find the money and take it! There's no way he saw Manuel give it to me, so why is he searching me now for the first time? Then I realize every other time I was in front of him, Sanchez was with me. He wouldn't try this shit in front of Sanchez, but now he has an opportunity.

-Puedes revisarme agente, pero todo lo que tengo es dinero. Si lo tomas, tendrás un problema con el Colonel. Él sabe que lo tengo. Si no me molestas, te daré mil pesos por ser amable. Tú decides hacia dónde quieres ir.

You can search me officer, but all I have is money. If you take it, you'll have a problem with the Colonel. He knows I have it. If you don't bother me, I'll give you one thousand pesos. You decide how you want to go.

I'm betting he won't take the chance that I go to the Colonel with this. It's not worth it. He can lose his job in a heartbeat. There are hundreds of cops in the courtyard who can replace him. The smart thing for him to do is accept my offer. Of course, I have no idea what the Colonel would or wouldn't do, but he doesn't know that. I'm hedging that he won't take the chance.

-Está bien, americano, no te revisare si me das dos mil pesos. Lo necesito para mi hijo Está enfermo y no tengo dinero para la medicina.

Okay American, I won't search you if you give me two thousand pesos. I need it for my son. He's sick, and I don't have money for medicine.

-Yo sé, amigo. Lo sé.

I know, my friend. I know it.

I hand him two thousand pesos from the money Manuel gave me. I don't want him to see the money I have in my front pocket in case another family member falls ill.

Chapter 16

Baseball Guys and Wife Beaters

"OKAY, I GO IN front of three Supreme Court judges. When will this happen?"

Victor and I are in Sanchez's office. I spent the last ninety minutes reviewing the situation, and I've made up my mind: I'm going. What choice do I have really? My kids are in Montreal, and my wife is locked up in Miami and on her way to New York. It's unrealistic to stay here to try and fight the Americans, knowing it will cost a fortune, to inevitably lose. No, I need to move forward. The sooner I get on with it, the sooner it'll end. I can only hope it won't be so bad. My life as I knew it is over. There's no way to salvage anything, most of all my reputation. I have to focus on my family and getting us back together for a new start and a better future, as hard as that seems right now.

"As soon as possible, probably within the next week," Sanchez says.

"Week? And where will I stay until then? Not in that stinking cell!"

"Unfortunately, there is nowhere else, Señor Stelman."

"Victor, there's got to be another way. Why can't I go back to my apartment and stay there under house arrest with a police guard. I'm sure that can be arranged."

"I think that's reasonable, Colonel?" Victor asks.

"Gentlemen, if it was up to me I would allow it. It is not possible for a few reasons. The Americans don't have a lot of faith in our ability to keep you if you are released. I personally find this insulting, but it has happened before, so I understand their concern. Secondly, we do not have the manpower at Interpol to keep you under guard twenty-four hours a day. Thirdly, there is nothing left in your apartment, and the landlord will not let you back in."

"What? What are you talking about? Where's all my furniture and personal belongings?" I ask incredulously.

"It was seized," Sanchez explains.

"Victor, you've got to do something! They're taking everything before I have a chance at due process! What about my wife's apartment and her car?" I ask Sanchez.

"The same, Señor. Seized."

"Victor?"

"Colonel, I need an inventory of everything you've seized along with photographs. I want to see everything with my own eyes. Where is everything being stored?" Victor asks Sanchez.

"Mr. Perez, I will look into this and get back to you. I will check with my superiors. Unfortunately, right now I must attend to a very pressing matter, so if that is all, I will have Señor Stelman escorted back by one of my men."

"Wait a minute, Colonel! What do you mean check with your superiors? What we're asking for isn't unreasonable. What's there to check? This shouldn't be a problem," I say.

"Señor Stelman, I am not in charge. I report to people. I am confident we will be able to provide what you are requesting, but I need to verify before I say yes. I have tried to help you in every way possible, Señor. I am your friend. You must understand, in some matters my hands are tied."

He's telling me not to make waves. I need him on my side.

"Colonel, I intend to defend my client's assets. Please provide the inventory I am requesting or I will petition the court."

"As I said, I will check with my superiors to see how this can be done."

"Okay. I expect the same for Mrs. Stelman's property," adds Victor.

"Mr. Perez, do you represent Mrs. Stelman?" he asks.

"Yes, I do,"

"You can provide a written consent from Mrs. Stelman appointing you as her attorney?"

"I don't have that yet, but I will provide it as soon as I am able to speak with her. I have also made a request to the FBI case officer," he explains.

"I see. Okay then, once you have that, I will present the matter to my superiors. In the meantime, I will ask how to proceed with your request for an inventory of Mr. Stelman's property. Is that satisfactory, Señor Perez?"

"Yes, thank you, Colonel."

I have a sick feeling everything we own already belongs to someone else. There's no way Interpol, who are essentially Dominican Police tasked to Interpol, made a list of everything and stored it for the Americans. No, I know better, they stole it all. Maybe they kept some of the obvious things like her car and a few pieces of furniture, but the wife of some Interpol General is wearing Lana's designer clothes as we speak. There's not a thing I can do about it either. They know it, and they will just delay Victor's request until I'm gone and forgotten.

"Colonel Sanchez, you promised me a phone call home. Please let me call now."

"Señor, I have no time right now. I will try to come see you before I leave tonight so you can make your phone call. It is the best I can do. I'm sorry."

"Colonel, why don't you let me stay here in the office until later then. It will save you the walk."

"Señor Stelman, you are only here because I'm here. No one else will take the responsibility for leaving you in the office. I need to go out. I'm sorry, you must go back."

When I got back to the cell El Lobo was gone. Big Man told me he was released two hours ago. I never asked him why he was there, but it must have been some petty charge that was dropped. Either that, or his family paid to get him out. There were some new faces, and they looked at me curiously but no one said a word, and I just took my place on the floor.

An interesting transition takes place when one finds themselves in a situation like this. It's a gradual depletion of your rights, your influence and ultimately your self-worth. You go from being someone who commanded some level of respect to someone who merely has to be tolerated and dealt with

I'm experiencing this right now as I become more aware of my powerlessness. I take the only pragmatic approach to my situation and accept my fate, hunkering down mentally, for whatever's in store for me. I know it won't be easy or nice. I know I'll be treated badly from now on, and I also know there's little I'll be able to do about it. However, for now, I do have some money, and with it, I can try to improve my current conditions. After all, Sanchez said I may be here for a week.

It's mid-afternoon when I walk to the cell door and shout for the guard. A few seconds later the door opens. He looks at me and says:

-Dime, americano.

Talk to me, American.

In a low voice I say:

-Escucha guardia, necesito que me compre algunas cosas. Te pagaré quinientos pesos.

Guard, I need you to buy me a few things. I'll pay you 500 pesos.

- ¿Que necesitas?

What do you need?

-Cuatro botellas grandes de agua, un paquete de papel higiénico, una pastilla de jabón, y arroz y habichuelas suficiente para todos. También, necesito platos, cucharas y vasos desechables.

Four large bottles of water, a package of toilet paper, a bar of soap, and enough rice and beans for everyone. I also need plastic plates, spoons and cups.

-Está bien, americano, tan pronto como pueda encontrar a alguien que me reemplaze por treinta minutos voy a ir.

Okay, American, as soon as I can get someone to replace me for thirty minutes I will go.

-Dame el dinero.

Give me the money.

Between the money Victor gave me and the money Manuel brought, I have eighty thousand pesos. I hand him twenty-five hundred. I feel nervous giving him the money, but what choice do I have? Last time it was a bribe. This time I need him to follow through. I hope he keeps his word.

At about four o'clock the cell door opens, and I'm hoping it's my stuff. A different guard brings in two new prisoners. I ask him where the other guard is, and he tells me he went to the store. Okay, that's good.

These two are loud and obnoxious and obviously still a bit drunk from whatever bender they were on. The shorter one is wearing jeans, a New York Yankees T-shirt and a Toronto Blue Jays baseball cap. He's about my height with broad shoulders that suggest he was in good shape at some point in his life, but now he carries a bloated pot-belly that hangs over his jeans. I figure late thirties but it's hard to know for sure. Life is hard for poor people in this country, and they often look older than they are. His partner is about five nine and extremely skinny. He's wearing a stained, white, wife-beater undershirt, a cap that says "Hollywood" and torn jeans. He's definitely younger, and I'd be surprised if he's a day over twenty-five.

Baseball Guy leads this act, because he's doing all the talking while Wife-Beater laughs at every joke and comment. These guys are trouble, so I move further down-wall to El Lobo's old spot and try to be invisible.

One of the other prisoners has a bowl of yuca, a potato-like vegetable, and some mashed plantain his wife brought this morning, and he's just closing the plastic lid to put it back in the bag when Baseball Guy asks for some. He explains he doesn't have enough because he already shared a lot of it earlier. What's left has to last him another day until his wife can come back.

Baseball Guy isn't happy with his answer and starts berating him in a threatening way. Wife-Beater joins in. They start moving towards him and this scene is looking awfully familiar. I'm hoping it won't go the same way as last time.

-Oye, déjalo. Él te dijo que no tiene.

Hey, leave him alone. He said he doesn't have. Big Man says from his place on the floor.

-No es tu problema Cabron. ¡No estoy hablando con usted!

It's not your problem, asshole. I'm not talking to you! Baseball Guy answers him.

Big Man gets up from the floor and walks towards the two of them. Then the Haitian, Gordito and one of the new guys stand up.

- ¡Te dije que lo deje, maricon!

I said leave him alone, pussy!

Baseball Guy, too stupid, too drunk and too belligerent to realize what's good for him, decides to challenge Big Man by pushing him hard in the chest and raising his fists to fight.

Big Man just looks at him and without any warning, punches him square in the face with a straight right. I think I see a tooth fly out of his mouth as he falls backward to the floor, stunned. I figure it's over, but then Big Man kicks him in the face brutally. For a second, there's nothing, then:

- ¡Mi nariz! ¡Está roto, hijo de puta! ¡Voy a matarte!

My nose! You broke it, you son of a bitch! I'll kill you!

This guy's nuts. He doesn't know when to shut his stupid mouth. Bloods oozing down his arms as he holds his nose, he's on his ass, and he's still hurling insults and threats at Big Man. It looks like Big Man wants to hit him again, but two others guys move between them and tell Big Man to calm down, it's enough.

Meanwhile, Wife-Beater is also shouting, so Big Man turns his attention to him. Then from nowhere, the Haitian grabs Wife-Beater in a bear hug and wrestles him to the floor. Another guy jumps in to help the Haitian, and thirty seconds later, Wife-Beater is surrendering and promising not to make trouble.

I'm watching this from the back of the cell trying to stay out of the way. I can't believe this is my new normal. I've been locked up four days, and I've seen three fights, one of them fatal. How am I going to survive this? I'm in a ruthless, savage, ignorant world, and I better adapt, because this is how I'm going to be living for some time. I begin to panic thinking about it. I feel nauseous so I walk to the back and lean on the wall close to the pipe, just in case.

I'm desperate for some water, and I'm hoping the guard will come back soon. A few minutes later the nausea passes so I walk back to the front to see Baseball Guy, nose still bleeding and Wife-Beater telling him to lie still. He won't listen and instead walks to the cell door and yells for the guard. The guard opens the door, looks at him, and after a few seconds passes him a dirty rag and shuts the door.

Why am I not surprised?

A couple of hours later it's getting dark. Sanchez never came, and I still haven't received my things, so I go to the cell door and call the guard. After what feels like five minutes the door opens, and it's the same guy. I ask:

- ¿El otro guardia todavía no ha regresado?

The other guard still hasn't come back?

-Regresará mañana, americano.

He'll be back tomorrow, American. Then he slams the door.

Motherfucker!!

Chapter 17

Carry-on Bag

THE NEXT MORNING AT seven the guard shows up with my groceries. He makes no excuses for being late and, under normal circumstances, I would express my irritation, but these circumstances are clearly not normal. I'm just so happy he came through, even if it is twelve hours later. Best not say a word.

Just like the previous nights, men come and go. Baseball Guy and Wife-Beater are gone, and now the guard calls for Big Man. It seems he's leaving too. The Haitian's still here, of course, and I ask him to walk with me to the back.

-Oye, probablemente van a venir por mí, así que necesito que mires mis cosas. Tengo comida para ti y cuando vuelva, si todo está allí, te daré doscientos pesos.

Listen, they're probably coming to get me, so I need you to watch my things. I have food for you, and when I get back, if everything is there, I'll give you 200 pesos.

-No te preocupes americano. Mantendré tus cosas seguras.

Don't worry, American. I'll keep your things safe.

There are eight of us now, so I share my food, leaving enough for another go around. I pass out one water bottle and make it clear the other three are for me; please don't ask. I don't want to use the water in case there's a change in my daily routine, and I really need it at some later point.

Even though I'll eat in a few hours, I want these guys to see me break bread with them, so I have some rice. I ask the Haitian how long

96

the rice and beans can stay good in this heat, and he tells me only a few hours. If I'm not back by then share what's left with everyone, I tell him. Don't let the food go bad.

At ten, one of Sanchez's men comes for me. Same routine. We make a stop at the bathroom. I tell him to be patient: it's going to take longer than usual today. I have my bar of soap in my pocket and after using the toilet, I undress to my underwear and wash myself in the sink as best as I can. It's glorious to feel clean again. If only I didn't have to put dirty clothes back on my body. I take the used bar of soap and conceal it on the inner frame of the window for next time.

At two, Victor shows up, and Sanchez comes out of his office for the second time today. He escorts us to the interrogation room, comes in and closes the door. Then he sits down and announces he has some news.

"Señor Stelman, Señor Perez, I received a call this morning from the court. Your extradition hearing is set three days from today on Friday morning at ten."

"I received the same call. I was about to tell my client," Victor says.

Okay, good then, progress. "What happens after that? I ask Sanchez.

"Well, I will be taking you to the hearing with two of my men. After, we will bring you to the prison in San Cristobal. It is better there. You will be happier."

"It won't take very much to make it better or make me happier, Colonel. Is it safe?" I ask.

"I think you will be okay, Señor Stelman," he answers.

"I hope so. Colonel, you never came last night. I waited for you. I still haven't called my family. You promised you would."

"No, Señor, I said I would try to see you. I couldn't. My oldest son had a baseball game. My wife called to remind me, and I had to leave right away. You understand the importance of being there for our children."

Is this guy a piece of work or what? He knows I'm desperately trying to speak to my own kids whose lives have been turned upside down, and he's preaching the importance of being there for children.

97

"I understand, Colonel Sanchez. Will you let me call today, or will you at least give Mr. Perez his cell phone so I can use it to call?"

"No, Señor, he cannot have his cell phone while he is with you. There are rules. I need to be present when you call. I give you my word I will escort you back this evening, and you can call then."

"Okay, Colonel, thank you."

"Señor Stelman, you had a lap top and carry-on bag with you when you were arrested. Both were taken by the FBI, but yesterday after hearing you agreed to extradition, they returned the carry-on bag. We will give it to you when we take you to prison. In the meantime, if you want to change your clothes, you can. I know there is some clothing in the bag. I will bring it in."

"Oh yes! Please! The clothes I'm wearing are filthy. Thank you."

"Yes, I know. We will try and have them washed for your hearing on Friday."

"Thank you, Colonel."

With that, he gets up and goes to retrieve my carry-on. I open it. My toiletry bag is there, and I suddenly remember I haven't taken my high blood pressure pill for four days now. That can't be good.

I look through the bag; there's stuff missing. I had a bunch of T-shirts, shorts, a pair of jeans, underwear, sneakers and a sports shirt. I also had a pair of prescription Fendi sun glasses I paid 600 dollars for, a couple of weeks ago. The only things I see is one T-shirt, underwear, one pair of shorts, and my old sneakers. I opened the toiletry bag and a brand-new tube of toothpaste, a roll-on deodorant, the medication, and my electric razor are also missing.

"C'mon Colonel! You can't be serious! Most of my stuff isn't here!"

"Are you sure?" he asks.

"Of course, I'm sure." I say, frustrated.

"I am sorry, Señor Stelman. That is how it was returned."

"So, the FBI stole my toothpaste, Colonel? I somehow doubt it."

"Señor Stelman, I don't know why things are missing, but at least you have some items. It is better than nothing, is it not?"

"Yes, yes," I say, exasperated.

"I can buy what you need and bring it for the hearing on Friday morning," Victor says.

"Colonel, can he do that? Buy me some things?"

"As long as they are permitted items, I see no reason why not. You don't want things confiscated at the prison." Sanchez warns.

"Are people allowed toothpaste, deodorant and clothing in the prison?" I ask.

"Yes, of course, Señor Stelman. That will be fine."

I give Victor a short list of things I need, and he says he'll have them by Thursday. I ask them to leave the room while I change, but Sanchez says I can't be alone in here without my hands restrained. I ask what the difference is between this room, the outer room or the bathroom, but he just shrugs. Instead, they turn around while I change. A few minutes later, Sanchez excuses himself and comes back with a plastic bag for my dirty clothes.

"Colonel, those are the only jeans I have. I hope they won't go missing."

He looks at me like I just accused him of embezzling money from Interpol accounts in Geneva and says:

"Señor Stelman, I am taking responsibility for your property. It will be fine. Your vehicle has been safe with me. I haven't let anyone touch it."

Unbelievable.

I spend another forty-five minutes with Victor who assures he'll visit me regularly once I'm transferred to the prison in San Cristobal. I stress he's all I have, and if he doesn't come, I'll have no money. He promises not to abandon me.

Chapter 18

Beat-down

ON THE WAY BACK to the dungeon I get my phone call. I reach Stephanie on her cell phone. It's great to hear her voice. We talk for about five minutes, and she updates me on Lana's situation. She's on her way to New York. The judge ordered the Bureau of Prisons to administer her Crohn's medication, but they haven't, still. She's getting sicker every day. The kids are really worried. I know from years of experience with her disease that this can end badly.

I explain my decision and how things will unfold. Two minutes into the call, overcome by fear and worry, she unravels and starts to cry. It's the first of many times to come that I can't take the time to comfort her because someone won't allow it. Sanchez has his hand out the whole time trying to get his phone back, telling me my time is up. At one point I lose my temper and remind him of the importance of being there for our children. I tell her I'll call again as soon as I can and not to worry about me. I promise I'm safe and being well treated. I tell her how sorry I am for everything and ask her to take care of her sisters and brother. What a responsibility to throw at a twenty-one-year-old. We hang up, and I hand Sanchez his phone, angry.

"One lousy call, Colonel, and you had to cut it so short?"

"Señor Stelman, you aren't supposed to use a telephone. I did what I could."

"Yeah, well, thanks for the call."

The guard's excited to see me and asks if I need to buy anything else. I tell him maybe tomorrow, but only if he delivers right away. He assures me the service will be more efficient next time. Then I think how ridiculous my demand is. It's not like I have options.

The same eight men are here, and they greet me with bravado. They've eaten what was left of the food and saved me some rice. Afraid it's spoiled or spoiling, I take it to the back, and I'm about to dump it down the pipe when the Haitian appears and asks for it. I tell him he may get sick, but he shrugs his shoulders and eats it with his hands.

Sometime after dark, notwithstanding the nagging pain in my shoulders and hips from the hard concrete, I manage to fall into a light sleep only to be awakened by the noise of men being ushered into the cell by the night guard and a few policemen.

From the light of the door, I see one guy resisting. He's refusing to go in and pushes one of the police. Another reacts by lifting his baton striking him on top of his head. He falls to the floor bleeding, and they drag him through the door by his arms. The cell door slams shut, and I'm blinded by darkness.

His friends attend to him as best as they can with help from illuminated watches. I can make out his form from across the room and, at one point, there's even enough light to see his face. He's bleeding heavily.

Someone asks if anyone has water so I answer. I tell the voice I also have toilet paper, if it will help. He asks me to pass it over. I ask someone to shine some light, so I can find what he needs. Then I pass a full bottle of water and a roll of toilet paper across the room. I ask them not to use it all. I need it. No problem, they say.

I lie back down and try to sleep, but I can't. My mind races with thoughts of my kids, my wife and my parents. I silently pray for them and ask God to keep them safe and give them the strength to live through this ordeal. Eventually, somehow, a restless sleep sets in.

In the morning after water call, four of the men I shared my food with are being released, so we say goodbye, wishing each other well. We're eleven now with the seven new guys from last night. I look across the floor and see the injured guy sitting, back against the wall, mouth open, snoring. His T-shirt and jeans are caked with dried blood, but he seems okay.

I see my water bottle and half roll of toilet paper on the floor next to three of the new guys, and I ask them to pass it back to me. One of them looks towards the other two bottles and toilet paper I have next to me and tells me I don't need it. I have enough. He's keeping this.

I explain I'm going to be here for some time still, so I need it. Please give it back to me. He looks at me, lifts the bottle to his mouth and begins to drink.

I don't know what comes over me. Probably a culmination of every injustice and slight I've been experiencing, or maybe I'm just sick and tired of people helping themselves to my things, especially after I've extended help. But definitely because of his total lack of respect. I lose my fucking mind.

I get up fast and walk towards the three of them and say:

- ¡Oye! ¿Escuchaste lo que dije? ¡Quiero mi agua y papel ahora! ¡Dámelos o los tomaré!

Hey! Did you hear what I said? I want my water and paper now! Give them to me, or I'll take them!

They jump to their feet, and the asshole says:

- ¿Oh sí, americano? ¡Tómalos entonces!

Oh yeah, American? Take them then!

His friends move closer, but so does the Haitian and my other friends. He puts the bottle on the floor and stands, ready. I don't care anymore, and I'm definitely not backing down. Fuck this guy! I'm going to kill this prick!

I feign a jab to his head, which backs him up, and hit him with a glancing right on the side of his jaw. I'm about to unleash again when I feel a burst of pain in my ear. Sucker punched! As I turn to face my assailant, I see his fist a hundredth of a second before it crashes into the bridge of my nose. A crush of pain and my eyes well with tears. I can't see. The Haitian's yelling and moves to separate us. I feel shoving and scuffling.

Then it happens again. Someone kicks me in the lower back, and the force sends an explosion of pain down my legs. I turn to see my attacker through watery eyes, but as I do, I get hit again, this time in the stomach—so hard that it knocks the wind out of me. I crumple to the floor, paralyzed with pain, unable to move, unable to breathe, gasping for air. Blood pours down my neck from my ear, and I taste blood in the back of my throat from my nose. I'm lying in a fetal position trying to get air as the Haitian struggles with one of them. Then it happens again. Someone kicks me in the back with the force of a mule. The pain is excruciating, and I start coughing. As I cough, I swallow blood which makes me heave. I cough harder, and then I vomit on the floor.

Everyone's fighting. The Haitian is hunched over hitting someone while the others are grappling. It's total insanity.

Suddenly the cell door opens, and the guard runs in swinging his baton at anyone he can hit. He's ordering everyone to get down on the ground, and they do. One guy tries him and the guard violently crushes his face with his baton.

I'm catching my breath now, and the paralysis is dissipating. My nose hurts, and every time I move, I feel a sharp electric jolt of pain down my legs. This can't be good, I think to myself.

Two black steel toed boots in front of my face, so I move my head thinking the worst but then raise my eyes to see the guard looking down at me.

-¿Qué pasó aquí americano?

What happened here, American?

-Nada. No pasó nada. Resbalé y caí.

Nothing. I slipped and fell.

-¿Quien hizo esto?

Who did this?

-Te lo dije, me caí.

I told you. I fell.

-¿Puedes leventarse?

Can you stand up?

-Dame dos minutos por favor. Quiero que mi nariz deje de sangrar.

Give me two minutes please. I want my nose to stop bleeding.

One of my friends offers to help me. He brings over the toilet paper and water bottle that caused this thing. I manage to sit up and hold some paper to my nose and ear. A few minutes later the bleeding stops. Sitting on my ass, I push myself against the wall.

The smell of vomit is sickening. It bothers the guard, enough so that he tells the Haitian to go and get the cleaning supplies. I'm just happy I wasn't wearing my new T-shirt. It's still on the floor laid out like a sheet. My shorts and sneakers are covered in blood. I'll have to figure this one out.

Twenty minutes later I'm at the guard's station being examined by a nurse. The guard called Sanchez and told him I had some trouble. Sanchez sent her to evaluate my injuries. She doesn't think my nose is broken. I concur. The pain shooting down my legs is pretty intense though, so she gives me a couple of pain pills that I swallow in front of her. Then she asks the guard to let me sit in his chair while she goes to speak with the Colonel.

Thirty minutes later three Interpol cops come for me. Sanchez wants me to go for an X-ray, and they're here to escort me to a hospital. I refuse, thinking about the quality of care in public hospitals in this country. I tell them I'm okay, feeling much better. I just need to clean up and rest. They call Sanchez, and he tells them to bring me to his office.

It's not an easy walk, but the more I move, the better I feel. By the time we get there, the pain has subsided quite a bit. They bring me into his office. When he sees me, he stands up and walks around his desk to examine my battered face. Maybe he was a doctor before he was a cop.

"I was hoping something like this wouldn't happen, Señor Stelman."

"Me too."

"Are you okay?"

"Well, I've been better, but I'll survive."

"Fighting is for men younger than you, Señor Stelman."

"I wasn't fighting. I fell."

"I want to know who did this."

"Not from me. I have to go back there. I fell."

"It won't happen again." Sanchez tells me.

"I know it won't. I'll be more careful from now on. Colonel, can I wash up and then lie down somewhere that isn't a dirty, concrete floor. Just for a couple of hours. Please!"

"I would like you to go to the hospital to be examined properly."

"There's no need."

"I would prefer you do."

"Colonel, may I be frank?"

"Frank?"

"Can I speak freely, openly?"

"Oh. Yes, of course, Señor Stelman."

"Why do you care about my condition? If you did, you wouldn't have put me in that shit-hole to start with. Stop pretending you're my friend. It's getting old and tiring."

"Señor Stelman, I am doing my job. I have nowhere else for you to stay. On Friday, after the hearing, you will be moved to a better place. I have nothing against you. I like you, and I'm sorry this happened. And...."

"And what, Colonel? What?"

"Well, it's just that you don't look good. I am concerned the judges will think we mistreated you."

Ah, so that's what this is about. He's worried about the hearing. He's afraid the judges won't grant the extradition order if they think I've been beaten or threatened or something. Leverage maybe? You know what? I'm losing the war. That's obvious. Maybe I'll win this battle.

"I can see why they may think that, Colonel. I'm sure I don't look good right now, and I'll bet it'll be a lot worse tomorrow."

"No one here laid a hand on you, Señor Stelman. I hope you wouldn't make that claim."

"You know Colonel, perception is everything. I won't have to make any claim. Even if I deny you hurt me, they'll have their doubts, thinking I'm afraid to tell the truth. Remember, I've lived in your country for some time now. I know how things work. They know how things work. It won't be a leap for them to suspect foul play, Colonel. You know it, and I know it."

"What do you want?"

"Very little. I know I'm up against an 800-pound gorilla, and I have no chance of winning this thing. I've seen how the FBI operates. I know what they told my sixteen-year-old daughter in the airport when they arrested my wife. They play dirty. What do I want? My hearing is in two days. Until then, I want to live better. I want to sleep in a bed, not on a filthy, bug infested floor in a stinking shit-hole dungeon. I want three meals a day, and I want to speak to my family for fifteen minutes every evening. I want a shower every morning and a toilet when I need one. And I want clean clothes to wear. That's what I want. And if I get these things, there will be no problem at the hearing. Those judges will know I wasn't beaten, tortured, coerced or threatened. You have my word. They will sign the order, and I will be out of your hair. Two days, Colonel, just two days."

"You are asking a lot, Señor. I have nowhere else for you to stay."

"Figure it out, Colonel. I know you can."

"We have a room here in the back with two beds that are used by staff. You can stay there during the day when we are here. I will arrange for a shower in the morning in the staff facilities, and I will buy you new clothes. We will feed you twice a day and you will be able to call your family for ten minutes in the evening, but I will be present. You can use the bathroom as needed during the day. At night you will sleep in the cell. That is the best I can do for you, Señor Stelman."

"It's not good enough. I'm not staying there."

"Señor, I am losing my patience. I am just a Colonel in the Policia. I am not the President of this Republic. Take what I have offered you."

"Five blankets. I want five thick blankets."

"I can do that."

"A light bulb. You have to fix the light."

"The light? I'm sorry, I don't know what you mean."

"There's no light in the dungeon. There's a light fixture but the bulb is burnt. You have to replace the bulb. There's no light at all once the sun goes down. It's pitch black in there."

"That shouldn't be a problem. I had no idea."

"They only turn the water on for fifteen minutes in the morning. It's not enough. It has to be on for two hours so men can wash themselves and their clothes."

"Fifteen minutes? I will fix that."

"Two hours, every morning. At the least."

"Okay, Señor Stelman. I will make sure the water is on for two hours a day."

"Even after I leave."

He just looks at me.

"Colonel, the Policia Nacional have a Haitian locked up in there for the past six months. It's criminal. Keep the water on. He's not an animal. He's a man.

He nods his head.

"I want your word, Colonel. Give me your word."

"You have my word, Señor Stelman."

"Then we have a deal. Keep your word, and I'll keep mine."

"Of course, Señor Stelman."

"Colonel, could I get some ice?"

"Yes."

"Thank you."

"Now please, have someone bring me to the bathroom so I can clean myself up and then show me that room with the bed. I need to lie down."

Chapter 19

Extradition Hearing

WE'RE IN THE PALACE of the Supreme Court in Santo Domingo. The building is adjacent to the National Congress, both very impressive structures. I've driven by them a thousand times but never paid much attention, until now.

I'm in an elegant office with teak walls, sitting at a spectacular mahogany conference table the size of a hockey rink. I count twenty-four chairs. A Supreme Court Judge's aid is sitting next to me as we review a document I need to sign, consenting to my extradition to the land of the free and the home of the brave. Victor is to my left and a professional translator sits across from us.

My appearance initially put them off. Their jaws dropped when they saw me, Victor included: they were aghast. My eyes are badly swollen, and the left one won't open. My cheekbones are black and blue and my upper lip is the size of my forearm. I look like a monster, but if you've ever experienced a good smash in the face, you know these things can look more gruesome than they actually are. In a couple of weeks, I should be gorgeous again. My lower back is stiff, but the pain isn't as bad. If you suffer from back pain, I recommend a couple of nights on a dungeon floor.

We're on the third reading of the document, just to be sure. The Dominican judicial apparatus is taking this very seriously. They really want to dot their i's and cross their t's. Maybe they've had issues in the past where extradition was concerned.

Sanchez and the two cops are waiting outside. Once this is over, they'll take me to Najayo Prison. "It is better there"; can't wait.

He kept his word and gave me everything we agreed to. Someone must have told him what happened because when I got back that evening, the culprits were gone. Probably shipped to an alternative dungeon or having their finger nails removed.

Once I sign the document I will have the formal hearing with the three judges. The translator just finished the last line, so I'm signing. Mazel-Tov they yell and begin dancing a hora. I suggest we invite Sanchez into the circle. He has the most to celebrate.

We're escorted to a magnificent, lavishly finished chamber. Three judges as advertised, two men and one woman. The woman is running the show. She wants to know who's in the room. She asks Victor first, and he identifies himself as my attorney. Then she turns her attention to the back of the room where the entire police contingent is standing, including my old golf buddy, Wendell. I turn back to look, and he smirks at my obvious physical discomfort. I ignore him like the piece of shit he is.

Sanchez identifies himself and the other two plain clothed cops as Interpol, and Wendell, proud like a peacock, announces he's with the United States Federal Bureau of Investigation.

Maybe I'm imagining it, but the woman's face turns red on hearing this, and seconds later, in a stern tone of voice, she orders him to leave the room, declaring this a Dominican Institution where the United States Government has no place. Nobody likes a bully, especially not Supreme Court Judges. She asks the Sanchez gang to wait outside as well.

She begins reading the request for my extradition, and when she's done, she focuses her attention on me.

"Mr. Stelman, are you volunteering to be extradited of your own free will?"

"Yes, Magistrado, I am."

"Have you been coerced, threatened, intimidated or physically harmed by anyone in order to get you to consent?"

"No, Magistrado, I have not."

109

"Are you sure, Mr. Stelman? You do not have to be afraid to tell me."

"Thank you, Magistrado. I assure you I have been treated well by the authorities."

"What happened to you, Mr. Stelman? You are badly injured."

"I had an unfortunate altercation while in jail. It is completely unrelated, I promise you."

"Mr. Stelman, we are very concerned that you have been unduly pressured in some way to agree to your extradition. Have you?"

"Magistrado, I have not. I want to go and face the charges and get on with my life. My wife was arrested for the same charges, and she is in custody in New York. I feel compelled to go there and get this over with."

"The FBI arrested your wife as well?" one of the other judges asks.

"Yes, Magistrado."

"Was she threatened in any way to force your consent?" he asks.

"I'm not aware of anything, Magistrado."

Then the woman says:

"You have not broken any laws in this country, and you have the right to oppose the extradition request. Are you certain you do not want to do so? You are waiving your right to oppose your extradition?"

"Yes, Magistrado, I am certain."

"Very well then, the order is granted. You will be held in our custody until the American authorities collect you and transfer you to the United States. This hearing is adjourned."

Just like that, it's over.

Chapter 20

Cartel

WE'RE DRIVING THROUGH SAN Cristobal, a small, densely populated city of about 275 thousand, home to Najayo Prison. Rafael Trujillo, the country's most ruthless dictator was born here in 1891. He ruled the country with an iron fist from 1930 until his assassination in 1961 by activists while driving home from the Capital. San Cristobal is also home to a long list of Major League Baseball stars, many of them pitchers.

I'd been here once before and planned to come back, but not for this reason. We're on a bustling, poorly maintained street, where cars and motorcycles park on one side, leaving just enough single lane space for travel in both directions. One-, two- and three-story structures host businesses, shops, and residences.

Sanchez is driving, one cop is up front, and the other is with me in back. We turn the corner onto a wider, two-way street, travel a few blocks, and it comes into view. An enormous light blue and yellow structure with twenty-foot high concrete perimeter walls, topped with barbed wire. Perched way above are four towers with armed guards, surveilling the prison grounds.

We approach the front gates where two black-clad, assault-rifle-toting policemen with German Shepherd guard dogs wave us down. They offer Sanchez a formal salute and ask for identity credentials. After checking inside the vehicle, they open the gates and wave us through. We drive to a second check-point where a prison guard sits

111

exposed to the hot sun on a wooden chair, M-16 across his lap. He comes to attention and salutes Sanchez.

Some brief conversation, and we're directed to the main office to find Señor Amado Peña who will receive me. Sanchez pulls up, and we get out. After a little wait, Sanchez sends one of the cops to find Peña.

To the left of the main office, there's a blue gate to somewhere. Curious, I walk over to look. It gives way to a corridor that runs thirty yards to a t-intersection. There's a mob of inmates moving through. Two guards stand in the middle with mini baseball-bat-like clubs directing the flow.

One inmate is screaming uncontrollably. Others laugh, shout back and push him out of their way. With no resources, poor people with mental illness are sent to prison. He sees me looking through the gate and takes off running towards me with his hand out, begging for money. Emaciated and dirty, rags hanging from his body, he has no shoes, and I see sores all over his skin. I step back for fear he'll reach through and grab me.

-Gringo dame algo! Ayuadame por favor! ¡Dame cien pesos! ¡Gringo! ¡Gringo! Por favor!

Gringo give me something! Help me! Give me 100 pesos! Please!

He cups his hand and brings it to his mouth in a gesture meant to mimic eating. I tell him I don't have money when one of the guards, a huge black man, begins yelling at him to come back. He ignores him and continues to beg even as the guard approaches. The guard shouts again, but he won't listen, so he swings his club hard and strikes him on the back of his legs across his hamstrings. The inmate falls to the floor from the force of the blow but continues to focus his attention on me. Through the pain, he still pleads for money. The second guard comes, and they grab him by his hair forcing him to his feet and drag him back.

I'm sick to my stomach. This is supposed to be better? I'm actually afraid. There's no way I can survive in here. I'll be mauled to death if I don't contract some terrible disease. I turn to Sanchez and say:

"Colonel, are you serious? You told me this place was better. You said I'll be safe here. Did you lie to me, Colonel? It looks like you lied to me."

"Señor Stelman, come away from there. You are going to a segregated area. We would not put you there."

I'm relieved but nervous.

"Colonel, how many people are in this prison?"

"I am not sure, but many. It is very crowded. It was built to accommodate 400, but there are well over one thousand. But as I said, you will be in a special area."

Moments later the main office door opens, and Señor Peña appears. He greets the Colonel and looks at me. Then he looks back at Sanchez with a head gesture that implies: What happened to him? Sanchez nods his head from side to side as if to say: Nothing, he's okay. Sanchez hands him a file and turns to me and says:

"Señor Stelman, this is where we say goodbye. I want to wish you good luck. Señor Peña will take you from here."

Sanchez holds his hand out, and I take it. We shake briefly, and I thank him. He and the two cops climb into his truck and drive off.

"Señor, you will be here until the Americans pick you up. You will be in a segregated area. Do you speak Spanish?"

"Yes, Señor Peña. I speak pretty well."

"Ah good. That will help."

"Right now, I need you to go to the medical office. They will examine you. It is down at the end of the building.

"Do I go on my own?"

"Yes," he says with a smile. "When you are finished come back here, and I will escort you to the unit."

"Okay, thanks."

It's the second time today I've thanked one of my jailers. Thanking someone facilitating the loss of my freedom seems odd, but they're just doing their jobs, and I'm grateful for being treated with a fair amount of dignity and respect. The alternative is far worse.

I walk to the medical office and go inside. There are three inmates in a waiting area. One has a gash over his eye that's bleeding. Another is holding his right forearm with his left hand, and I can tell his wrist is broken. The third is coughing uncontrollably, so I stay as far from him as possible and use the bottom of my T-shirt to cover my nose and mouth.

About fifteen minutes later, a pleasant but tired looking nurse dressed in a baby blue uniform with soft white shoes appears and tells the inmate with the broken wrist to go to the front gate where guards are waiting to take him to the local hospital. Good luck, I think to myself. She asks the guy with the cut to follow her into the back room and, twenty minutes later, he appears with his eye taped.

I'm expecting her to call the cougher spreading air-borne diseases next, but she calls me instead. I follow her to a sparsely furnished room. There's a warped steel examining table in its center and a few medical instruments in a steel wall fixture. She takes a seat at a small wooden desk. The wheels of her torn vinyl chair squeak as she adjusts her position.

She asks me to sit on the examining table while she does some paperwork. I look around and notice peeling paint and a large water stain on the ceiling.

When she's done, she gets up and gently places her hand under my chin turning my head softly so she can examine my injuries. She asks if I have pain, and I tell her mostly discomfort. She suggests I ice my eye and lip to bring down the swelling. I thank her and ask how I can get ice. I can buy it inside, she says. She asks if I have any other injuries, and I tell her about the pain in my back. She suggests I ice my back as well. Then for the next five minutes she tries to check my blood pressure with a tattered blood pressure cuff that has trouble inflating.

-Creo que necesitas uno nuevo.

I think you need a new one.

-Sí, pero esto es todo lo que tenemos.

Yes, but this is all that we have.

I nod understanding. She finally manages to get a reading and delivers the news.

-Tu presión es alta.

Your pressure is high.

-Sí, no estoy sorprendido. Sufro de presión alta y no he tomado mi medicamento en diez días. ¿Tienes medicina aqui?

I'm not surprised. I suffer from high blood pressure, and I haven't taken my medication in ten days. Do you have medicine here?

-Desafortunadamente, no Señor. Tendrá que comprarlo usted mismo. Si tiene dinero, puede pedirle a uno de los guardias que lo compre para usted.

Unfortunately, no, sir. You will have to buy it yourself. If you have money you can ask one of the guards to buy it for you.

-Si no tengo dinero, ¿qué haría?

If I don't have money, what would I do?

She just shrugs her shoulders. I suspect they have a high mortality rate.

She asks me a bunch of questions about my medical history while she fills out a form. Do I have HIV or tuberculosis? I say no to both, but she has to draw blood to screen for them anyway. I watch carefully as she takes a brand new hypodermic needle from its package and pulls on a brand-new pair of latex gloves. I'm relieved.

- ¿Hay mucho VIH y tuberculosis en la prisión?

Is there a lot of HIV and tuberculosis in the prison?

-Tratamos de controlarlo, pero ya sabes, es difícil.

We try to control it, but you know, it's hard.

Just wonderful.

When the examination is complete, I thank her and walk back to find Peña.

He asks me to follow him, and we make our way through the same corridor I saw earlier.

It's chaotic. There are inmates moving in every direction while guards look on, clubs at the ready. Everyone shouts; the noise is mind-splitting. There's no prison uniform, everyone wears street clothes. Many are shirtless and many without shoes.

All eyes are on me as they pass. Peña walks quickly, and I struggle to keep up with him as inmates walk between, separating us. I brush away hands clutching at me hoping for a hand out. One grabs my T-shirt and won't let go so I twist his hand and shove it forcefully. I call to Peña who's twenty yards in front of me. Either he doesn't hear or doesn't care. I'm petrified I'll get left behind and swallowed by this mob.

I catch up to him when he stops at a gate where a pleasant female guard is stationed. He asks her to unlock the door. As we pass through I notice a lot of flies; in the air, on the walls on the floor. The further we walk the more there are. The buzzing sound is unnerving, like something out of an Alfred Hitchcock movie.

We turn a corner and what I see shocks me. A mountain of garbage three feet high spread out in an area at least 300 square feet. The obvious source of the flies, and they literally blanket everything.

In the middle of the heap are three naked Haitians shoveling the garbage into large drums. Their bodies are covered in filth and sludge. The flies buzz around their heads and stick to them like wall paper, yet they work undistracted.

Well away from the garbage, about 100 feet back, a guard stands, talking to two other inmates. He stops for a second and yells at the garbage men to work faster. One slips and falls, and when he stands up, he's covered in a brown filthy liquid. He picks up a rubber hose from the middle of the pile and rinses himself down. The water makes their job more difficult. Now I understand why tuberculosis is a problem.

On the other side of the garbage pile are two gates that open to an empty outdoor recreation yard. I see four basketball courts, all in a state of disrepair. One has rusted and bent baskets with steel chains for mesh. The others, just backboards. The paved surface is warped and broken in many places. There's garbage everywhere. A set of bleachers on the far side of the yard has broken and rusted seats. Behind the bleachers, a green area that runs a hundred yards to the back-perimeter wall of the prison. At second glance, it's a massive cropping of wild bushes and five-foot high weeds. Swarms of insects hover above.

We continue, passing a large open area to our left where men lie on the floor. Peña tells me most sleep here because they can't afford to pay for a cell. It's only 100 pesos a week to use the floor and that gets them four one-foot tiles to sleep on.

We turn a corner and head down a long corridor with cells on both sides and arrive at a gate where another guard sits. He stands, greets Peña and unlocks the door. We walk through to a staircase that ascends to a second floor. Two inmates are preparing food on a grill under the staircase, and the smell engulfs me as I'm reminded how famished I am. I hope I get to eat today.

At the top, chain-link windows offer vistas of the outside. A couple of inmates are standing and smoking, looking out to the streets that are visible above the wall. They look at me, and I say hello. They greet me back.

There's a short hallway with a bathroom on one side that has a real toilet and sink. Okay, so far so good. Sanchez was right; this is already better.

We walk onto a large rectangular tier forty-foot-long by fourteen-foot wide. Six cells line each wall with two more at the back. A long wooden bench offers a place to sit and there are several tables with plastic chairs where inmates are playing dominoes, cards and eating. They all lift their heads to look at me. I also notice three small freezers; two are locked.

Peña takes me to one of the cells and knocks. Seconds later a tall heavy man with long, black and grey hair, tied in a pony-tail, opens the cell door. Evidently, he was expecting us because he says:

"Okay Peña, I got it."

"You the Canadian?"

"Yes."

Peña says goodbye and walks away.

"I'm Cartel. I call the shots here." New York accent.

"I'm Warren. Nice to meet you. You from New York?" I ask.

"Formerly. I was born here but grew up in Queens. I was in the NYPD for fifteen years. Now I'm here. They want me, but I'm doing my best not to go. I'm looking at a lot of time if they send me back."

"Shit," I say. "What's a lot of time?"

"At least twenty-five."

"I understand your reluctance to go."

"No shit."

"Cells need to be clean by eight thirty every morning for visiting. After eight thirty no walking around without a shirt. Watch how you talk when visitors are on the unit. No swearing. We try to be respectful. Sunday is family day. Kids come. Girlfriends can come on Tuesdays and casual friends on Thursdays."

"Casual friends?"

"Hookers! Only Thursdays. We don't want them around when wives, girlfriends or children are here."

"Got it. I doubt I'll be entertaining though."

"Don't care what you do as long as you follow the rules."

"Okay."

"You have a visitor, you get one hour alone in the cell with her. Only an hour. If one of your bunkies has a visitor you leave for an hour. Works both ways."

"So conjugal visits are allowed?"

He just looks at me like I'm stupid. I guess it was a stupid question after what he just explained.

"You need anything from the street you see me. I'll get what you need. I charge 15 percent. That's in addition to the 185 percent that goes to the Colonel and the guards."

"Hundred and eighty-five percent to each?"

"No, in total. Basically, anything you want costs triple. That's non-negotiable."

"Okay."

"You can get whatever drugs you want but no heroin. Don't need no junkies here."

"I don't do drugs."

"Good for you."

"You have money?" he asks.

"Not right now, but I will when my lawyer comes. Should be tomorrow." I'm reluctant to say I have money until I figure this place out.

"Alright, you eat with me tonight until you're set up. He's coming tomorrow, right?"

"He promised."

"Okay then."

"Hey, thanks, Cartel."

"You're staying in that cell," he points across the tier. "I know you're just waiting to get picked up so you won't be here that long. It's a big one, and there are three other guys in there right now. C'mon, I'll introduce you."

Cartel knocks and opens the cell door. A man gets up from his bunk to greet me. His name is Oscar, and he's been here for five years. He's from Santiago and was a private investigator until he tried to extort a politician with photos of him with an under-age girl. I find out a couple of weeks later that he left out the part about trying to have the guy murdered when things went bad.

The cell is divided into three sections. The area we're standing in has three sets of wooden, three-level bunk beds. Oscar points to a lower bunk and tells me I can sleep there. He also mentions I can rent the mattress for two thousand pesos a week. It's not much of a mattress, but it's better than a hard surface, so I offer 1000 for a month, and we settle at fifteen hundred. I'm not expecting to be here for that long anyway.

Oscar sleeps in the lower of the bunks in the middle of the cell, and he uses the second and third to store all kinds of things.

An accordion door in the corner opens and a heavily muscled black man comes out to greet me. He introduces himself as Sapo. He's a Columbian serving a thirty-year sentence for three contract murders in the Dominican Republic. He has ten in, but he'll be released in five because the law only requires you do 50 percent of your sentence.

His bunky also comes out. He's a Mexican who calls himself, surprise, Mexico. He's here for cocaine trafficking for one of the cartels. He's been here for nine years, and he has another three to go. They get a little more privacy because of the length of their sentences, although I don't know who decides that. They can't afford to live in a one-man cell like Cartel who pays thirty thousand pesos a month to the Colonel running the prison.

On the left side of the cell through a doorway is a small area with a sink and table surface that holds a hot plate. Dishes, cutlery and drinking cups are stacked on a shelf above. Beyond that is the bathroom with toilet and shower.

Oscar tells me I have to contribute to the cost of electricity for air conditioning, Direct TV and the cell rental which is paid to the Colonel. I tell him I don't have too much money, and he assures me we'll figure it out. Nice guy. I wonder how much of his nut I'll be subsidizing. He explains we take turns cleaning the cell and washing the dishes or hire someone and pay them to do it.

I notice everyone has a cell phone so I ask if they're allowed. They tell me not technically, and if there's a shake down, they'll confiscate them.

Over the next few hours I meet everyone on the unit. The majority are here for drug trafficking in some capacity. I count three cartel pilots amongst us, one of who is also serving thirty years. A few are here for homicide, and there's a young American who had a pot-selling ring on the North Coast. Most are fighting extradition to the US while some are on this unit for their own protection. I seem to be the only one who is actually waiting to get picked up.

Cartel warns me that for the time I'm here, I should take care of any business I need to take care of. Once you're in the US you won't be able to do anything to help yourself. Here there's some freedom.

A few offer the services of their US lawyers, waxing poetic about how great they are. I suppose it's part of the discount referral program.

Inmates from general population work as personal butlers, washing clothes, cooking meals and cleaning cells. I arranged to have my clothes washed for 200 pesos. Living large again.

Chapter 21

Man Down

"THEY TOLD ME ANY day. I'm hoping by next week."

We're in Cartel's cell. His "cell" is a generous sized room plus a bathroom. In addition to the small sofa we're sitting on, there's a bed, coffee table, flat screen with Direct TV, wall-mounted air-conditioning unit and an inverter for power failures; an everyday occurrence in this country.

Considering it's prison, he lives well. He's not the only one either. Earlier this morning I met a Russian named Dimitry who immigrated with his family when he was very young. He's locked up on an infamous cocaine trafficking case that was in the news for over a year.

Dimitry invited me for coffee and a Krispy Kreme donut. The donuts are delivered fresh every morning from Santo Domingo. Dimitry has money. His cell is like a miniature hotel suite with living room, kitchenette, bedroom and a bathroom finished in Italian marble. There's a stand-up fridge, air-conditioning unit, inverter, microwave, small stove-top and a forty-inch flat screen. He paid to renovate everything and pays the Colonel 1500 dollars a month in rent. I can only imagine how well the Colonel lives with all his rental income.

Dimitry tells me one of his co-defendants has a private house on the prison grounds that puts his "cell" to shame. He also tells me there are two Canadians downstairs in an apartment converted from four large cells. He'll introduce me later.

"You'll be here for at least a month, maybe longer," Cartel says.

Ridiculous that he calls himself Cartel, I think to myself, but I won't tell him. I have to believe anyone involved in a drug cartel wouldn't want to advertise. On the other hand, he is here, so there's that.

"Man, I hope not."

"Why not? You're better off here where you have more freedom. You should hope it takes them a year to come get you. You'll get credit for the time because technically you're in US custody. Everyone tries to stay. There you suffer, my friend. It's hard time."

"Hey, listen, they have my wife, and I feel I should be there to support her. I don't know if it's the best thing to do, but it feels right," I say.

"Support? They'll have you locked up twenty-four hours a day. You can't support her. You won't even be able to talk to her."

"I understand, but just knowing I'm there will give her courage. Anyway, too late now."

"Yep."

"Cartel, I saw my lawyer this morning. He brought me some money, so I'd like to pay you for last night's dinner."

"C'mon, don't insult me. I told you it was on me."

"Are you sure? It's really no problem."

"Keep your money. You're gonna need it."

"Thanks, I appreciate it."

"Can we ever leave the unit?"

"You can shop in the prison store but don't go alone if you don't want to get robbed. You need to walk through general population. It's a motherfucking jungle down there. If I'm going, I'll let you know. Oscar can go with you."

"Alright. I have to buy food anyway because we're splitting the food between the four of us."

"And we go to the yard every second day. Today's our day, so if you want, be ready at two."

"Oh, okay, be nice to get a change of scenery. Is that the yard I saw on the way in, where all the garbage was?"

"Only yard there is. Couple of other units go at the same time. You got sneakers? You'll need some if you want to play basketball."

"No, just these loafers. I'm not playing. I just want to get some sun and air. Get out of here for a bit."

"Let me know if you want to play next time, and I'll find you a pair of sneakers."

"Thanks."

At two o'clock, we leave. We walk through the garbage to get to the yard. There wasn't as much of it as the other day, yet the flies seem more aggressive.

I'm shooting a basketball at one of the back boards with a guy named Alvarado, a Dominican from Florida. Nice guy, early fifties. He stays in shape by running up and down the stairs on the unit every morning.

He flew drug planes and now the US government wants to extradite him on conspiracy charges. He insists they have a weak case for extradition. He's been in Najayo fighting for four years, and it's costing him a lot of money.

He used to pay for a private cell, but he can't afford to anymore so he bunks with two other guys. It makes me wonder how he's going to beat the US government once he runs out of money. Sparring with an 800-pound gorilla is an exhausting proposition. Besides, I can't imagine the US going easy on a guy they deem as "uncooperative," but what do I know? If it was up to Conroy or Wendell, he'd get the death penalty.

On the main court, the only one with nets, teams are forming. There are enough players for four teams, so they split the rec time and run two games. There's arguing about the make-up of the teams, and I sense bad feelings between many of the players.

Alvarado explains long-standing, bitter rivalries exist here that carry over from the street, so satisfying everyone isn't always easy. Watching this, I'm more content with my decision not to play. I'm pretty sure bitter rivalry is a generous term for bad blood between drug gangs.

Five minutes later, teams are formed, and they're ready to start the first game so Alvarado and I clear a place on the bleachers and sit down to watch. One inmate is refereeing. He's wearing a bright yellow T-shirt and has a whistle he loves to blow.

He calls the teams to center court for the jump. The tallest guys from each side take the toss and barely land on their feet when a fist fight breaks out. Everyone's involved. Some try to contain it while others push, shove and hold each other. The ref blows his whistle repeatedly trying to restore calm.

It reminds me of a bench-clearing brawl in an NHL hockey game. Once everyone settles the game resumes.

It's more like a roller-derby match than a basketball game. Flying elbows, pushing, shoving, punching and tripping are as much a part of the game as dribbling and shooting. As basketball goes, these aren't the most skilled players I've watched. It's absurdly comical, as long as you're on the side-lines.

The game continues uninterrupted for the next ten minutes until a second fight erupts, leaving one guy with a bloody lip. I look over at the guards on the opposite side of the yard. They see what's going on, but as usual, don't care. I also notice three guys off to a corner in a very heated discussion. I don't recognize any of them, so I assume they're from another unit.

As our two hours of recreation comes to an end, I've tallied six fist fights, a spattering of arguments and multiple shoving matches.

The guards open the gate, call everyone inside and walk ahead. Most of the inmates on the yard leave quickly. Alvarado tells me the water runs out at this time of day, so they all want to get to the showers fast.

He and I are walking towards the gate. I'm on the left, and one of the guys I saw arguing earlier is walking in front of us.

When he's about twenty yards from the gate, I notice two inmates turn back to face him. Then from behind someone bumps into me lightly, passing on my left. He's walking in a calculated and purposeful manner. I'm pretty sure he's one of the others I saw arguing earlier.

I notice something in his right hand. I'm trying to process what's going on, but it's happening way too fast. Alvarado understands though, because he puts his arm out to stop me, and then I understand.

He catches up to the guy walking in front of us just as the other two raise their arms and with lightning speed strike at him with knives. One of them stabs him in the top of his chest just below his shoulder, and the other sticks him deep in his right side below the rib cage. He's screaming for the guards, cursing, trying to defend himself, but they're too much for him. Then the guy who bumped me moves in and stabs him repeatedly in the back and sides.

-¡Coño! ¡Diablo! Ayudame alguien! ¡Coño!

Fuck! Someone, help me! Fuck! He mutters and falls to the ground.

As fast as they attacked, they disappear through the gate. Alvarado pushes me forward and yells:

"Go!"

I move quickly, and as we pass him lying on the ground, I see a large pool of blood under him. His eyes are closed, and he's moaning.

Alvarado and I go through the gate, stamp through the garbage and walk quickly down the corridor towards the unit. I look for the guards, but there aren't any. Strange.

When we reach the unit, the gate is open but no guard. Alvarado practically pushes me up the stairs and, at the top, he grabs me by the elbow and pulls me hard towards the bathroom. For a split second, I get nervous and resist until I realize he just wants to tell me something.

"You didn't see a fucking thing, right?"

"No, man! Nothing! Not a fucking thing!"

"These people don't play! Don't talk about this, ever! Forget it! Just forget it!"

I look at him, understanding the gravity of the situation. I have no idea what it was about, and I don't want to know.

"Alvarado, I didn't see a thing. I didn't see a thing. I just want to go lie down, brother."

He looks at me for a minute, straight in my eyes as if he's looking for truth and says:

"Go man. Go chill."

I head to my cell and fall on my bed. I'm shaking, breathing heavily. It takes me a long time to calm down. I think of my wife, kids, and parents. I ask myself for the thousandth time how this happened? I wonder how it's all going to end. Will we be okay? Will we survive? My eyes begin to well with tears. I turn over and face the wall so no one will see. I ask God to carry us safely through this nightmare. I ask God to keep Lana safe. I ask God to keep my children safe. I ask him to keep me safe. Maybe after what I've done I have no right to ask.

Chapter 22

Oscar

I'VE BEEN HERE TWO weeks now, and I'm getting antsy. I wake up every morning and get ready to leave. I'm the first one to shower and the first dressed. Then I wait.

I'm running out of money. I bought a cheap cell phone and use it to call home every couple of days. Between the cost of pre-paid cell phone minutes, food, laundry service, medication and cell rental, I'm spending what I have fast.

To make matters worse, I experienced my first shake-down two days ago. Cartel warned it might happen. One of the guards tipped him off.

How do you prepare for a shake-down? Start by cleaning and organizing the cell. For some reason, it's supposed to deter them from turning it upside down. As you do, hide anything you shouldn't have, things like cell phones, weapons and, in Oscar's case, jars of fermenting fruit he uses to make his famous hooch.

He's proud of his hooch-making skills, acquired from an older inmate when he was first locked up. Every time he cooks up a batch, he recounts the story to me. I've heard it ten times in two weeks. I realize he's a bit off.

He makes vodka and rum and apparently both taste like they should. I tell him I don't drink, but he tries hard to get me to order anyway. He charges ten dollars for a sixteen-ounce plastic bottle of Oscar's finest. Truth is, he can't make enough. He's always sold out.

You can buy real liquor from the street but with the smuggling surcharges, it's too expensive for most.

Anyway, back to the shake-down. They hit the unit fast and hard. There were twenty of them led by a fierce looking Captain who carried his club at the ready. I could see the propensity for violence in his eyes. Dark skinned black man about six-foot tall, built like an NFL fullback. I made sure not to look at him or at least let him see me looking at him. He was deadly serious and yelled the whole time. It was obvious the other inmates were afraid of him.

They tore the unit apart. After two hours of intimidation and searching, all they took was our cell phones. They knew where to look.

They didn't touch the machete Sapo keeps under his mattress or Mexico's electric drill or Oscar's cache of dangerous tools like assorted hammers, wrenches and plyers. They didn't even bother with his chain-saw. Yes, that's right. He has a fucking chain-saw in the cell. They even left his fruit jars. Interesting.

There were a lot of upset inmates, and Cartel was working hard to mitigate their displeasure. He was in closed-door meetings most of the afternoon and, on two occasions, left the unit to go see the Colonel. He returned from the second meeting with great news. We can all get our cell phones back for a thousand pesos. He reminds us it's only because of his great relationship with the Colonel that he was able to arrange this.

The Colonel, for his part, doesn't want unhappy or frustrated inmates which can lead to bigger problems, so he agrees to release them. Right.... So, what did I do? I paid the thousand pesos. I need the phone.

I couldn't help notice Cartel had two bottles of Johnny Walker delivered to him later in the evening. In fairness to him, he did offer me a glass.

I call Victor every day and ask him to bring me money. He keeps promising to be here tomorrow. It's been four days and still no Victor. He apologizes profusely each time, citing the distance, the traffic and his busy schedule as reasons he hasn't been able to get here. Tomorrow, for sure, 100 percent, he promises. I remind him he's all I

127

have, and he assures me he'll be here. Out of sight, out of mind, and all that.

The last thing I want to do is call my family to ask them to wire money, but living here without money isn't an option. I don't even want to think about it, yet it's always on my mind.

I worry so much that I'm back to eating only once a day now. I wait until seven o'clock every night to order a pizza. We can actually order in food from local restaurants that deliver, providing we tip the guard. I found the restaurant's number written on the wall next to an out-of-order pay phone. They charge eight dollars for arguably the worst pizza on earth. There's sugar in the tomato sauce.

I wait downstairs by the gate to the unit for the delivery man. He's always happy to see me. I pass the money through along with his "propina," his tip, and he, in turn, hands me the box sideways through the bars. I also hand the guard outside the gate 100 pesos. I go upstairs and spend the first minute re-proportioning the toppings that shifted to one side before I eat it.

I really look forward to eating that pizza, as bad as it is. I'm reminded of a story my father told me about his time in a forced work-camp in Siberia during the war when he worked in an armaments factory.

"There vasn't food and for one whole year all ve had vas potato. I don't mean baked potato or fried potato or mashed potato. No, raw potato. Ve had nothing to cook with. But I vas lucky. You know vhy?"

"No, Dad, why?"

"Because I smuggled grease from the factory in my crotch, and I used it to cook the potato. But ve didn't eat the whole potato either. Ve peeled them and used the peel to make hamburgers for days vhen there vere no rations."

I hope it doesn't come to that.

Later that night I'm in the cell with Oscar, Sapo, another guy from our unit and one of the guards. We're watching a movie on DVD that we bought earlier from a street vendor who comes in to sell his wares every once in a while.

I've seen "The Bourne Ultimatum" before, but I really enjoy watching it. I read all the Bourne novels. Robert Ludlum is one of my favorite authors. The movie's in English with Spanish subtitles, and I keep turning the volume up to hear. Oscar keeps turning it down.

It's becoming clearer to me how twisted he is. He's constantly doing things to annoy. I feel like he wants to get a rise out of me, but to what end or for what reason, I don't know.

I'm not the only one he irritates. He keeps shutting the air-conditioning claiming it's not working properly, and Sapo keeps turning it back on claiming it is. There may be something wrong with it because it's not blowing very cold air, but it's providing relief from the heat. This small, confined cell is unbearably hot. It may even rate worse than the dungeon.

It's like an insane asylum scene from "One Flew Over the Cuckoo's Nest," another old favorite of mine. Oscar turns the volume down, and seconds later I tell him I can't hear, so I turn it back up. Then he closes the air-conditioning and places the remote on a chair which Sapo takes and turns back on. Oscar argues it's not working, and Sapo tells him it is. A few minutes later, he lowers the volume again, and I look at him and say, "Oscar, I can't hear. I'm turning it up."

Minutes later, he closes the air-conditioning again. Sapo grabs the remote and turns it back on.

This dance continues for the next hour until our guests leave. I can tell they're having trouble enjoying the movie with all the insanity.

Exhausted from dealing with Oscar, Sapo packs it in and goes into his cubby hole and closes the door. The second he does, Oscar closes the air again. Mexico is already sleeping, so it's just Oscar and me. I decide to talk to him about his behavior.

"Oscar, I understand you've been here a long time, but I'm paying my share of the rent while I'm here, so you need to respect that. I paid my part for the DVD, and I want to watch it just like you. I can speak Spanish okay, but I can't read and understand the sub-titles well enough to follow the movie. I need to hear the volume."

"Yes, but you make it too loud," he says.

"Oscar, it's not too loud. When you turn it down, I can't make out a word."

He says nothing.

"You may have a point with the air-conditioner though. I think the unit may need service, but it's still working enough to keep the cell cool. Why don't we leave it on, and tomorrow we'll try to get someone to look at it?"

"It's not working right, and I don't want it to break completely. I'm keeping it off."

"Oscar, it's too hot in here without it."

"You can use a fan."

"I don't have a fan, Oscar."

"I have one I can sell you."

"Oscar, I'm not buying a fan from you. I could be leaving tomorrow morning. I'm not spending money on a fan. You know what, let's just watch the movie."

"It's eleven, we're going to bed," he says.

"Oscar, there's only fifteen minutes left in the movie."

"We go to sleep at eleven. We can watch the rest tomorrow night."

With that, he closes the television and stands on the edge of his bed reaching for the top bunk. After a few seconds of fishing around, he brings down a large fan and positions it on the floor so it blows directly on him. Then he removes his pants, locks the cell door, hits the light switch and gets in his bed.

"Oscar, would you turn the fan outward a bit so I can get a little air please?" I'm on my bunk sweating. It's stifling.

"No, I need it on me."

"You know what, Oscar? You're an asshole!"

I can't believe I said it. It just came out. For a second, I prepare myself for the worst, but then he says:

"Give me 500 pesos, and I'll let you use the other fan I have for tonight."

"Fuck you, Oscar!" Shit I did it again.

"Okay," he says.

I'm pissed. I don't know what to do. He wants to grab as much money from me as he can before I leave, and I refuse to give into this prick. I'll speak to Cartel tomorrow to get into a different cell, as far away from this lunatic as possible. It's just a matter of time before the problem escalates into something more serious. My bad temper aside, I don't want trouble with him. I know what he's here for. I've already seen what can happen in a heartbeat when there's a beef in this place. Fights on the unit are so common that I don't even pay attention anymore.

An hour later, I'm still awake. I have a headache from the heat, the bad diet and lack of fluids. The headache is getting worse, and I decide I'm better off trying to sleep outside on the tier where there's a bit more air flow.

I get up quietly, take my make-shift pillow of rolled-up clothing and leave the cell. I'm happy to see everyone has gone to bed and I'm alone. I close the door gently, leaving it slightly ajar, and lie down on one of the benches.

Someone is tapping me hard on the leg. I open my eyes and see Sapo standing over me. Usually a pretty happy guy, he doesn't look it right now. Mexico is behind him.

"What? What's wrong?" I ask.

"What are you doing?" he asks.

"I'm sleeping here because I can't breathe in there. Oscar won't keep the air on, and I don't have a fan. It's too hot."

"You left the cell door unlocked! Are you stupid?"

"Stupid? Why? What's wrong? I'm right here," I say.

Suddenly he reaches down and grabs my arm squeezing hard. I struggle to get up, worried he may do worse.

"Get off of me! What the fuck are you doing? Leave me go!"

I grab his wrist and turn it, making him release me and jump up fast. I still don't understand what this is about. I'm afraid they're going to jump me.

"What the fuck are you doing? Why did you do that? What did I do? What's wrong?"

"I have enemies in this prison. We lock the door when we sleep. Never leave the cell door unlocked at night. Do you understand?"

"Shit, I'm sorry man. I didn't know. Someone should have told me."

"Now you know!"

131

With that, they walk back into the cell and lock the door, leaving me on the tier until morning.

The next day Alvarado tells me there were already three attempts on Sapo's life. The last time they almost succeeded. Someone got onto the unit late one night and attacked him while he slept. He was stabbed eight times but lived.

"Didn't you notice he never leaves the unit. It's not safe for him to be anywhere in the prison except here."

"No, I never really paid any attention. Why do they want to kill him?"

"One of the murders he's doing time for was the youngest brother of a big narco boss in Columbia. He put a 250-thousand-dollar contract on his head. Lot of guys in here want that money."

Now there's a thought. Maybe I won't have to call home for money after all.

Chapter 23

Back in Santo Domingo

I'M BACK IN A dungeon. This is the worst one yet. Worse because it's very small, and I'm feeling claustrophobic. Just down a hallway a guard sits at a desk. He thought he was being nice when he tried to hand me a dark, blood- and crud-stained pillow that was once a much lighter color. I didn't want to touch it and told him to throw it on the floor. It's still lying where it landed.

Taking a shower early yesterday morning turned out to be for naught, because once again, I'm lying in filth, and dealing with bugs and the occasional rodent. The good news is I have my trusted carry-on bag with me. I packed my clothes in large plastic bags which seems a God-send right now because I used the plastic to cover the filthy mattress that's on the floor. I'm hoping the sweat-slicked plastic will protect me from whatever diseases the mattress hosts. What a snob I've become complaining about the quality of a mattress.

The cell's only redeeming feature is it has bars instead of a solid door, so I have a view of the concrete wall facing me. There's no toilet, not even the hole in the ground I've come to expect. That's probably because I'm on the second floor. Instead, I have to wait for the guard to let me use a sort of shower room that has no showers but does have the standard wall spittle a foot off the floor, offering a slow flow of cloudy water. Of course, the floor is covered in feces.

I was brought here with two other guys also being extradited to New York for running the same scam. They showed up on the unit a week ago. One of them is from Montreal, and I know him, but we were not involved together. His wife was also arrested, but she's still in the woman's wing of Najayo. I don't know the other guy.

I spoke to Stephanie who told me the newspaper back home ran a story that implied we all worked together. We didn't, but I imagine the husband and wife spin seemed more appealing to the reporter and his editor. What we do have in common though is Roland Ross who worked with the two of them a few years back.

We were picked up by the Policia Nacional yesterday morning. I rode with three policemen in the back of a pick-up truck. I considered escape, realizing this might be the best chance I'd get. Then I thought about what it must be like to die in a hail of bullets, so I decided to pass.

I thought I was on my way to the airport, but instead, I was brought here to DNCD headquarters, the Dominican version of the DEA. They put me in this disgusting cell. Apparently, I have to wait here until the US Marshals land, and then I'll be taken to the airport to meet them. It should be sometime today.

Other than the regular fights between inmates, my last week in Najayo was uneventful. What's interesting is that the violence is becoming so normal that I'm beginning to view it with nonchalance. One fight, however, was particularly disturbing.

An inmate from Peru serving a long sentence came back from the rec yard one afternoon to find two inmates from another part of the prison visiting one of his cell mates. They were sitting on his bed drinking rum and having a good time.

The problem was, these two were part of the gang that met the cocaine smuggling boat he was working on when it landed in the D.R. to deliver its cargo. Instead of paying for the drugs, the Dominican buyers stole the cocaine after murdering everyone on board; or so they thought. He was the lone survivor and miraculously crawled away with his life and eleven bullets in his body. He was found on the side of a road by someone who brought him to the hospital. Somehow, he survived.

I understand why he was unhappy finding two of the assassins who tried to kill him in his cell, on his bed; disrespect at an unprecedented level. He, however, made his dissatisfaction known by attacking the two of them with a small machete. I didn't see the attack, but I heard it. What I saw was the gruesome aftermath when both were carried away. They were alive but gravely injured. The Peruvian was beaten badly by the mad Captain and two of his hand-picked guards in front of everyone and dragged off the unit. I didn't see him again.

Victor finally shows up with money, albeit not as much as I hoped for. He does promise to come back again but can't say when exactly. I suspect he can't wait for me to leave so he can keep what's left as complimentary compensation. For my part, I'm not really making a fuss because there isn't much I can do about anything.

During his update to me on the hopelessness of my situation, he confirms what I already know. My bank accounts were frozen by the Dominican authorities at the request of the United States Attorney General's office. I ask if there's anything he can do to get them released, but he says he doubts it. I knew he would say that, so I already granted a power of attorney to a woman lawyer I met on the unit. She claims to have a lot of experience with such things and promised to get my money released for the low price of 30 percent. I've pretty much thrown in the towel anyway, instead focusing all my energy on digging down deep so I can get through whatever lies ahead. For now, all I can do is wait and hope the marshals get here quick so I can get the fuck out of this hole.

Chapter 24

MCC

THE SOUND OF KEYS. I jump off the metal slab and go to the three-inch thick cell door to try and see. It has a tiny six by ten-inch window. It's designed for them to see in, not for me to see out. I can't look left or right, just directly in front of me to another cell. The black guy in there is still doing burpees. He never stops. He's shirtless, ripped and covered in tattoos; just like the movies. He's tried to talk to me a couple of times, but I can't really make out all he's saying through the two cell doors. I told him my name, but I don't know if he understood. He keeps calling me "Yo." I understood his name perfectly: Murder. He looks a bit crazy to me, but who knows what I look like to him.

"Guard! Guard! Hello?" I shout.

No answer.

"Guard, I need a blanket. I'm freezing in here!"

I hear the keys. He's closer. He's coming, thank God.

He looks at my ID card on the door.

"What is it, Stelman?" Military type. Flat-top, clean shaven, with a mean scowl.

"Guard, please, I need a blan…."

"I'm not a fucking guard! I'm a CO! Correctional Officer! You address me as CO, inmate!" he shouts.

"I'm sorry, CO. I didn't know. I'm…I'm new to this. I didn't mean to offend you."

"What do you want?" he asks.

136

"I need a blanket. I'm freezing. I asked the other guard…I mean CO who was here earlier when he brought my tray, but that was hours ago. I'm so cold. Can I please have one? I saw a whole rack of them outside the main door when they were bringing me in. Can I get one please?"

"He told me you asked for one before he left, but I've been busy. Still am. I'll get you one when I have a chance," he says.

"CO, it's been hours. Please, I'm freezing. I'll even take one from another cell. I don't care if it's dirty. Could you grab one while you're here?" I ask, almost begging.

"I can't right now. I'm doing rounds. Night watch will be here in a few hours. Ask them." He walks away.

What a prick! Rounds consist of looking through every tiny window to make sure no one is dead.

It's early fall and still very hot outside, but the air conditioning is cranked so high it feels like forty degrees in here. I wet chunks of toilet paper and stick them to the vent, but it's not working. I'm wearing a paper-thin T-shirt, boxer shorts and a jump suit that's three sizes too big. Everything is bright orange, even the cheap canvas shoes, which are too big; part of the punishment. They have hundreds of pairs in every size. I saw them, but the CO said he didn't have mine.

I'm miserable. I have a pounding migraine from caffeine withdrawal, and I'm very hungry. The tray they slid through the door slot in the cell door at five fifteen this morning had hardly any food; stale cereal, pint of milk, piece of hard breakfast cake. That's it. Well, there was a rotten banana, so I didn't eat it. Now I wish I had.

I'm in the Special Housing Unit: the SHU, the box, the hole, on the ninth floor of the Metropolitan Correctional Center in downtown Manhattan, New York. It's the most secure super max detention center in the country rivaled only by USP ADX in Colorado where the worst of the worst are serving their sentences, locked in underground cells twenty-three hours a day. It's also been described as worse than Guantanamo Bay. The indictment was filed here in the Southern District of New York, the Second Circuit, so the marshals brought me here to face justice. I arrived two nights ago. My wife is downstairs on the second floor in the woman's unit.

Four US marshals escorted me. We flew commercial from Santo Domingo via Atlanta to New York. It was unlike any flight I'd ever taken. Handcuffed, I had the privilege of pre-boarding from the tarmac and placed in the back row where the seats don't recline. I had an armed marshal on each side of me lest I somehow remove the handcuffs and take control of the aircraft. The other two marshals sat two rows up.

When we got here I went through intake. Now I'm waiting to be placed in general population. House-keeping didn't make it here before my arrival because it's still dirty from the last guest. The only source of natural light is a sliver of heavily frosted glass, caged behind bars. There's a one-piece stainless steel toilet-sink combo a few feet from the rack. Next to that is a metal table top surface, not big enough to write on, and an attached round metal stool. Truth is, I'm happy to have a toilet and sink of my own.

There's a total of sixteen two-man cells on this tier, eight on each side. I'm not alone because all day and night I hear guys shouting to each other up and down the tier. I can't sleep a wink. I'm hoping after I get some food in me I'll get a few hours.

I really need a shower too. It's been three days since my last shower in Najayo. In Atlanta airport, the marshals let me wash up a bit in a secured private bathroom obviously designed for detainees because there was a ceiling camera, and the steel door locked from the outside. I was in handcuffs though, so I couldn't really clean myself properly. I'm told I have to wait two more days until I can take a shower because I missed Friday's shower call. No one told me, and the room service information card is conveniently missing from my accommodations. Next chance, Monday.

I hope to have better luck with a shower than I'm having with a blanket. I smell really bad. They gave me a plastic bag with toiletries, and I tried to wash in the sink, but the water only stays on for a few seconds, so it's impossible really. I'm using the towel they gave me placed on top of my canvas shoes for a pillow. McGyver would be proud. Baby steps. Start with some food. All I can do is wait until the slot opens, and they slide it in.

Chapter 25

Shower Time

I FINALLY GOT MY blanket from night watch around two in the morning. At first, when he kicked my door and woke me up from my restless sleep, I was pissed. But when he slid the blanket through the slot, I was ecstatic. Receiving it was at par with driving off the dealership in a new car.

I find myself talking to God again. I've been doing that lately. I remember reading there is evidence of negative psychological impact on detainees after only three days of solitary confinement. I believe it. I no longer react to the sound of keys and slamming doors in the same way. The disappointment is too crushing. If they come, they come. It's day four, and I'm adapting. Not knowing how long it will go on for is the hardest part. If I knew it would be one week, one month, or even two, I could prepare myself mentally. Not knowing adds to my desperation and despair. I need to find a way to suppress it though. My time in the Dominican Republic gave me some experience with this sort of thing.

I've been thinking a lot about my father, a holocaust survivor. Growing up, he was the toughest man I knew. Nothing's changed. There was a side to him that was scary. He never seemed to fear anything. When I was a teenager, I traveled to Israel and met my father's only family who survived a Siberian work camp, largely due to my father.

Alex, his younger cousin by ten years, met me at the airport. I'll never forget what he said after the first few minutes: "Your father lived like a wild dog. He's the reason I'm alive." At the time, Alex was a little boy and my father provided food scraps and physical protection to him and his mother. To this day, my father still measures everything by "having food to eat."

I doubt it compares, but in these jails, I do what I have to do to survive. Because of the experience, I have a better appreciation for extreme conditions and what my father must have lived through.

It all seems surreal right now as I discover a different type of hell. Try to imagine being locked up in a space the size of a large closet for just a few hours, let alone days, weeks, months and for some, years. I understand now why Murder doesn't stop doing burpees. He's either doing them to remain sane or because he's already insane. I've started doing push-ups and sit-ups. It helps.

The highest point of the day is when the door slot opens, and they slide in a food tray. For one, I get to see someone else other than my friend, Murder. The ten-second distraction is a break from the boredom and loneliness. The food's terrible, but I've learned to expect it. I also know to eat, no matter how bad it is. I think about that scene in "Castaway" when Tom Hanks loses his soccer ball companion. I understood it then, but it really makes sense to me now. I've said almost nothing to Murder, and we know nothing about each other, but he's now my friend. Madness.

There's a sudden flurry of activity on the tier. It's shower time. When they passed out the breakfast trays this morning, I shouted at the CO through the slot. He promised I'd get mine today. I never wanted anything so bad. I pray he keeps his promise. If he doesn't, what can I do? I can't call the front desk to complain.

An hour later the CO shows up. He kicks my door. Why do they have to do that? It's all about the power.

"Stelman! Shower time. You want one?" he asks.

"Yes, CO, please!" I answer.

"Turn and face the wall, hands behind your back!" he orders.

I do as he says, and I hear the lock disengage. (He's going to cuff me? For a shower? Why?) He slaps the cuffs on me roughly and pulls hard on them for effect.

"Okay, let's go!" he orders and turns me around by my shoulders.

I see other inmates looking at me as we walk the ten yards to the end of the tier. This shit is beyond ridiculous, I think to myself.

The shower stall has a cell door, but it's only one third the size of a cell. The CO tells me to walk in and face the back wall. He removes my cuffs and says "You got ten minutes!" as he walks away.

I yell after him, "CO, where do I put my clothes? There's no hooks to hang them."

"Just leave them on the floor," he tells me.

"On the floor? They'll get all wet. I'll freeze to death in my cell! You can't be serious!"

"You want a shower or not?" he asks.

"Yes, of course but...."

"Stop complaining, and take your fucking shower!" he screams.

I immediately close my mouth. I know for sure if I say one more word, this prick is going to take me back to my cell. Crazy!

I learn days later that there are no hooks in the showers because they don't want to give inmates the opportunity to hurt or hang themselves. I guess freezing to death in wet clothes is okay.

I undress and place my clothes in a ball, shoes first, on the floor in the corner closest to the door to try and shelter them from the water. I turn the faucet on and, for the first time in close to two weeks, I stand under the water. It's wonderfully hot, and I almost cry because I'm so happy. I scrub the dirt and stink off my body and quickly repeat the process two more times, carefully counting the seconds and minutes in my head so as not to go over ten. When I get to nine, I towel off and get dressed. I'm not happy I have to wear the same clothes, but it is what it is. I'm not about to complain. When I pick them up, I'm surprised they stayed reasonably dry. More blessings.

Ten more minutes pass, and I'm standing in a wet shower stall fully dressed. I feel like an asshole, and I'm beginning to get extremely anxious. The stall is moldy, and I'm getting claustrophobic. I've yelled for the CO twice, but no one has shown, so I wait. I hear two COs talking, and I keep calling, but no one cares. After what feels like a half hour, the calming effect of the hot water and lack of sleep from my ordeal have caught up with me, and my eyes start closing. There's nowhere to sit, but I can't hold my head up, so I kneel down and lean my head against the wall. I'm terribly uncomfortable yet terribly sleepy, so I succumb to the conditions and sit on the shower floor resting my head against the wall. I must have nodded off because some time later I wake up to the CO kicking the door.

"Let's go, Stelman! You've been in here for almost an hour! I said ten minutes!" he barks.

"I was ready in ten minutes, but you never came! I kept calling you. Didn't you hear me? I heard you talking to someone," I tell him.

"No, I didn't. You didn't yell loud enough. Turn around and face the wall!"

Liar.

He cuffs me, walks me back to my cell and locks me in.

Truthfully, I'm so happy to be clean, he can't even get to me right now. Maybe I'm getting used to the mental abuse. I fall on my rack as if it's a king bed at the Waldorf Astoria and sleep soundly for the first time since I was arrested. Be grateful for small things. They really do matter.

Chapter 26

The Bullpen

A HEAVY DOOR SLAMS shut. Loud voices, lots of activity. I open my eyes. Still dark.

What time is it, I wonder? I've barely slept. My shoulder and hip ache from the hard metal rack below me. Every time I drift off, the soreness wakes me. They're opening door slots. Feeding time. I sit up just as the food cart approaches. The CO unlocks my slot, and the orderly slides a tray through.

"Stelman, you're going downstairs. Ten minutes!" he barks.

"For what? I can't get ready in ten minutes!" I'm getting sick of these pricks with their stupid orders. Fuck him!

"You're going to court. Hurry up!" he says with little regard.

"What time is it?" I ask.

"It's five fifteen. Move it!" he says and walks out of sight.

"What time does the court open? I'm sure not before eight-thirty. I need more than ten minutes to eat and get ready!" I yell through the cell door, incredulously.

"Too fucking bad! I'll be back in ten!" I hear from down the range.

I brush my teeth with the four-inch brush and tiny tube of toothpaste they gave me. I'm grateful for them. I splash water on my face and open the tray. The milk is frozen stiff, so I stuff it under the bed for later, even though I don't know if I'll be back. I eat the stale cereal with my hands. The cake is hard and dry, and I practically choke on it. I drink a few sips of water from the faucet. The orange is great. I eat it and wish I had another one. I also wish I had coffee. The headache hasn't stopped. I never realized how powerful a drug caffeine is.

How long has it been? Five minutes? I place the tray on the floor and sit on the toilet. I don't really have to go, but I try anyway. I don't know when I'll get another chance. Plan ahead. After a few minutes, I get up. No luck. Santo Domingo already taught me that I can't shit under pressure. Murphy's law will kick in later.

After much more than ten minutes the asshole is back.

"Put your hands through the slot!"

"I thought you said ten minutes. What time is it now?"

"Five forty-five! Hurry up, you're late!"

Don't say a word. He's trying his best to get a rise out of me. I smile at him and put my hands through. He slaps some cuffs on my wrists and tightens them. They hurt.

"C'mon, CO, loosen them a bit. They're hurting me!" I say, very annoyed. He got me in the end, after all.

"Can't do that. You'll be fine." He smirks.

I say nothing, no point. He'll just make it worse somehow.

"Move back!" he orders.

I step back, and he unlocks the cell door. "Let's go!"

He walks me to the main door where two other guys are cuffed and waiting.

"Special Housing. Main. Three to go!" he says into his radio.

The door opens, and we get on the elevators. At the basement level, we go through the door to R&D (Receiving and Departure). I was here two nights ago when they brought me in. This is where I met the in-take officer who finger printed me and took a DNA swab for the third time since my arrest.

R&D is a large room with a service counter manned by two COs. Behind them, on the wall, are all form of chains and restraints. There are several other rooms and offices branching off the main one. We're not placed in one of the offices nor offered coffee while we wait. Instead they move us to a fifteen- by fifteen-foot holding cell with benches along the walls.

The two guys I'm with are both black and look far more experienced. One is late thirties and the other mid-twenties. Both wear the standard tattoo sleeves. The older guy has a tear drop under his left eye and a tattoo on his arm that says RIP Troy 1977-2005. There's more, but I can't decipher it. He sees me looking, so I nod.

"I been done this shit yesterday. Motherfuckers is so fuckin' stupid. I told them my hearing was postponed till today, but they wouldn't listen. Motherfuckers! I sat in the bull pen the whole fuckin' day. Stupid motherfuckers. Shit got me tight!" he says to both of us.

"Dats how dey do," adds the younger one.

"Dey more fucked up dan de State. I been on de island for six months and den dey tell me dese Fed niggas picked up my case. Dis shits crazy! Five grams o' crack. Dees motherfuckers is vicious!"

I just listen. He's talking about Rikers Island in New York. He was there facing state charges when the Feds delivered an indictment. They continue to talk to each other for a few minutes, and then the younger one who calls himself B turns to me and says:

"What dey get you for?"

"Fraud."

"Oh, yeah? What, like bank fraud? Credit card fraud? Dat shit?" he asks.

" No, it was something else," I answer.

"You from New York?" G Rock, the older one, asks.

"No, I'm from Canada."

"Oh, yeah, supposed to be nice in Canada. Where in Canada?"

"Montreal."

"Where that at?" he asks.

"It's North of New York City, just over the Canadian border."

"Dat where Drake from?" asks B.

"No, he's from Toronto," I say

"Oh, yeah, Raptors up there in Toronto too. Hear it's nice. I want to go there when I get out," says G Rock. "I was locked up in Raybrook right near Canada in 2003 on my first bid. There was some Canadian niggas there on the treaty transfer. One of them was my bunky. His name was Pierre something. Big weed dealer. You know him? Good nigga, crazy as a motherfucker," G Rock says.

"No, I don't. Lot of people in Canada. But it sounds like he may be where I'm from, because his name is French. Where I live it's mostly French Canadian."

"I hear jails in Canada is sweet," says B.

"I don't know. This is my first time in trouble. I've never been in jail before. I wasn't in Canada when I got arrested either. I was living in the Dominican Republic with my family. I was extradited here. I can guarantee you that Dominican jails aren't sweet though," I say with a smile.

"No shit, day come and get you all da way dere?" asks B.

"Yeah," I say.

"You was getting' that money. But if you wasn't in the United States, why they get you?" asks G Rock.

"Because there were American victims," I answer.

"Oh, yeah, makes sense."

"What dat like, the Dominican Republic? I hear the bitches is like dat. My boy from der. I plan to go der when I get done. He lives in the city," adds B.

"Do you know what city? Is it a big city? Santo Domingo maybe, or Santiago?" I ask, just to sound like I give a shit.

"Yeah, yeah, I think dat de one," he says.

The door unlocks and eight more inmates walk in. B knows two of them from the street. It's like a family reunion. They perform some ritualistic hand shake which I assume is gang proprietary, but I can't be sure.

They are a mix of blacks and Latinos. There's one other white person.

Since that first night in jail in Santo Domingo, I've been learning how to carry myself in this environment. Less is more, so I only talk if someone talks to me and make sure to be polite and respectful, but with an air of indifference. An "I don't need any more friends" type of vibe.

A Latino guy asks me something, and I answer in Spanish. He's a Puerto Rican from the Bronx, and he's surprised I speak Spanish. He asks me how I speak Spanish, so I tell him, and he turns to another guy and says:

"Hey, Javi, he's your homey, my nigga! He lived in Santo Domingo. He's from Canada."

Javier is Dominican. He's from Washington Heights, New York, home to a million Dominicans. He's here for drugs. He's only been to the D.R. once in his life when he was young so he's full of questions about the country and amazed at how much I know. We're like brothers. I want to ask him if he knows my friend, Murder. If he does I'll consider it divine intervention.

Just then the door opens and, one at a time, our names are called. We have to recite our Federal registration number.

"Stelman!"

"Yeah, 91903054."

"Okay, follow those guys over there."

We are led to another changing room and ordered to pick clothes in our sizes. This uniform is blue and comes in two pieces; top and bottom. It's for court appearances. Once dressed, we're placed in another holding cell to wait. By the time the process is complete, there are about twenty-five of us waiting.

At this point the marshals take over. They enter like Rock Stars, dressed in business suits, smiling and waving hello to the lesser BOP workers. They cuff and chain us together in groups of ten and herd us, one chained group at a time, into an elevator that goes to a subterranean level. We are instructed to follow a painted red line on the floor that leads us through a long tunnel. On the other side of the tunnel, we take another elevator up and then pass through a door that reads "Federal Court House." Once inside, we're placed in holding cells. There are guys waiting who were brought from other jails. I hear several refer to this place as the bullpen, and I'm reminded what G Rock said earlier. This is where you wait for a court appearance, and that wait could be all day. It's only seven-thirty, and court won't open for another hour.

A marshal passes with a cart, handing out brown paper bags for each of us through the bars. I open mine to find a ham and cheese sandwich, an apple and a pint of milk.

It's supposed to be lunch, but most guys eat theirs immediately. I know I'll be hungry later, so I eat the apple, drink the milk and save the sandwich.

I count fifteen and can't help but notice for the third time today that most are Black and Latino. Conversations are about common acquaintances, previous bids or venomous complaints about the FBI, the judge, the prosecutor or their own defense attorneys. I'm amazed at how comfortable some of these guys seem to be with their situation. Most claim to be here because someone told on them. I do my best to stay out of any conversations as I conclude there's nothing to gain by discussing anything.

About two hours later, I cave to the hunger and eat my sandwich. My eyes are beginning to close so I take my shoes off, place them on the bench and use them as a pillow. I actually doze off for a bit until I hear my name being called down range.

Chapter 27

Marty

HERE WE GO AGAIN. The marshal cuffs me and escorts me through a door and down a long corridor. I'm placed in a small room where I sit in a wood chair in front of a tempered glass window just like I've seen on TV cop shows. I assume I'm here to see my government appointed lawyer paid for through the "Criminal Justice Act" program. To ensure everyone being prosecuted has representation and access to fair and balanced justice, the government hires private lawyers to represent defendants.

When I was in Najayo, I interviewed a couple of New York criminal lawyers by telephone and quickly realized the only thing they would be good at is extracting money from me. Having experienced Lana's Miami lawyer, I saw how quickly the money goes. He met with her twice and appeared in court once, and it cost me ten thousand dollars. It also didn't help that I didn't trust a word they said which ranged from "I know your judge very well, you're probably looking at six months" to "Don't worry, you'll be okay, I just need a twenty-five-thousand-dollar retainer to get started." None of what I was hearing aligned with what guys awaiting or fighting extradition were telling me about "the land of the free," so I decided not to try to borrow money to pay for my defense just yet, at least until I learned more.

After about fifteen minutes of sitting in total discomfort, a tall, heavy set man appears at the window. He looks late sixties with a bald head.

"Hello, Mr. Stelman. My name is Marty Clayman. The government appointed me to represent you. Your wife is okay. She's being represented by another lawyer. I know him. He's a good lawyer."

"Okay Marty, nice to meet you, although I wish the circumstances were different. Will I be able to see my wife?"

"Yes. We'll be able to set up a co-defendant meeting at some point with her lawyer present. We'll do that as soon as possible."

"Okay, good. Marty, can you tell me a little about yourself? I'm assuming you're very experienced, right?" I ask, hoping to be impressed.

"I'm sixty-eight years old, and I've been practicing law in New York for over forty years. I'm in private practice, but my firm is accredited for CJA cases, so I've been appointed to handle your case. My normal fee is 500 dollars an hour. The government only pays 125," he explains.

I'm not sure why he's telling me this but it sounds an awful lot like "I don't want to work too hard on your case." At first, I was happy when I realized Marty was Jewish. I can just tell. One of the tribe sort of thing, or in prison speak, "my homeboy," but now I'm not sure. The way he's looking at it, he's losing 375 dollars an hour, and he's holding me responsible for his loss. Great.

"Marty, you don't sound happy to be working on my case. Is it a problem? I need to know."

"No, no. Of course not. I work the same whether you pay my full rate or if the government is paying. I'm a professional," he assures me. "It's just that I got here at eight thirty this morning, and it took me three hours to get to see you. The security here is ridiculous, but that's fine."

"Okay, that's good then. I just find it funny that you even mention it is all. I mean about the fee," I say.

"Oh no, please…I'm just explaining how the system works. They really don't pay us enough, especially when I waste a whole morning trying to get in."

"Well I'm sorry about that Marty. But let me ask you a question. Why then are you part of the CJA program? I mean, are you obligated to do it, or is it voluntary?"

"Oh no, in fact you have to qualify to be accredited to participate. Not every lawyer makes it. I do about two every month. Helps pay the office overhead," he explains.

"Makes sense. So, in other words, you take these on when you have no other paying client, right? Or to top-off your existing case load. Found money, so to speak."

"Well, I suppose you can put it like that. But, understand, I treat all my clients and their cases the same, no matter what."

The fact that he said it again confirms that he's only focusing on the reduced fee the government pays him. Fuck! Just what I need, a lawyer who isn't just doing me a favor, but worse, feels like I'm costing him money. Can it get any worse? Nothing much I can do about it at this moment, so I'll see how things go. If I get the sense that he's not serving my interests I'll figure out what to do. In the meantime, I'll try and find out what options I have.

"Marty, talk to me. I want to know what I'm looking at here," I say all business-like.

"Okay. I spoke to your prosecutor, and I have to tell you she really doesn't like you. She's tough. In forty years I never had such a difficult conversation with a prosecutor."

"You're pulling my leg, right, Marty?"

"No, I'm serious. She even told me she won't speak to me on the phone any more. Only on the web."

"What do you mean 'on the web? What does that even mean?"

"Through the email. She sent me some on my phone, but I didn't know how to open them. That's why I called her, but she said she won't take any more calls. She said she only uses the email and the text messages."

"Marty, can I ask you a question? Do you know how to use electronic communication? Are you comfortable using email and text messaging? Tell me the truth please, Marty."

"Well, not really. I just started using it. My secretary prints them out for me, and I tell her what to write, and she sends them. I have trouble opening them. I'm still learning, but I'm getting better."

"Shit, I hope so. Okay, Marty, what happens now?"

"We're going in front of the judge to enter a plea. For now, plead not guilty. Then we'll make a decision on how to proceed. The process will take some time, at least a few months."

"Alright. How well do you know my judge? Stolberg, right?"

"Ralph Stolberg. I know him well. I need to be honest with you. He's not a good judge to have. He's very tough. He's one of the toughest judges in the second circuit."

I just look at him, speechless. Then: "So, Marty, you're telling me I have the worst prosecutor you've seen in forty years and the toughest judge in the second circuit. That's wonderful. How are you going to help me, Marty?" I ask.

"I'll do everything I can to help you. Your best course of action is to take a plea. There is something else. Let me ask you something. Did the FBI ask you for help with anything?"

"Help? What kind of help would they need from me?" I know where he's going, but I want to see how he gets there.

"Information. Did they ask you for any information you have that would help them?" he asks.

"They kept asking me about the location of one guy and about the people who sell leads. I told them I have no information, and I can't help them. I don't know anything."

"Okay, listen, Warren. I must tell you, the best way to help yourself is to cooperate with the government. I'll speak to the prosecutor and see if she's willing to cut a deal if you can help them with information they need. She did allude to something like that on the phone. That's your best bet." He announces this like he just delivered the final round answer on a TV game show.

"Hold on a minute, Marty. I'm not doing anything like that. I won't cooperate against my wife. Is that what you're suggesting? I won't cooperate against anyone else either. Forget that!"

"Right now, you should be worried about yourself. The prosecutor told me she calculated your guidelines, and you're looking at twelve years at the lowest," he says.

I can't believe what he just said, and I lose my temper. "Twelve years! Are you out of your mind? Twelve years? That's insane! I stole some money, I didn't kill anyone! I deserve to be punished but twelve years? No fucking way! No way! Hey, you know what, you can't help me. I want another lawyer! Someone who's ready to work hard and help me, not sell me out."

"Calm down, just calm down. Please stop shouting. I know this is a difficult situation to be in. That's her starting point. It's a process. I'm just telling you that the best way to help yourself is to help them. That's the way it works. Calm down. If you don't want to, fine. I'll work hard on your case. Just calm down. I wouldn't be doing my job if I didn't tell you your best course of action. Okay?"

"Okay, Marty, sorry. Sorry for yelling. Look, Marty, my wife and I, we have four children. We're good parents. I was a businessman all my life. I never broke the law before. I've never been in trouble. This is the first time. Our first time. We made a terrible mistake. There were extenuating circumstances that led us to this. It's not an excuse, and it doesn't excuse what I did. I understand that. I can't go to prison for twelve years or even five years. That's a very long time. Do you understand?" I ask.

"I understand what you're saying, but I must tell you you're not being realistic. Without cooperating you're going to be doing some time. It's not that bad."

"What's not that bad? Going to prison? Are you serious? What are you talking about? It's bad! It's bad for us. It's bad for our children, our parents. It's terrible! It's already terrible! Marty, do you know anything about my case? Have you received anything from the government yet? I understand in a fraud case the time you can get relates to the amount of the fraud. Have they provided anything yet? Do we even know what the case consists of?"

"No. I just have a copy of the indictment. I received it yesterday afternoon."

"So, all you have is the indictment, and on the strength of that you're trying to get me prepared that I'll be going to prison for a long time? Two years is a long time to me. Marty, what about innocent until proven guilty? Isn't this America? Isn't that how it's supposed to work? What do I need a lawyer for if all you want to do is get me mentally prepared to go to prison? That's not going to happen so easily. I'm going to fight this thing. Are you ready to do that, to fight for me? Or do I find another lawyer?"

"Yes, of course I'll fight hard. I'm a professional."

"I know you keep telling me that. Okay, I plead not guilty. Then what happens?"

"They take you back to MCC and we wait on a trial date. In the meantime, we'll get the discovery from the government, and the whole process begins. Once we know exactly what they have, we can decide how to proceed. Listen, I need to get into the court room right now. I don't want to upset Stolberg."

"Okay, but when will I see you again?"

"Probably sometime in the next few weeks."

"How do I reach you?"

"Oh yeah, here's my business card. You can email me."

"Will you be able to open an email?"

"Of course."

"It's just that you said you're still learning how to. Should I call instead?

"Yeah, that's probably better."

"Okay, Marty, fair enough. I'll call you."

Chapter 28

Not Guilty, Judge

ONCE MARTY LEFT, I had a few minutes to think about my situation. I was arrested by Interpol in a foreign country on behalf of the US government after what had to be an expensive investigation. The US then instituted extradition proceedings in the Supreme Court of the Dominican Republic. I made it easier for them, and hopefully myself, by agreeing to extradition, but that remains to be seen. The four marshals they sent to escort me spent the weekend in Santo Domingo, so there was salary, over-time pay and expenses, plus the cost of commercial flights. Now I'm here in New York in Federal custody, facing criminal charges, and I'm being represented by an attorney who is being paid by the very same government.

Conflict of interest? You think? To make matters worse, my attorney is so unhappy with his fee, he can't help but repeat this sentiment more than once. Then there's the matter of the judge and prosecutor. I may not be the smartest guy around, but it's pretty clear the deck is stacked against me.

I've learned that most federal prosecutions end up in plea bargains, contributing to the government's 97 percent conviction rate. For white collar crime, it's 99 percent. So, I have a 1 percent chance of not being convicted. If I go to trial and lose, the sentence will be very harsh as the government punishes people who take them to trial: sets the tone for the next idiot who tries. So, I'm going to prison, I get that. What I need to do is make sure it's for as little time as possible.

The marshal escorts me back to the bullpen where I eat the sandwich I saved. It was right there where I left it. As expected, I need to use the toilet. In the corner of the cell, tucked behind a three-foot dividing wall, providing some semblance of privacy, is the toilet-sink combo. Thankfully there is toilet paper, and I use some to clean off the seat and sit down on the cold stainless steel. I go about my business with nine other men in the room, flushing continuously during the process. What's crazy is this is getting easier to do each time. No one bats an eye. Everyone's been in the same situation. I wash my hands with water; there's no soap.

There's a continuous flow of prisoners to and from the bullpens for their court hearings. It's now eleven thirty, and I'm still waiting. A marshal brings back a prisoner who left first thing this morning. He doesn't look happy. I heard him talking earlier. He's been at MCC for nine months on pre-trial for a drug conspiracy, and he was surprised they brought him here this morning. He didn't know why he was coming. Now he does. He's about twenty-seven years old, and he's from the Bronx. He's also a "Blood."

"Yo, VG. What's wrong, my nigga?" asks Slim, another Blood.

"These Motherfuckers is vicious, my nigga!" he says with contempt.

"They superseded six of us niggas. Someone told. They put a body on us, my nigga. I ain't do nothin'. I don't know nothing 'bout no body, my nigga! These niggas wanna fry me, my nigga. This shit's crazy. These motherfuckers don't play, my nigga. I'm lookin' at life, my nigga."

I tune it out. I can't believe I'm here. I can't believe the mess I got myself into. How does a fairly intelligent, educated, responsible, otherwise decent person, end up where I am? Fear and greed, that's how. Fear of failing and greed to get back what I lost. To put it in current terms, I'm one stupid motherfucker, my nigga.

I close my eyes and think of my children. A lot of good I will be to them now. Instead of helping them, they'll have to help me. I'm dying inside. I thought things were bad before, now I wish I had those problems.

They're calling me. Somehow, despite all the noise, I dozed off. The marshal appears, opens the door and cuffs me. We make our way to a different elevator which takes us to the court room level, and he locks me in a small holding cell. Fifteen minutes later, he's back, and he walks me into the court room. Just as I enter, he whispers in my ear "no trouble."

It's much bigger than I expected. About twenty people sit in the audience section at the back. I wonder if any are related to my case. I hope not. Marty is sitting at a table on the left side of the room, and he motions for me to join him. I pass another table on the right side where a man and a woman are sitting. I assume they're the prosecutors. In front of us is an elevated station where the court stenographer works. Behind her, on a higher elevation, is the judge's stage.

Minutes later, the court clerk announces:

"All rise for the honorable Judge Ralph A. Stolberg."

We do, and as he enters and takes his place, he directs us to be seated.

So far, the television shows I've watched seem bang on.

The formalities are handled, and the judge calls on the government. Anna Gabro, the Assistant United States Attorney and the worst prosecutor Marty has ever encountered, stands up and tells the toughest judge in the Second Circuit she's there on behalf of the government. Marty confirms he is here for me.

Judge Stolberg then reads the charges against me.

One count of conspiring to commit wire fraud, in connection with a telemarketing scheme that victimized 10 or more persons over the age of 55 in violation of Title 18, United States Code 1349 & 2326(2).

One count of committing wire fraud through a telemarketing scheme that victimized 10 or more persons over the age of 55 and targeted persons over the age of 55 and aiding and abetting in the same, in violation of Title 18, USC. section 1343, 2326(2).

One count of conspiring to launder the proceeds of the conspiracy to commit the wire fraud telemarketing scheme in violation of Title 18 USC. section 1956(a)(1)(B)(2).

157

I'm not a lawyer, but the first two counts sound awfully similar to me. I mean how do you "do" something, without thinking about it. I'll have to ask Marty about this. It's the first time I've heard the charges against me.

Judge Stolberg explains that these charges carry a combined penalty of zero to forty years imprisonment. Did he say forty? Really? Forty fucking years? I begin to sweat profusely, feeling ill. It's so outrageous it's as if I'm watching this scene unfold from somewhere else. I heard it, but I can't grasp it. If forty is the high end, what's a good deal? Where will this land? Holy Fuck! I feel nauseous.

Stolberg orders me to stand up and asks me to address the court.

"Mr. Stelman, do you understand the charges against you?"

"Yes, Judge, I do," I say in a quivering, barely audible voice, because I'm doing everything possible to keep the vomit down.

"Please speak up, Mr. Stelman, so the court can hear you."

"Yes, judge, I do."

"To the charge in the first count, how do you plead?"

"Not guilty."

"In the second count, how do you plead?"

"Not guilty."

"In the third count, how do you plead?"

"Not guilty."

"Of course, you do," he says sarcastically.

"Okay, Mr. Stelman, you can be seated. I'm setting trial for November 15, 2013. Is that good for the government, Miss Gabro?"

"Yes, Judge, that will be fine."

"Mr. Clayman?"

"Judge, let me just check my calendar please."

With that Marty starts fumbling in his suit pocket for his agenda. He spends the next two minutes trying to decipher what he's scribbled while everyone waits impatiently. I'm watching Stolberg watch Marty and it's becoming clear to me that he may like Marty even less than he likes me.

"Um, okay Judge, just give me a few more seconds here." A few loose papers nestled in the center pages of his agenda fall to the floor and, when he bends down to pick them up, he bangs his shoulder against the desk and loses his balance. I reach over to steady him.

"Are you okay, Mr. Clayman?" Stolberg asks.

"Yes, Judge, thank you. I'm sorry about the delay. I think I got it. Yes, yes, I do. Judge, I will be out of the country at that time. I would ask that we set the trial for the last week of February as I am in court for the first two weeks of February."

"I don't want this to drag on, Mr. Clayman. You may have to reschedule your trip. This court is very backlogged. It is unable to accommodate everyone's schedules. But, considering, I will set trial for January 15th. I trust that will be suitable?" Almost daring Marty to say no.

"Hmm....15th January you say? Let me check. Another thirty seconds that feel like thirty years. Stolberg is getting pissed, and I am feeling the water rise to my neck. Finally, "Judge, that will be fine," Marty says defeated.

"Happy that works for you, Mr. Clayman." Marty is still writing the date in his agenda and grumbles something. He's beginning to make me sick.

"Miss Gabro?"

"That works for the government, Judge. Thank you." Already sounding victorious.

"Excellent. Court adjourned," Stolberg says with a powerful bellow as he rises to leave.

Just like that, it's over. Marty tells me he'll be in touch. Thinking about the cost of parking in Manhattan, he can't wait to get out of here.

Chapter 29

11 North

THEY BROUGHT ME BACK to the SHU after court. It's mid-afternoon and the CO just unlocked my door and told me to walk to the laundry area to change from orange to brown; the first indication that I'm moving. When he hands me a bed roll with a blanket, sheet, towels and a face cloth, I have no doubt.

We take the elevators to the eleventh floor, and he directs me to the right where a large steel reinforced door reads eleven north, across the hall, eleven south. Glass panes next to each reveal men moving freely inside. Okay, housing units.

"One package for eleven north at the door," he says into his radio.

A few seconds later a buzz, and the lock pops. He walks me inside to the officer's bubble, a secure work station enclosed in tempered glass where the unit officer can escape to, if necessary. We pass a kitchen area along the way. It has stainless steel counters, a large double sink and two microwave ovens.

I feel the eyes of inmates on me. They look tough, like hardened criminals. I act like it's nothing, like I've done this before, trying to project an air of confidence and indifference. I glance around. The unit is a large triangular shaped common area with three tiers running off it. Each tier splits into an upper and lower level with sixteen two-man cells on each level. Steel barred doors at the entrance to each level are used to lock down the tier.

The main floor has three televisions. Inmates listen to the TVs through radio head-sets. In one corner of the unit floor is a separate glass enclosed room that serves as a gym with an exercise system of bars for pull-ups, dips and sit-ups. Another TV is mounted on the wall in the gym. Outside the gym, a staircase rises to a mezzanine level that houses computer work stations for email access. There are also offices for the unit manager, counselor and case manager. Three inmates lean over the railing above me and stare.

Some watch TV surrounded by others who are talking, laughing and shouting. Two guys play ping-pong on a table set up in the middle of the unit floor. I look to the tiers and see men sitting at tables playing cards while others eat. Across the floor on two-tier, a group of guys sits on the stairs as if they're outside a building on their block in the Bronx. They listen to one of their homies rap as they bob their heads and clap their hands to the beat. It's very loud in here but preferable to my last address.

Of the ninety-six inmates the unit holds, most are Black and Latino. I see three telephones on the wall and realize it's going on two weeks since I've spoken to my kids. I'm sure they're worried about me. I'm worried about them, and I want to hear how my wife is doing.

It feels good to be around people again, but I have no idea what to expect. It isn't fear, but it's definitely more than nervous.

The unit CO asks for my ID as he writes something in his duty book.

"Says here you need a lower bunk."

"Yes, that's right." I answer. With a top bunk I have to climb up and down for stand-up count and to use the toilet; a real pain in the ass. "Why don't you have a lower bunk pass then?" he asks.

"I don't know. What's that? How do I get one?"

"You get it from medical. The medical intake officer who wrote this didn't tell you that?"

"I don't think so. I would remember that. But I need a lower bunk because I suffer from acute vertigo, and I had a heart attack in 2010."

The heart attack story comes in handy again. The acute vertigo is creative freedom. I just came up with it and don't even know if it makes sense, but it sounds very medical. Enough for him anyway.

"Alright. I put you in a lower bunk for now, but you need a pass from medical, or you'll lose it."

"How do I see medical?" I ask.

"Watch the call-outs. You should be scheduled by next week."

"Okay." I have no idea what the call-outs are, but I'll find out.

"You're in tier three cell seven, that way." He points to the right side of the unit.

I grab my ID and head to my cell. All eyes are on me as I walk down six steps and straight to the back of the tier. My new house is the second to last cell on the right. The door is open, and a Latino guy is moving his property to the top bunk.

"Hey, what's up?" I ask, trying to break the ice.

"The police told me I have to move up top. That's what's up. I don't like the top bunk."

"Sorry, man, I have a medical condition. I can't sleep on top," I say looking for his buy-in.

"I'm Warren, from Canada. I just got out of the SHU."

He tells me to call him "Cash." He's twenty-five and Puerto Rican. He's here on a drug conspiracy and homicide case. He's a Latin King.

Jackpot! I'll be sleeping in a locked cell with a pissed-off murderer. Like I don't have enough on my plate. It's his first Fed bid, but he did two years in the state when he was eighteen. I ask him a bunch of questions about how things work, and he gives me a bunch of short answers.

I take my bed roll and make up my rack. The mattress is a lumpy, cracked, foam-filled piece of garbage, and I realize that I'll have to find a solution for it if I ever hope to sleep at all. It's worse than the one I slept on in the hole. I ask Cash what he thinks I should do, and he tells me to wrap it tight with a blanket to compact it. I don't know exactly what he means or how to do it, but I will deal with it tomorrow.

A few minutes later, I hear a female voice calling my name from the unit floor.

"Stelman! Stelman!"

Cash sticks his head down from his rack and says:

"That's you, right? Stelman?" He looked at my ID while we were talking.

"Yeah," I answer.

"Pill line. Go get your meds. Take your ID with you. Hurry up."

"Oh, okay."

"Stelman! Last call! Pill line!" I hear as I grab my ID and head up the stairs to the main floor of the unit.

A nurse is standing impatiently behind a pill dispensary cart.

"You Stelman?" She sounds pissed off.

"Yes."

"You didn't hear me call pill line?"

"I heard something, but I wasn't sure what it meant. I'm new."

"Well, now you know. Next time you hear pill line get here fast. Don't keep me waiting. I have a thousand inmates to see. You're not special."

"Yes, Ma'am, sorry."

She hands me my pills in a Dixie cup and a second cup with water. She tells me to swallow the pills and then open my mouth wide and stick out my tongue. She needs to be sure I didn't squirrel them away in the back of my mouth or cheek for some reason. One pill is for acid reflux the other high blood pressure.

Meanwhile, a few black guys are gathered on the stairs to tier one and two of them are laughing at my predicament. I don't like it and decide at that moment to let them know. This is something I knew would happen eventually. My jail time in the Dominican Republic taught me a few things and I imagine it's not too different here. I don't want to fight, but I will if I have to. Growing up both English and Jewish in a predominantly French-Canadian neighborhood in Montreal wasn't always easy. My brother and I had to fight when we were young. Get picked on and beaten up enough and you eventually learn to defend yourself. You also lose the fear. I wrestled for a while in my teens, and I practiced martial arts very seriously for a long time. I hate bullies. Anyway, both of them look twenty-something and I decide on the louder of the two. His arms are covered in tattoos, but strip that away, and he doesn't look so threatening. I wonder if he would be laughing at me if I had tattoos on my arms, or even better, on my neck, like Murder. He looks out of shape to me.

I walk towards him, stare coldly and say:

"What the fuck is so funny?"

He's caught off guard. He didn't expect this. While he's wondering about me, I'm silently praying this goes my way. I have no idea who these guys are. It's a calculated risk. I'm assuming everyone will see or hear about this. I hope it turns out well but, if not, a fight won't last long and for the most part, I'll manage. Anyway, win or lose I'll give it my all.

"Chill, OG. We're just messin' with you," he says with a smile on his face. He's calling me an Old Gangster, a street term.

Checkmate. I know he won't be any trouble, so I decide to step it up a notch for the sake of the show.

"I'm not in the mood, and I'm definitely not the one!" I say all tough-like.

"Hey, OG, I don't want no smoke, chill. Just funny how she did you," he says.

"Not to me. I don't find it funny, and I don't like being laughed at. I'm not the one bro!" I repeat for dramatic effect hoping I'm not going too far. If I push too hard in front of everyone, he may feel like he has to do something about it. Fine line. I have to make him believe I'm a threat and not worth the trouble. This, after all, is a performance.

"My bad, OG," he says.

I know when to quit. It won't get better than this. In fact, it can only get worse if I persist, so I walk away acting more pissed and less nervous than I am. A lot of guys heard the exchange. I hope the news will spread that the new guy has balls.

I go back to my cell and lie on my rack. When the CO calls four o'clock count, he locks the cell doors. Once count is cleared, the CO unlocks the doors and we go to the kitchen area one tier at a time to pick up our trays. A couple of inmate orderlies pass them out while two others stand by dumping the contents of eaten trays into garbage cans.

After I've eaten and returned my tray, I go back to my cell and fall on my rack. I'm exhausted.

"Canada!" I hear someone calling in my dream.

"Canada! Wake up! It's count time! Wake Up!"

I realize where I am, but it's definitely not Canada. Oh, I'm Canada. He's Cash, and he's trying to wake me. I stand up a bit confused and look at him.

"It's count time. They're on the upper tier. You better stand up, or you'll be going back to the box, nigga."

"Shit, thanks Cash. I must have been tired. I actually fell into a deep sleep on this piece of shit mattress."

"That's the last time I wake you for count, cabron. I'm not an alarm clock."

"I appreciate it, Cash. By the way my name is Warren. You can call me Warren."

"No, too hard to remember. I can remember Canada. Raptors are from Canada."

Raptors, again.

"Okay, Canada works."

So that's me, Canada. My name for as long as I'm here.

Chapter 30

Miss Edwards

"LEGAL LIBRARY! LET'S GO! Legal library! The CO shouts. Miss Edwards, a tough black woman from the inner city has been working our unit on day watch.

I jump up, slip on my blue canvas shoes, button up my overalls and grab my ID. I've been on eleven north for almost two weeks, and I've been waiting to go to the law library. Last week it was cancelled. They didn't say why. They never do. I have no idea what the law library actually is or what I'm going to do there, but anything is better than what I'm doing here. I'm going crazy on this unit twenty-four hours a day. Any chance to get a change of scenery is a blessing. I also feel like I need to do something to advance my situation. Maybe I can learn something that will help me and my wife.

"Fifteen only. First fifteen for law library only." Miss Edwards says as I approach the door. There's already a group of guys in front of me, and I quickly count eight, relieved that I made the cut.

She asks each inmate for their name and number and references some paperwork she has on a clip board.

"Stelman, 91903054."

She looks down at her paperwork and, without looking back at me, she says:

"No."

"No? What no?" I ask.

"No. No library for you," she says.

"Why not?"

"Seps."

"Seps? What's that? What does that mean?"

"Move to the side! I got no time to argue with you!"

"I'm not arguing, Miss Edwards. I just want to understand. I don't know what 'seps' means."

"I said MOVE! Do you know what MOVE means?"

I figure I better get out of the way and let her clear the inmates behind me. When she's finished, she asks Control to crack the main door, and they file out of the unit and into the elevator, leaving me behind. Then she closes the door and heads to the bubble, ignoring me. With the door open, she sits down and picks up the telephone.

Unbelievable, I think to myself.

A few seconds later I hear her talking.

"Hey girl, whatcha doin'?"

I stand there agitated. After what seems like forever, she hangs up and starts flipping through a People magazine. She knows I'm standing there. She's making an effort to not look at me. I wait a few more minutes, and then I get up the nerve.

"Miss Edwards?" I approach timidly.

No answer.

"Miss Edwards," I say, a bit more loudly.

"What? What do you want? Why are you bothering me? I'm busy."

Here we go again with this bullshit. From what I've seen so far, none of these COs are ever busy.

"I'm sorry, Miss Edwards. I just want to understand why I can't go to the library. What does "seps" mean?"

"It means you have someone in the building you can't be near. A co-defendant or someone who can be a threat to you. You can't be in the same place as them. You are separated. That's what seps means."

Co-defendant. My wife is my co-defendant.

"My wife is on the second floor in the woman's unit, but I'm sure she isn't scheduled in the library the same time as us. Besides, I can't see her anyway because men and woman can never be in the same place. By default, we're automatically separated."

The women's unit is on the second floor along with medical, the library and commissary. The elevators open to the medical waiting room. If men are on the floor waiting to be seen, and the women have to be moved, to the library, for example, or to take the elevators to the roof for rec, the men are locked in a room out of sight of the passing women. Once the women have gone, they clear the men and let them go back to the waiting room. This is called a "controlled move" and it ensures that inmates never cross paths. They do the same sort of thing to move an inmate to and from the SHU.

"Hey, listen, Stelman. I don't give a shit 'bout none of that. Says on my paper you have a sep, so you don't go. That's what I know."

"So, I can never use the library because she's on the same floor? Is that what you're saying?" I ask again, amazed.

"I'm saying you can't go to the library. You have a sep. Now get away from the bubble before I lock you up."

She's talking about sending me back to the hole. This woman's crazy!

"Lock me up? For what? I'm not doing anything wrong! I'm just asking a question. I need to use the law library. I have the right!" I say.

She stands up abruptly. I'm looking at her, and it's as though her face is going through some form of physical change. Her eyes open wider than the average sized forehead, and her brows curve downward to meet in the middle of her nose. She slams the door to the bubble and walks right up to me, peering in my face and begins screaming at the top of her lungs. Everyone on the unit is watching and listening.

"The right? You have the right? You think you have rights? Get the fuck out of my face, or the only right you'll have is a shower every third day and meals through the door slot. You understand? Get the fuck out of my face! Move!"

Everyone on the unit has stopped what they're doing, and they're watching this lunatic spew her venom at me.

I think to myself, she's insane. I also know she's serious. This deranged woman is about to hit the deuces and send me to the box. She actually wants to do it. I have nothing to gain by standing here trying to reason with her.

"Yes, Miss Edwards. Thank you for your time and professionalism." I say with a little sarcasm as I walk away. Now I have a new problem that I need to resolve or I won't ever be able to use the law library.

I go back to my rack and lie down frustrated. Another obstacle. My thoughts drift to Lana. I pray she's okay. I've asked some of the COs how she's doing, but the only answer I ever get is "We can't give you any information. If there's a problem your family will be contacted."

The judge in Miami ordered the Bureau of Prisons to administer her medication immediately but, not surprisingly, they ignored the order. Ten days later when they transferred her to New York, she was so sick they had to rush her to New York Downtown Hospital where she underwent emergency surgery to remove seventeen centimeters of her small intestine.

If she was taking her meds, the whole thing would have been avoided. It got worse when a few days after the surgery, they brought her back here to MCC. Her wound had to be cleaned and re-dressed twice daily, but they refused to clear the second floor of men so that she could go to medical. Instead, they gave her gauze and scotch tape from the CO's bubble to change her own dressing. The wound became badly infected as a result, and the site of the surgery became abscessed. She was rushed back to the hospital where they discovered she was septic and placed in intensive care for eleven days. She almost died. Now she's back at MCC, and no one will tell me how she's doing.

I know all of this through my kids who speak to her by telephone and relay the information to me. It's torture knowing what she must be going through and just as bad knowing what our kids are going through. Their peaceful, happy lives have been turned upside down. I know they are terrified that something bad will happen to Lana, and there is nothing anyone can do about it. We have no control over anything. The feeling of helplessness is overwhelming, and the despair is paralyzing. We all try to give each other strength when we speak, but it actually hurts inside every time I hear the fear in their voices.

The one consolation is that I have never met anyone stronger than Lana. Her threshold for pain and her strength are unparalleled. She's dealt with Crohn's disease for almost twenty-five years and has been through multiple surgeries, being so sick that you wonder how she made it. Yet Lana always does. I know her, and I know she's too strong and too tough to let this beat her. She will survive this ordeal no matter what they throw at her. That's what I keep telling the kids and what I keep telling myself.

I pray now every morning when I wake up. These desperate situations have a way of making you turn to a higher power. I know we're being punished for what we've done, but I pray that prison and everything that comes with it will be the extent of the punishment. I ask God not to let anything happen to my family. I ask that Lana get better. I ask that He watch over and protect my children and parents. I ask that I get to see my parents again. After that, whatever will be, will be. Take it out on me. I will endure whatever I have to. Just keep everyone safe.

Chapter 31

Cast of Characters

IT'S BEEN A MONTH, and I'm trying to settle in, but it's not so easy. Since the altercation I had on day one, I stay out of the way. No one bothers me, but that can change in a heart-beat. Truth be told, it's a difficult existence. With ninety-six men living in such a confined area, it's ripe for conflict. It's like walking a tight-rope. I have to stand up for myself or else guys will take advantage. At the same time, I don't want to get into trouble. If I get into a fight and get caught by the police, I'll be back in the box and receive a shot, an incident report.

There are four levels of shots. The 400-series (low) the 300-series (low-moderate) the 200-series (moderate) and the 100-series (high). The 100-series shot would be written for rape, murder, rioting and drug dealing. The 200-series shot for stealing, fighting and drinking. The 300-series shot for disobeying a direct order, getting caught with contraband or being out of bounds (somewhere you aren't supposed to be). The 400-series shot for being late to your prison job or running a business. A fight will get me thrown in the hole and a 200-series shot as well as a hearing with DHO, the Disciplinary Hearing Officer who has the option to take away my telephone, email, and commissary privileges.

I try to stay positive, but surrounded by all the hypocrisy, misery, desperation, intimidation and violence, this place is chipping away at me. I worry constantly about my family and my future. I especially stress over Lana's situation. The burden is almost too much to contend with.

There's a lot of tension. You can cut it with a knife, and there are few outlets other than one hour of recreation on the roof of the building every three days, and one hour of library time each week. Because security trumps all, both activities are cancelled at least 50 percent of the time with no explanation, leaving everyone frustrated and adding to the tension.

A lot of guys in here have serious problems. Besides their own legal troubles, they have issues out there, on the street, with family. Wives, baby mamas, and kids, all with their own problems, exacerbated by the situation. In here, guys are helpless to do anything about the issues on the street and because of that, the smallest thing can set them off. There are a lot of arguments and lots of fights. When one pops off, the CO locks himself in his bubble and hits the deuces, his body alarm.

***

The unit is stormed by cops, like a swat team, deadly serious, ordering everyone down on the floor. Take too long to drop on your stomach, and they'll pepper you. The guilty parties get dragged off to the box, leaving us locked down for at least two days until they're satisfied that the trouble was contained and won't lead to something bigger.

This is a pre-trial detention facility, so there are no inmate security classifications. After they're convicted some will be going to pens and others to mediums or lows. Make no mistake about it, everyone will be convicted.

This being New York, there's a large gang presence. The Bloods, Trinitarios and Latin Kings are dominant. The Trinitarios are Dominican and the Latin Kings mostly Puerto Rican. The Bloods are predominantly Black. The power on the unit shifts weekly depending on who has the most numbers. The Spanish gangs stick together to counter the sheer number of Bloods.

Of course, the administration is aware of who they populate the units with and tries to maintain a cold-war-like balance of power. We have a few Paisas from Mexico and some really high profile Mexican and Columbian cartel bosses. Then there's the wise guys and their Russian and Albanian counter parts. There are at least two narco-terrorists on the unit, which I think means they sold drugs to fund terrorism. MS-13 is also represented and so are the Ñetas from Puerto Rico.

Across from me is a five-foot four-inch-tall Puerto Rican, with a French last name. LaPlante looks like he never jay-walked, but he's facing life in prison for contract killings. He would never admit it, but we're sure he's been cooperating. He's been here for seven years, which almost certainly means he's helping the Feds, and they'll keep him until they can make cases and arrest the people he's giving up. It's his path to less time when he gets sentenced. He is obsessive compulsive, and his hustle is cleaning cells and waxing floors. Maybe he's subconsciously trying to clean the blood off his mind, who knows.

One cell over is Marco, a formerly successful pharmaceutical drug distributor out of Atlanta who was indicted for aggressive sales tactics and price fixing. He loves to talk about his money, his ex-stripper wife, and especially his case. He hired what he calls a "dream legal team" of the best lawyers in Atlanta and New York to represent him. He talks about them like they're going to deliver him from the bowels of hell to the gates of heaven. He's already spent over half a million dollars on legal fees, and he's barely started.

I think he's nuts. In the end, for a couple of million, they'll convince him to take a plea like the rest of us. If he goes to trial, the government will slay him. I try to avoid talking to him about his case because it's exhausting to listen to. We can be talking about Monday Night Football, and he'll find a way to compare it to some aspect of his case. I think he mistakes me for his psychologist. I'm not interested. I have my own problems.

His bunky is a Dominican drug dealer who goes by the handle "Barrabas," like the character in the New Testament who was imprisoned and set free instead of Jesus. I wonder what that infers about him and his case. Every night at around eleven o'clock, this lunatic sings reggaeton music at the top of his lungs when everyone's trying to sleep. He sounds like a dying pig. We've all asked him to

173

knock it off, but he doesn't give a shit. I heard a few guys talking about shutting him up "for real."

Preacher, an over-weight black drug dealer in his late thirties who has spent most of his life in prison, was recently re-born. He spends his time teaching bible classes and schooling us on life. He makes me uncomfortable because he thinks he knows everything. I respect his religious beliefs, but I have a hard time with his know-it-all demeanor. Then, when he has to, he falls back on his gangster persona. The other day someone tried to get into the shower ahead of him and he went to his cell to put on his shoes, which means he was getting ready to fight. Lots of guys in here turn to God with sincerity and deep devotion, but I sense, in Preacher's case, it might be a charade for the probation office's sake. He knows I'm Jewish, and he's always asking me questions about the Torah and the Kabala. I tell him I don't know much, which he takes as his cue to try and educate me. From the little I do know, he must be reading a different Torah.

Aladino is a Dominican drug dealer. He was busted with a ring that imported cocaine into New York from the Dominican Republic. He's also our local handy-man. He fixes radios, head-sets, does tattoos and sews laundry bags together to make clothing storage bags. The things he can do are actually quite remarkable. I have no doubt he can craft a hydraulic lift out of paper clips.

For twenty fish, he'll even perform surgery and implant a small stud called a pearl in the shaft of your penis. Yes, that's right, he surgically implants it in the shaft of your penis by cutting you open and letting it heal without stitches. Sound like a good idea? It's supposed to give your girl more pleasure. He makes the pearl out of a filed down Domino piece or a plastic hair brush handle.

He'll swear on a stack of bibles that the procedure is sanitary and sterile because he wears latex gloves he got from the facilities workers: the inmates who do the building maintenance. When he proposed the surgery to me, I couldn't believe what I was hearing, but in true entrepreneurial form, he called over two of his ex-patients to assure me and to attest to their satisfaction with the procedure. I thought they were all insane. I mean, some of these guys probably won't be with a woman for the next ten years, at least, and this is what they're thinking about. To Aladino's disappointment, I declined the operation.

Nick is Albanian. On most mornings, we play cards. He's a funny guy, and he makes me laugh which is golden in here. According to him, he was driving in a car with another Albanian who owed him money. They were on their way to the bank, so the guy could pay him, when the Feds busted them. They had a warrant for the other guy. Nick just got swept up. Bad luck, wrong place, wrong time, he claims. I still don't understand what they charged him with, and he has trouble explaining it. He expects to get bail and then have the charges dismissed. He constantly argues with his lawyer about his expectations. The story sounds suspect to me, but what do I know? I'll believe it when I see it.

Gino Vitale is a wise guy with one of the New York families. He's been charged with extortion. The government claims to have a taped conversation of him threatening his victim on the telephone. He says that's their entire case against him, and when he received the government's discovery, a CD with the conversation was included. He claims the tape is unintelligible; you can't make out five words being said. I counter by saying they couldn't possibly arrest him and indict him on the strength of a tape that can't be understood, so he lets me listen to it. He's right, you can't make out a thing. He says he's going to trial. I hope he knows what he's doing. That rarely works out.

Aram is a thirty-five-year-old Armenian who grew up in the former Soviet Union. He came to the United State on a student visa and was studying to become an engineer. When his visa was expiring, he tried to obtain a green card through illicit means. He met someone who claimed to be a former mercenary and CIA operative who could help him get one. After a few months of courting, the guy asked Aram if he had any contacts in the former Soviet Union who could help him buy a rocket launcher. Aram, trying to impress, told him he did, and he made a phone call to a childhood friend who was in the military. This started the case against him. Turns out the mercenary was a confidential informant for the Feds, and he set Aram up. He was arrested, charged and sentenced to twenty-two years.

The prosecutor asked for life but the judge, recognizing that Aram was "a petty criminal at best," who never had the means or the wherewithal to complete the transaction, felt bad for him and mercifully gave him the low end of the sentencing guidelines. Twenty-two years. What a gift. He was never in trouble before in his life. He has already done eight in Victorville Medium in California, and he's back here for re-sentencing after winning an appeal challenging the sentencing guidelines. His original judge retired, so he's waiting on the new judge to call him for his hearing. It's already been seven months.

I like Aram a lot. He's smart, and he's a guy I could be friends with. We work out together. He's physically big and one of those guys with super-human strength. No one in here will try him. The last guy that did ended up in the hospital when Aram was here on pre-trial over nine years ago. Aram earned one year in the box for that deed. He's always telling me how bad this place is and assuring me that when I get to a "real spot," actual prison, it will be much better, a brighter future and such.

Across from me in the corner cells are the real heavy hitters. Jose Reyes is a boss in a Mexican drug cartel. He's a quiet, mild mannered man of about forty-five years old who speaks in low tones. We talk over coffee and breakfast cake early every morning. He has offices and homes in Columbia, Panama, Guatemala, and Mexico City. His family lives in the United States. He was entering one of his offices at seven o'clock in the morning when he and his body guards were overpowered by eight masked men, clad in black. They handcuffed him and put a black hood over his head. He was driven to an airport and put on a plane. When they removed his mask ten hours later, he was in MCC New York in the SHU. His loyal pilot of twenty years set him up.

Apparently, the country he was kidnapped from doesn't have an extradition treaty with the United States so the government kidnapped him instead. I learn that they do this sort of thing all the time. He's been here for almost two years now, and he forfeited many millions of dollars that the US government seized from bank accounts linked to him in several countries. His indictment charges him with conspiracy to traffic hundreds of tons of cocaine. That's right, tons! Enough to get him multiple life sentences, but he expects to only do three to four years in total. He's not embarrassed to suggest he's cooperating. When I ask him how he expects to live in peace after, he says the business has changed and, if caught, it's now accepted to give someone else up, and they will do the same. A form of paying tax is how he put it. Another thing I find hard to believe. In every Ponzi scheme, someone ends up losing.

His bunky is another cartel guy. To me he looks like a janitor, but apparently what he cleans up isn't property. According to Jose, Miguel's family works in the enforcement division of the cartel. Miguel's indictment charges include over seventy murders. I don't know his deal, but I assume that if he's bunking with Jose, he's also cooperating.

Then there's Luis Obermann. Even though Jose has known him for many years, I sense tension between them. He hasn't told me why. If it was serious, the government would have placed "separations" on them, and they wouldn't be on the same unit. Obermann's family charges the cartels a tax to transport their product through the territory they control. His German last name irks me, and it makes me think that someone in his family may have been a Nazi that escaped after the war. I could be wrong.

A few months later they bring the former President of a South American country to MCC. I wonder who helped with that. Hey, this is the Southern District of New York, the pride and joy of Federal prosecution. It doesn't get bigger than this. I'm living what most people watch on television. If my friends could see me now.

Chapter 32

Pressure Cooker

ADMINISTRATIVE POLICIES LEAD TO unnecessary problems on the unit. A good example is how the microwave situation is managed. The food is terrible, and there's very little of it. To augment nutritional intake, inmates buy food from the commissary. Once a week, we fill out a commissary order form. The following day, the orders are delivered to the unit and handed out.

Inmates then cook the food they purchase in the microwave. The cooking is done in "cars," pooling the food to make meal time a culinary extravaganza.

Items like pre-cooked instant rice are a big crowd pleaser. The "pre-cooked" label on the packaging is misunderstood because hours are spent "cooking" the pre-cooked rice in a variety of different ways. Another crowd pleaser is "nachos." Nacho chips, covered in salsa, beef log, pepperoni slices and oozing with mozzarella cheese, are meticulously prepared, incorporating the nacho chip bags turned inside out and joined together as the serving platter.

The problem: Only one microwave works. The other one has been unplugged for months, according to inmates. There's no hot water dispenser either, so the one microwave is used to heat water for coffee, tea, or another huge seller: instant Ramen soup. This puts a lot of demand on the appliance. We've asked the counselor for another microwave to replace the broken one, but she says they have no money. Maybe they should have sent three marshals to escort me from Santo Domingo instead of four.

"Warm up! I need a warm up…two minutes," says Skinny, a gang member from the Bronx. He just wants to heat up some water and is hoping that whoever's cooking will let him go in. He doesn't notice the line of guys waiting.

"My nigga, we's all waitin' on warm ups. Gutter last…you after him," says Trinny, a gang banger from Brooklyn.

There are six of us. I'm third. The two ahead of me are waiting to heat water also. I want a cup of coffee. It makes me think they should refer to the act as a "heat up" not a "warm up," but what do I know.

"You ain't givin' warm ups? Who in there now?" Asks Skinny.

PB from New Jersey turns around as he opens the microwave door to stir the rice he's cooking. "I'm in, I'm cookin'. Can't let you in right now…fryin' rice…need another fifteen minutes." He's frying the rice in a cut out box of snack crackers. "I been waited two hours. You needs to wait," he tells Skinny.

"Yo my nigga, I ain't tryin' to hear that. No need to talk like that. Watch your mouth!" Skinny answers.

PB stops stirring his rice and turns to face Skinny. "Who you talkin' to, nigga? I just sayin' you gotta wait. I been gave seven warm ups already. I wanna finish cookin' my shit. Dat a problem?"

"Nah. No problem. Just watch your mouth is all I'm saying. No need to be disrespectin' niggas."

"I ain't disrespectin' nobody, my nigga! You a disrespectful motherfucka, Skinny!"

PB slams his fist on the stainless-steel counter top and moves towards Skinny with his arms at the ready.

"Hey PB….chill…I don't want no smoke…just try and talk better, my nigga…sounds disrespectful the way you come at me. I'm a grownass man, my nigga!" Skinny says.

I can't believe I have to listen to this shit again. All day, every day, same crap. This time it ended peacefully, but it usually doesn't. These stupid microwave related confrontations can easily be avoided. All they have to do is put two more microwaves on the unit. Then we could have two dedicated to cooking and one for warm ups. They won't, though, and I'm starting to understand why. They want trouble. It's good for job security.

Another example, the telephones. There are four, but only three are working. Obviously, the administration could fix or activate the fourth one if they wanted, but for some reason they don't. Each inmate gets 300 minutes of calling time per month. Each call can last up to fifteen minutes before the line disconnects. The telephones are only operational during certain hours, and every day after four o'clock count, everyone wants to use the phone to call family.

Again, the queue system goes into effect. Because the wait is so long, guys will get a place in line and then go off and do other things after confirming with the person in front or behind that they are "next." Problem is, they may come back too late and both guys already used the phone, so they try to jump the remaining line.

The gangs will send one guy in line with a list of other gang bangers to follow. A sort of proxy representation. You can oppose their methods if you want, but you won't be going in front of a grievance committee or a tribunal to get a fair hearing. Another phone or two would alleviate most problems. Or at the very least open them up for more hours in the day.

At first, I couldn't understand why the administration lets such things happen, especially when there are such simple solutions to such potentially dangerous situations. Slowly, I began to understand, it's by design. They want these problems to exist because it feeds the machine. Problems and security issues require staffing and paperwork. The units are feeders for the SHU. On any given day, between all the units in the building, guys are carried off to the SHU. It's a vicious circle. Make living in the units as intolerable as they can legally get away with, and in the name of security, they create an explosive environment. When something happens, their jobs are rationalized and justified. Then they punish by taking things away, declaring things like microwaves a privilege, not a right, causing even more misery and anger.

"I don't get it. We were already locked down for two days, so why take the microwaves? The guys who fought went to the hole. Why punish the rest of us?" I say to Aram.

He just chuckles.

"No, really, man, why do they do this shit? Why punish the whole unit when no one else was involved? I wasn't fighting, neither were you."

"There you go again with the questions. You've been here six weeks. Give it a little more time, and you'll stop asking or caring," Aram says.

"Maybe, but I just don't get it. What's the point? It makes no sense."

"It doesn't have to make sense to you. It makes sense to them. That's all that matters."

"What do you mean by that?"

"My God! You're driving me crazy! You're a smart guy. Figure it out."

"It just creates more problems because everyone's frustrated. Don't they see that?"

"They don't care."

"We were locked down last week because they threw that guy down the stairs from the second floor because of an argument over the microwave. Did you see that? There's no way that guy lived. His brains were leaking on the floor. Over a microwave for fuck's sake!"

"Yeah, I saw. That's what the cops want. They wouldn't get away with it in a real spot. They would never use the microwaves as a punishment like they do here. The cops are more respectful because they know something can go sideways on them. Here they don't give a shit," Aram says.

"What do you mean? What's the difference?"

"In the medium or the pens, there are a lot of guys doing life. They don't give a shit. They will fuck a cop up in a heartbeat. They're gonna die in prison anyway, so they don't care. Prison is their home. It's the only place they'll ever be until they die. They'll fight for a better existence. The cops know that, and they're scared. Shit, even in the lows guys have come down from pens and mediums and have done real hard time. They can be doing twenty years in the low. So, in prison they treat inmates with more respect. They want to do their shifts and get home to their families safely. They don't sweat the small stuff."

"Yeah, but there are a lot of real bad dudes here too. A lot of them are going to pens. This place is full of murderers," I say.

"Yeah, that's true, but they want to be on their best behavior here because they haven't been sentenced yet. They think good conduct in pre-trial will help them when they're getting sentenced. They'll fight but not with a cop. The cops know that, so they aren't afraid to do things or treat us in ways they wouldn't in prison. Fight with a cop or hurt a cop here, and they'll get charged and their sentence will be much worse."

"I see what you're saying. So, you think the cops see it as a free pass to mistreat us?"

"I don't think. I know for sure."

"But what do they get out of doing it?"

"They just enjoy it. They do it because they can. A lot of them are miserable, and they hate their own lives. Abusing us makes them feel better."

"Okay, but it still doesn't explain this group punishment thing."

"They think that if they punish everyone, we'll police ourselves. In prison that will happen, but not here. If I do something wrong in the medium that affects everyone, my own people will discipline me."

"What do you mean your own people?"

"Say I did something wrong that disrespected another group like the Blacks. It can lead to a very serious problem, maybe even a riot. Before that happens, the shot-callers will make things right. My own people will judge whether I was wrong and, if I was, they will fuck me up or run me up top. This way, there's peace on the yard and things are contained."

"Run you up top? What does that mean?"

"Force me to check in to PC, protective custody. I tell them I fear for my safety, and they put me in PC. I'll stay in PC until I get shipped to another spot. If I tell on my own people, it'll catch up to me eventually. Someone in the new spot will find out I told, and I'll have problems all over again. So that's how we police ourselves. By the way, that is the least of what can happen."

"So, if someone does something that brings heat on everyone, then the group deals with it. I understand. But that isn't really happening here."

"No, and the cops know that, but they enjoy creating a stressful environment. It's as simple as that. They view us as sub-human."

"That's fucked up. It's hard to believe," I say.

"It'll be different once you get to a real spot," he assures me.

There's that reference to my brighter future again. I can't wait.

Chapter 33

Rabbi

"DID YOU TALK TO the counselor?" Aram asks. We're having coffee. It's seven o'clock in the morning.

"Yeah, I spoke to her. She said she couldn't do anything about it. She told me to talk to the case manager so I tried. Man, she's special. She made me come back four times before I could ask her, then she blew me off in one second. I won't get any help from her. They don't do anything to help us, do they?" I say.

"No, they aren't here for that."

I don't want to ask him what he means because I don't really care to hear the answer. First sign they're starting to turn me, I guess.

"I don't understand it. If I can use the phone, why won't they give me email access? I'm just emailing my family, the same people I'm speaking to on the phone. It's all monitored anyway. It doesn't make any sense."

"They like to make things difficult even when there's no valid reason. They're also lazy, so they don't want to do any work. They can probably resolve it, but it would require a little effort. That's if they wanted to. Let me ask you something, have you heard of Rabbi Mintzer?"

"Who? No, why? Who's he?" I ask, surprised that he mentions a Rabbi of all things.

"Well, you're Jewish, right?

"Yeah, I'm Jewish."

"He's a Rabbi that has a prisoner outreach program. He helps Jewish prisoners. He's really good too. He must have a lot of power or powerful connections because he gets shit done. I've seen it. You need to reach out to him."

"Aram, you're not Jewish. How do you know about him?"

"I heard about him when I was pre-trial nine years ago. I was with some Russian Jews who were in contact with him. I wrote him a letter. I told him I'm not Jewish, but I may be interested in converting, which is true. Since then, we've stayed in touch. He sent me some Jewish religious books in Russian. I suggest you write to him and introduce yourself. Tell him about you and your wife, and ask him to help you with your email. He may be your best bet."

"Okay, I'll do that. Give me his contact info please."

Two weeks later it's one thirty in the afternoon on a Tuesday. I just finished working out and showering. I'm lying on my rack when I hear the CO calling my name, so I go out to the bubble.

"CO, you called me? Stelman."

"You need to go downstairs."

Downstairs. Shit, Marty must be here. Finally.

I go and change into my best dress overalls, the only pair I have, and meet the CO at the main door. He pats me down, waves the metal wand across my body and radios Control to tell them to pop the door.

The CO working the elevator has a miserable look on his face. He orders me to face the back wall as we descend. What an asshole. At the basement level he says:

"Turn left, and go to the Lieutenant's office."

The Lieutenant's office? I wonder what this is about. As I turn the corner, I see the Lieutenant waiting for me.

"You Stelman?"

"Yes, Lieutenant."

"Okay, follow me." We go down a corridor and arrive at his office.

"Sit down here and wait. Captain wants to see you."

The Captain? What the...he runs security for the institution. Man, I hope I'm not in trouble.

185

A minute later, he's back. He tells me to follow him, and we turn a corner to the Captain's office.

We enter a reception area where the Captain's secretary sits.

"He's here to see the Captain," the Lieutenant says to her.

"He's waiting for you, go on in," she instructs.

The Captain is sitting behind a large mahogany desk. The name plaque on the desk reads "Cole." He's on the telephone, so I take a quick look around. His office is like a baseball shrine. There are pictures of players past and present, including a few of him playing softball. There's a shelf full of trophies. There are no pictures of his family, which is probably smart, given his line of work.

He's about five feet six inches tall with a compact, muscular frame. He looks powerful and appears to be in good shape. He's black. His head is shaven, and his scalp slick and shiny. He's wearing gold, wire-framed glasses. He hangs up the telephone and orders me to take a seat across from his desk. The Lieutenant moves to my left and stands, lurking over me.

"What's up with your email?" the Captain asks, as if I've done something diabolical with it.

Oh, so that's what this is about. Maybe Aram was right about the Rabbi.

"What email? I don't have email, Captain," I answer.

"Why not?" he asks.

"I was hoping you might tell me, Captain. I have no idea why not. Both my wife and I are here. She's on the second floor. We have four children. Two are minors. I just want to be able to email my family."

"I see. Wait outside!"

"Okay, Captain."

After about fifteen minutes, the door opens, and the Lieutenant calls me back in. I take my seat again and wait to hear something.

"Stelman, we have some new information." He's looking at me as if he just solved a twenty-year-old cold case. He glances at the Lieutenant and then back at me. I feel like he's waiting for a confession, but he doesn't get one, so he says:

"What are you here for?"

"I guess for my email issue," I offer, hoping I have the right answer.

"No, I mean your crime. What did you do? Why were you arrested? Why are you here at MCC?"

"Oh, sorry. I thought you would know that already. I've been accused of telemarketing fraud."

"Exactly! That's the reason you have no email. It's because of your charges. You used a computer to commit your crime. That's why your email is restricted. That's why you can't use a computer."

"Captain, I said telemarketing. That means using a telephone, not a computer. I don't know how to use a computer for anything other than what one is commonly used for. I send email, I surf the web, and I use Microsoft Office. I'm not a computer hacker if that's what you're suggesting."

"Oh, so you used a telephone to commit your crime. We can restrict that also."

What the fuck is this guy talking about? I'm here to resolve my email issue, and he wants to take away my telephone too. I look at him in disbelief and say:

"Captain, I just call my children and my parents. Don't do that please."

He looks at the Lieutenant and then back at me and says:

"Go wait outside."

Unbelievable. Is this guy serious? How complicated can this be? I get up and walk out. Even his secretary looks perplexed. This time, he leaves me waiting thirty minutes when the door opens and the Lieutenant calls me back in. I sit and the Captain looks at me.

"Stelman, I read your file. This is the first time you've been locked up."

"Yes, Captain, that's right." It sounds like it's a strike against me.

"Why didn't you follow the chain of command?"

"Captain? The chain of command? As you said, it's my first time. What do you mean? I don't understand."

"Cut the bullshit, Stelman! Why did you go to the region? I don't like inmates going over my head and not respecting the chain of command! That's what I mean! Don't bullshit me! The warden got a call from the region. He doesn't like that either!"

He stands up for dramatic effect, probably thinking he's taller than he is.

"Captain, with all due respect, I don't know what you're referring to exactly, but let me explain. I went to my counselor, and she said she couldn't help me. I went to my case manager, and she wouldn't help me. I wrote you two "cop outs" explaining the situation, and you never responded. I wrote two more to the Warden, and he never responded. If that is not respecting the chain of command, then I'm not sure how to follow the protocol. I never went to the region. I don't even know about the region. All I did was write a letter to my clergy explaining what was going on because he has experience with the system. I told him I'm worried about my children, and I need email to communicate with them. That's all I did, Captain."

He looks at the Lieutenant in a "good cop, bad cop" type of way. I feel like I've been here before.

"Go wait outside, Stelman."

You've got to be kidding. No wonder this place runs so poorly. This idiot runs it.

"Yes sir," I say and walk out.

This time the wait is short. Five minutes later, the Lieutenant calls me back in. I can see by the look on his face that even he's getting tired of this. I take my seat, and the Captain says:

"Okay Stelman. Your email will be on in an hour. Next time though, you better follow the chain of command. Do you understand me?"

"Yes sir, chain of command. I got it. Captain, Lieutenant, thank you. I do apologize for any inconvenience this may have caused. I'm sure you have children. I love my children, and I need to be there for them. The telephone isn't enough. It's also too expensive to call Canada. Captain, why is it so expensive anyway? The rest of the world pays pennies for long distance today, yet here, I'm being charged a dollar a minute. It's kind of predatory, over-charging inmates who have no source of income." I'm pushing my luck.

"I have no idea about phone rates, Stelman. That's decided somewhere else. Anything else, Stelman?"

"No sir, that's all. I just thought I'd ask. Just seems abusive charging so much. Thanks again."

A week later I still don't have email. I've sent cop-outs to the counselor, the Lieutenant and the Captain. Chain of command. I'm frustrated. I decide that if I don't hear anything in forty-eight hours, I'll have my daughter call Rabbi Mintzer. Screw the chain of command. What choice do I have?

The next day at lunch, a parade of officials comes to our unit during main line. The Warden, the Captain, two Lieutenants, our counselor and case manager are all standing to the side, responding to inmate concerns and problems. It's customer service for the incarcerated. Looks good, but it's all bullshit. I take the opportunity to approach the Captain who is acting like the consummate professional around the Warden.

"Excuse me, Captain. We met last week in your office. Stelman, about my email, do you recall?"

"Yes, Stelman, I remember. What can I do for you?" he says in a sweet tone of voice. Wow, what a difference. I feel like asking him to bring my car around.

"Well, Captain, it's the same thing. When we finished, you promised that my email would be activated within the hour. That was over two weeks ago. I still don't have email. I did as you instructed. I followed the chain of command. Did you not receive my cop-out?

"I've been out of the office. I haven't checked. What do you mean, you don't have email? Why isn't it working?" he asks me.

My fault again.

"I don't know, Captain. I don't control it."

"Give me a minute."

He talks into his radio and tells someone to call him at the local extension in the officer's bubble. A minute later, the phone rings, and he answers. When he returns, he tells me to go and check the computer right now. I go upstairs and log in. I have email! Yes! Finally! I'm ecstatic. I go back downstairs and approach him. He's talking to the Warden, so I wait off to the side. When he's finished, I go up to him.

"Captain, my email is activated. I want to thank you for your help. I really appreciate it."

"No problem, Stelman. Now make sure you stay out of trouble, do you understand?"

Unbelievable.

"You won't get any trouble from me, Captain. Not if I can help it. I'm low maintenance." I give him my brightest smile and walk away before he can respond.

Chapter 34

Jailhouse Lawyer

"I READ YOUR INDICTMENT, and it's a good thing I did. There were no victims in New York. The indictment's defective. There's no jurisdiction in the state of New York. You need to file a motion to have the case thrown out. You'll get the case dismissed, 100 percent. This is a bullshit indictment. If you want, I can prepare the motion for you and file it. You're going home."

I'm talking to a black guy named Reese. He's a jail-house lawyer, someone who does legal work for other inmates because they can't rely on or afford lawyers to do work on their behalf. Every jail has them. Some of these guys shouldn't be taken lightly. They practice law, mostly through trial and error, and some can boast successful outcomes at times. I was talking to him the other day, and he asked me if I ever had anyone look at my case. I told him no, so he offered to look it over and give me his thoughts. We're sitting at a table on D tier. It's his office, and my indictment is lying on top of a pile of legal papers that he's working on.

"What do you mean no jurisdiction? I don't understand what you're talking about. Can you explain what you mean?"

"It's simple. There was no crime committed in the state of New York. There were no overt acts committed in New York. They should never have used New York as the jurisdiction to indict you. It's defective. The court has to dismiss it. You're going home. Pack your shit."

"Going home? Reese, I committed my crime. You think the government will just let me walk out of here because of some technicality? It sounds too good to be true."

"Do I think? Canada, I don't think! I'm positive! Look, you need to understand, the government makes these sorts of mistakes all the time. It's just that most guys don't know their rights, and most of their lawyers don't give a shit. The ones that are being paid want to drag the case out so they can bill a lot of money, and the public defenders or CJA lawyers don't want to work. They're in bed with the government anyway. I know what I'm talking about. I've had cases dismissed for the same reason."

"So, you're telling me that if we file this motion, my judge will have to dismiss the case. That's what you're saying?"

"That's exactly what I'm saying."

"What if the government indicted me in a state where a...what did you call that? Something act? What was it you said?"

"Overt...overt act," he answers.

"Yeah, overt act. What if they filed the indictment in a state where an overt act was committed?" I ask.

"Then the indictment would be valid. There were no overt acts committed in New York, so there's no basis for the indictment. That's the law, plain and simple. They should have filed in a state where a crime or overt act was committed, but they wanted to prosecute you here in the second circuit for some reason. Big mistake..."

"Okay, assuming you're right about what you're saying, two questions come to mind. If the indictment was deemed defective by the court and they had to dismiss it, couldn't they just re-indict me in another jurisdiction?" I ask. "I mean, I don't see them just letting me go."

"No, they're not allowed to do that."

I don't know much about the law, but I know they retry cases all the time, so why wouldn't they just re-indict while they have me in custody. I'll need to check this out. I really don't know Reese, so I have to be cautious. Guys will do a lot of things for money in here and most jailhouse lawyers have no practical experience.

"Okay, my second question is what if you're wrong? Won't it piss my judge off?"

"Who cares what it does to your judge. Stolberg's a motherfucker anyway. On the contrary, when he sees you know your rights, he'll know he has to dismiss. I'm telling you, this isn't a maybe, this is 100 percent. You're going home, Canada."

Why does his pitch sound so familiar? He's telling me exactly what I want to hear. Then again, he doesn't know who he's talking to. That's what we were doing, telling people what they wanted to hear, what they wanted to believe. It's what got me here. Reese is looking for a "mooch." I use the word "mooch" to describe someone who wants to believe something so badly, they'll ignore every shred of evidence, every logical conclusion, their own instinct that suggests it isn't so. It's a fascinating psychological disposition.

Our victims wanted to believe the bullshit we were feeding them. There was no other way it could have worked. We told them they won a sweepstakes, and we were a courier company delivering their winnings. It's what they dreamed of hearing. In the last minute, we'd call them back and tell them we didn't get the final waiver to release their winnings because the processing fee wasn't paid. That's how it started. It took some convincing, but not much. You know why? They wanted to believe they won, that's why. We told them to send the processing fee via Western Union or MoneyGram to the notary's office quickly, so we can get the final waiver "to release" their funds. We have their winnings with us and we can make the delivery, but we need the waiver. If not, we have to return the envelope to the sweepstakes company. It's up to them, but it has to be done right now because we have other deliveries to make, and we can't keep the envelope after today. Once they sent the money, we got them to send more. Unbelievable, right? Not really.

They're gamblers who play all sorts of sweepstakes. They fill out entry forms and mail them in with amounts of money ranging from ten to thirty dollars for each sweepstake. Many, or most of them, fill out and mail away multiple entries every week. The "sweepstake companies" own multiple banners with multiple offerings. Once someone replies to one of their mailers, they inundate them with sweepstake opportunities. They make their money through entry fees and by selling the data (name, telephone number, address) to lead brokers, who then sell the names to people like us.

Everything, and I mean everything, was bullshit. The sweepstakes companies were bullshit, just doing the minimum required to operate legally. The lead brokers were bullshit, knowing exactly what we were using the information for and staying in the boundaries of the law by requiring a copy of a legitimate sales pitch which they keep on file along with a terms-of-use contract. We supplied a bogus but legitimate sales pitch from a bogus company to satisfy their minimal legal requirements. Then we used the leads to contrive our bullshit.

The craziest part of all, what always amazed me, is I never once spoke to someone who hadn't already sent money somewhere before. That's right, this wasn't the first time, and it wouldn't be the last. You'd think once or even twice would be enough to learn. As long as the pitch was switched up enough to give them something to sink their teeth into, they believed it.

The government called them "vulnerable" victims, and they were, but not because of their age, senility, or loneliness. Most of the people I spoke to were very capable and in control. No, what made them vulnerable, was their desperate desire to win money and their willingness to believe they won. There were seniors, for which I am even more ashamed, but there were also business owners, professionals and, in one case, a retired judge.

Why do people send money for the latest diet craze, or the stomach band that's supposed to make you lose weight just by wearing it? Because they want desperately to believe these products will give them what they so badly want. Guess what, it won't happen! You only lose weight by burning more calories than you take in. Cut down on food and start doing a lot of real hard exercise. That's how you lose weight. What about miracle creams that are supposed to reverse the effects of aging in weeks for only seventy-nine dollars? Mooches buy, because they want to believe it will work. It doesn't.

You probably think you're not a mooch, right? Wrong! We're all mooches in some form, at some time. We all have something we want to believe so badly, we ignore the obvious and re-purpose the evidence to support our belief. It doesn't have to be anything major either.

A pretty girl in a store tells you the shirt you're trying on makes you look slim and really brings out the color of your eyes, and you buy it. You want to believe it's true. You're a mooch.

Or a handsome salesman tells you the dress you're trying on is really slimming, even though it's not. You buy it knowing it doesn't look as good on you as he suggested, but you ignore that thought, wanting much more to believe in what he said.

We've all had experiences in our lives where we want to believe something so badly, we ignore all the contradictory evidence to support our desired outcome. Mooch!

I ask myself for a second whether there's something to what Reese is saying. Hold on schmuck! Don't be a mooch! Still, a part of me hopes he's right. Enough so that I'm prepared to investigate further, but thankfully not enough to dive in.

"Reese, how much will you charge for preparing and filing this motion?" I ask. Now there's a buying question. It just came out.

"Not much...100 bucks. You can have your people put it on my books or send it to my people on the street," he tells me.

"Okay, give me a few days to think about it. I want to check with my lawyer then I'll get back to you," I tell him.

"Waste of time. I know your lawyer. He doesn't know anything about this, even though he should."

Sounds an awful lot like me telling someone on the phone not to listen to a family member who's telling them it's a scam... "They don't know because they don't play the sweepstakes".

"How do you know my lawyer?" I ask.

"Clayman? Shit, I've known him since the nineties. I used to do paralegal work for his firm when I was on the street. He's a real crook," he says.

"You used to do paralegal work for him?" I ask.

"Man, that's what I did out there. I'm from New York. I had a paralegal services company. I used to do research and prepare motions and briefs for small firms that don't have their own in-house lawyers to work on that stuff. I did a lot of work for his firm in the mid-nineties. He defended a lot of Columbian drug guys back then. He made a fortune. He'll tell you the jurisdiction defect is bullshit, but he doesn't know. Besides, he doesn't make any money getting the case dismissed so quickly. It's in his interest to bill the government."

"Hey, Reese, I have a question. If you're a paralegal, why are you in jail?" I ask.

"Got greedy. I was doing work for a lawyer whose clients were on a drug case, and I prepared some motions for them. I got the case dismissed because of inadmissible evidence. Anyway, two years ago, they caught another case, so they got in touch with me. The government seized all their assets, and they had no cash to pay me, so my dumb ass got involved in a conversation about taking my fee in cocaine. I was never gonna do it, but we talked about it. One of them ended up telling the Feds, and I got caught in the mix. The Feds hate me 'cause how many times I beat them in court, so they jumped all over it and indicted me."

"Makes sense," I say. Oh my God, what bullshit. Every fiber of my being is telling me he's concocting this crap as he goes along. Guys like Reese can easily prey on gullible and uneducated inmates who desperately want to believe he can help them. I see him doing legal work all the time, but I haven't heard of one successful outcome yet.

"Reese, I have another question. I could have sworn I heard you talking to that dude Sweat on B block last week at medical about you being in three other prisons. When was that? I mean if you were running a paralegal company on the street, when were you in prison?" I ask.

"Man, I did a nickel before this indictment. I had the paralegal company before I went to prison on that case," he tells me in a "what don't you get" tone of voice.

"Makes sense too." This guy's unbelievable. "Drugs also?"

"No man. I'm not a drug dealer," he says in an insulted tone. "Insurance fraud, but I was innocent. They fucked me!" he says sounding all righteous.

"Oh, okay Reese. Thanks for clearing that up. Hey, like I said, give me a few days, and I'll let you know if I want to file the motion."

"Okay, Canada. Hey listen, I'm starting work on a big case next week, so I'll be busy for a while. Let me know ASAP. I can prepare your motion before I get busy with that one. If I get the money, you'll have it the next day, and I won't charge to type up the motion. I have a new typewriter ribbon."

"Oh, okay Reese. That's very nice of you. I appreciate it."

Chapter 35

Speaking the Local Language

WHEN I FIRST GOT here I had trouble understanding what people were saying even though they were speaking English. The New York street dialect, vocabulary, and expressions were foreign to me and threw me for a loop. I've been listening carefully though, and I'm beginning to understand.

The two most common nouns are "nigga" and "motherfucker." Both are used indiscriminately to describe all things and in all manner of sentences.

"Nigga" should not be confused with "Nigger," which is offensive, derogatory and racist. When I first heard someone use it I was appalled. When they used it to address me I began to understand it has a different meaning than what I first assumed.

"Nigga" is practically a term of endearment. It's typically used in place of "man," "guy," or "friend."

Example: "Hey, my Nigga," which means: "Hey, my man."

Or "Those Niggas is crazy," which means: "Those guys are crazy."

Or "He's my nigga," which means: "He's my friend."

I think it important to point out that while the term is used by black inner-city people, it isn't exclusive to them. Puerto Ricans, Dominicans, Columbians and even some white people use it freely here.

"Motherfucker," which on the surface seems self-explanatory, is rarely used in its literal sense. Rather, it is used in almost every situation as well as to describe things good and bad.

Example: "That po-lice is a motherfucker!"

Or to describe food, like nachos: "They's some bad motherfuckers!" which means they taste very good.

It can also be used to describe itself: "That motherfucker is a motherfucker, my nigga!"

Which means: "Well, actually I'm not sure. Give me some more time. I'll get back to you.

"You do you" or "I do me" means to worry or take care of one's self.

Example: "My nigga, that's cool, you do you." Which means: "Do what you have to do."

"Stay in your lane" means "Mind your own business."

"He's my son" refers to someone you've taken under your wing to teach or care for but at the same time implies a subordinate position.

Example: When playing a sport or game, a player beating another player may refer to the loser as "his son."

When I first got here, a group of us were sitting around and "shooting the shit" when one Puerto Rican talking about his homie, said: "He's my son!" to which I replied, "You don't look old enough to be his father." Everyone broke out laughing. I was serious.

The word "smash" is used to describe "beating someone badly" in a fight, a sport or a game. It can also be used to describe how you might perform intercourse on a female. "I'd smash that."

When working out hard, "you get money."

When playing a sport and leveraging another player's weakness to score easy points, you say "there's the money," similar to "easy money."

"Baby Mama" is the mother of one's child. Most guys in here have multiple baby mamas. It is interchangeable with "my bitch."

The word "liked," as in to have liked something, takes on an extra "ed" and will be used as "I likeded that shit."

A more common and well known one is "aks," which replaces "ask" as in "Don't aks me that."

"Like that" means great, or fantastic or really good. It can also describe a person. "She's like that" as in "she's hot."

Or "that car is like that" or that pizza was "like that" ...well you get it.

"Tight" means angry, pissed off as in: "That motherfucker got me tight, my Nigga."

"Out the way" means minding my own business or staying low key or in the background.

Example: "Hey, I'm out the way, my nigga."

"How they do" implies "what they do." Example: Regarding how unfairly the COs may treat us, one will say: "That's how they do."

"How you do me" means how you treat me. Example: I failed to include you when cooking a bowl of nachos, so you might say: "That's how you do me, my nigga?"

"I'd put a baby in that" is a pronouncement made when one sees a woman he would be prepared to have a long term, lasting relationship with. By impregnating her, he will mark her as his property or conquest, and it is a statement of how much she means to him. The fact that there will be a child to care for and support, thereafter, is secondary and of little consequence.

"Blanking out" means "losing one's mind."

"Burnt out" is another one. Guys who do a lot of time are often described as "burnt out," usually because they are so institutionalized that they are nearly impossible to deal with. "That nigga's burnt the fuck out," would be the proper use of the expression.

"Joint" is a noun and can be used for anything:

"Did you see them joints?" referring to pictures or magazines or clothing, or new chips on commissary.

"My nigga, I watched that new joint last night."

Or: "That joint's like that."

Or: "I got these joints for sale."

"Mad" is used for emphasis of quantity or quality... "They got mad phones on that joint," talking about contraband cell phones on another compound. "That food was mad good."

One I found really interesting is how the past participle of the verb "To Be" is used as some form of auxiliary verb.

Example: "I been heard that" or "He been done that" or "They been seen that."

The word "holler" is used in the place of "talk."

"Yo, my nigga come holler at me when you got a chance" or "Can I holler at you a minute?"

"Ain't tryin' to hear that" is synonymous with "I don't accept that" or "I'm not interested in that" or "Don't tell me that." It is dismissive of the other's position. "Yo, my nigga, I ain't tryin' to hear that shit."

"More better" is used in place of even better. "It's more better if you holler at him."

"Good looking" isn't describing someone's physical appearance. Rather, it means thanks for looking out or thanks for doing something. I gave my bunky Cash a package of Ramen soup when he was hungry, and he said "good looking." I said "thank you." He seemed confused.

"For real, for real," means "for sure" or "really."

Example: "For real, for real, I been said that."

There's still more to learn, but with this basic understanding I have the foundation I need to communicate.

Chapter 36

Co-defendant Meeting

"STELMAN, GET DRESSED. YOU'RE going downstairs." The CO is standing at the door to my cell. I dozed off, Grisham book on my chest.

"Okay, CO...be right there. Do you know what for?" I ask.

"Legal. Must be your lawyer."

"Oh shit, just give me a few."

"Alright, but hurry up. I need to call in the census numbers. I'll clear you first."

"I appreciate that, CO," I say as I put on my jumpsuit.

A few minutes later, I head to the bubble so the CO locks the door and starts walking to the main door, talking into his radio.

"One for legal, eleven north."

"Ten-four." The door buzzes and disengages.

I'm happy Marty's finally here. I really need to speak to him, and I need to see Lana. He can arrange that. The physical imprisonment is bad enough, but it pales in comparison to the inability to defend yourself when you are locked up in a pre-trial facility.

Everything is designed to impede any effort to that end. You can't meet with or speak to your attorney freely when you want to. You can't have fair, unfettered access to the law library or legal resources. People working on legal briefs are forced to use antiquated typewriters and forced to pay exorbitant prices for typewriter cartridges. To make photocopies, you have to buy a copy card at commissary for seven dollars and fifty cents but you only get five dollars' worth of copies. The impediments are too many to list, and in totality, insurmountable to overcome.

Despite what Marty said about being able to email him, he hasn't accepted me on the BOP CorrLinks email system. The system only allows an inmate to communicate with an email recipient through a formal invitation and acceptance. I sent him an invitation the day my email was activated, but he hasn't answered. Without that we have no connection. Speaking of that email, I fought so hard for, it has a seventy-two-hour delay. If I send an email on Monday, it isn't received until Thursday. If I send it on Friday, it's delayed by two more days. In many cases, I can send a physical letter through the postal service, and it will arrive faster. I've tried to find out why, but no one will tell me. No other inmate has this problem. They have the standard two-hour delay. I saw the Captain on the unit a few days ago and asked him about it. He said he'll look into it, which means he'll do nothing. I'm at the point where I'm just accepting it. That's what happens. It wears you down. I won the battle but lost the war.

When I speak to my kids I ask them to call Marty for me, but all they can do is leave a message with his office. He rarely calls back and when he does, he tells them he'll see me soon. I've tried calling, but he's never available and obviously he can't call me back. It's not just me either. Everyone in here has the same trouble seeing or speaking to their lawyer whether they are paying them or not. For those that are paying, it seems once they are deeply invested with a lawyer, they get jerked around as much as the guys using legal aid or CJA attorneys. I'm starting to realize this whole justice system is a charade, designed to give the appearance of fairness, but is the furthest thing from that.

So, hearing he's here makes me feel like I've won a lottery.

When the elevator hits the basement level where legal meetings, R&D and the administrative offices are located, I'm directed through a thick glass door. Two COs are sitting at a desk.

"Name?"

"Stelman"

"Number?"

"91903054"

"Put your ID on the desk and walk through the metal detector."

I do and nothing happens, so he says:

"Go down the hallway and turn left. Last door on the right."

"Thank you," I say.

As I head there, the second CO follows behind me which makes me think, why didn't he just say follow me instead of giving me directions? Another thing that makes no sense.

As I approach the meeting room, I see Lana through the glass doors. The room is small; ten by ten with a meeting table and six chairs. She's wearing a blue two-piece uniform like the one I wore to court. She looks pale and tired. When she sees me, her eyes well up with tears. Marty's sitting in one of the chairs, and there are two other men across from him, sitting on each side of Lana. I go in and take Lana in my arms and hug her tight.

"No touching!" the CO says from behind me. He's standing in the doorway.

"What? CO, she's my wife. Can't I give her a hug?"

"No! Touch her again, and I'll terminate the visit!"

I look at Lana, and she turns her eyes downward, appearing sad. She doesn't seem well. I've never seen her so defeated. I look to Marty for help, and he says:

"Listen to him, he'll do it. He can."

One more abuse. Damn these people.

I back away from Lana and Marty says:

"Warren, sit here next to me.

"Warren, this is Stewart Leiter, Lana's lawyer and his junior counsel, Joseph Tarpman."

I reach out to shake their hands, wondering if this will terminate the visit, but the CO doesn't react. I take a seat next to Marty across from Lana.

The CO says, "Okay, take all the time you need," and leaves.

What a wonderful guy, I think to myself. I turn to Lana and say;

"Lana, are you okay?"

"Warren, I was so scared. They treated me so bad. I was so sick. I almost died. I just want to see my kids again. What's going to happen, Warren?"

"Lana, listen to me. Everything will be okay. It's hard to believe right now, and things may get worse before they get better, but they will get better, I promise. We'll get through this. The kids will get through this. We're a strong family, and we all love each other very much. You just have to stay strong, like always. You need to fight and never give up. The only thing they can't take from us is our spirit. Do you understand me, Lana?"

"Yes," she answers with a little more life in her voice.

"I promise you we'll all be together again, and this will just be a bad memory. You have my word."

"Do you love me, Warren?" she asks.

"Yes, Lana, I love you. I always have."

"And you promise we'll be together again?"

"Where else will I be? I promise," I say and smile.

"Okay, Warren, I'll be strong. I'll fight. I was so scared, Warren. You have no idea."

"I can't even imagine, Lana. But we're here now. Lana, give me a smile. I want to remember you smiling when I have to go back upstairs."

She smiles and begins to cry. It's like the flood gates opened. I was dying inside, but I knew that letting it out was good for her.

"It's alright, Lana," Stewart says.

"I'm sorry. I'm so sorry," she says sobbing. "I'm okay."

Marty takes this as his cue. "Okay, listen. We need to talk about a couple of things. I only have thirty minutes. I have to be in court in Brooklyn in an hour and a half for a murder trial. I'm cutting it close."

I can't believe what I'm hearing. I look hard at him and say, "Thirty minutes? What's thirty minutes? Are you serious? I've been waiting weeks to see you, and all you can give me is thirty minutes?"

"I was prepared to spend two hours. I came at eight o'clock, but they didn't let me in until nine thirty. The security is ridiculous. I can't stand coming here. It's so unpredictable."

"Can you imagine how we feel? We live here," I say.

Marty looks at me oddly, something he never considered.

"This is crazy. How can we defend ourselves if we can't see our lawyers?" I ask.

"Warren, you're wasting precious time," Stewart says annoyed. "This meeting was set up primarily for you and Lana to see each other."

"And we appreciate that, don't we Lana?

"Yes, of course. I'm so happy."

"What time did you get here, Stewart?" I ask.

"We got here at seven forty-five. We were lucky. They let us in right away. It's not Marty's fault. This is the most secure building in the country. You just never know," he tells me.

I hope he'll defend Lana as mightily.

"So, you've spent time with Lana?" I ask.

"Yes, we've been with her for over an hour now."

"Maybe I should hire you, Stewart. You're easier to see than Marty."

I don't give a shit what they think. This is my life on the line.

"That's not possible, Warren. I'm already defending Lana. I can't represent both of you," Stewart answers. "Marty is an excellent lawyer. Let him do his job."

"Stop it please, Warren," Marty says, sounding insulted.

"Marty, when you leave in twenty-six minutes, will I be able to stay and spend time with Lana?"

"No. Without me, you can't be here."

"Listen," Stewart says, "I have Joseph with me, so I think it'll be okay. They just count the lawyers. I've done this before, should be okay."

"Alright then. That's good. We appreciate that, Stewart, thank you, and thank you Joseph."

"Yes, thank you," Lana adds.

They tell us it's no trouble at all.

"Are you okay, Warren?" Lana asks. "I was so afraid for you. I worried so much about you in the Dominican jail. Was it bad?"

"It was terrible, Lana, but I made it. We'll talk about that another time; it doesn't matter now. Marty has to leave soon, so let's get to what he wants to discuss."

With that, my attorney, Marty Clayman, clears his voice, places his hands on the table and says:

"Okay, so we received some discovery material from the government. It's not complete because they said there's more to follow, but there is a list of victims and their losses. We need you to review it. As you know, fraud sentences are related to loss amounts. The court uses loss amounts to set guideline ranges. If you plea out, the parole board studies your case and then prepares what is called a PSR or Pre-Sentence Report. They take all the information from the prosecution, the FBI and interviews with you personally, and they prepare their report with the guideline range to be considered. Now, the court isn't obligated to sentence within the guidelines. They can sentence below or above the range, which is referred to as a variance. For now, what you need to do is study the discovery material, particularly the loss amounts and victims, and give us your feedback on them. It is all on a disk and I will make copies of it and mail it to you."

A discussion about our possible innocence isn't tabled, so I assume that they assume we're not.

"Marty, how will I look at the disk? The laptop I ordered hasn't arrived yet," I say.

I'm being an ass, but I'm frustrated with the lack of time I'm getting from my lawyer.

Marty looks at me for a few seconds trying to figure out if I'm serious. Lana, who knows me, gives me a dirty look, while Stewart says: "Warren, we're here to help you. Stop it."

"I understand Stewart, and I apologize. Marty, I'm sorry. I'm just so frustrated. I can never speak to my lawyer and then when you come to see me, it's always so rushed. We really can't get anything done. Surely you understand. And speaking of that, why didn't you accept me on CorrLinks?"

"What's that?" he asks.

"It's the BOP's email system. I sent you a request to accept me in order to establish the link between us, but you never approved me. You're the one who told me I can email you. If you don't know what it is, I'm assuming you never used it, right?"

"No, I've never used it. I'll find out how and accept you," Marty says.

"You've never had to use it before with other clients?" I ask.

"No, I never used it before. I don't like using their email. They monitor everything. I don't like to talk on the email or the telephone."

"That actually makes sense, Marty, but we don't need to discuss anything sensitive. We can just use it as a means to schedule meetings and stay connected. For that, it's very useful, and I would feel much better having contact with you.

"Lana, Stewart, are you guys connected?"

They confirm they are. I say to Marty: "You see Marty, we should use it too.

"Marty, is it possible to print out everything from the CD and mail it to us? This way we'll be able to get to work. There is one computer on my unit that has a CD rom reader, and it's supposed to be used for legal, but half the time it isn't working, and the other half, it's used to watch porn."

"Porn?" Stewart asks.

"Yep, porn. I don't know how they get it in, but they do."

I used to see guys huddled around the computer, and I thought they were reviewing the discovery from their cases. One morning I was walking to the counselor's office to ask a question. As I walked behind two guys who were on the computer, I noticed they were watching porn. I recognized it because I've seen it before. They noticed I noticed, so they said: "Mind your business, my nigga!"

That's when I realized, notwithstanding the most secure jail in the country part, people find a way.

"Anyway, forget about the porn. I think if we get hard copies we can be more efficient, given the physical limitations," I say.

"Okay, of course. I'll have it printed and mail it to you tomorrow. You should have everything the day after. Then we can meet again in the next week or two to go over everything."

"That's great, Marty. I think that's a good start. Will Lana have it as well, Stewart?" I ask.

"Yes, we'll send it out this afternoon. Joseph will you please take care of that."

Joseph makes a note and says: "Done."

"Have either of you had any further conversation with this Anna Gabro?"

"I tried to call her again, but she won't take my calls. She insists on email. She's very difficult," Marty says.

"Yes, she's really difficult," Stewart adds. "I've been emailing her, and we've been texting. I'm trying to soften her up a bit and trying to get her to move on her position, but she's adamant. I'm pretty concerned. She claims that the loss amount is over two million dollars. She's also claims there are close to 100 victims. Anyway, it's all in the discovery material you're getting, so you need to go over it carefully."

"Alright, Stewart, that sounds like a good plan. Hopefully, it will be sooner than later. Are we going to meet together? Is that what you're saying?"

"Yes, I think that will be the best course...you agree, Marty?" Stewart asks.

"Yes, yes, I agree. We'll try to meet again late next week or the week after," Marty says impatiently.

"And Marty, by then we'll be connected on CorrLinks, and you can let me know when exactly."

"Yes, absolutely," he says and puts his legal pad in his file folder. Then he stands up to leave.

"I have to go right now. Who knows how long it will take me to get out of this place. I can't be late."

Marty leaves and the rest of us stay behind. For the next thirty minutes Lana and I catch up on what happened since that day at the airport in Santo Domingo. At one point, Stewart left the room to see another client and, surprisingly, the COs didn't break up our meeting with only Joseph present. Sometimes their laziness can work to our benefit.

Chapter 37

Trouble with Six

"YO, CANADA. YOUR NAME'S Stelman, right?" an inmate called Cuba asks me.

"Yeah. That's me."

"She's lookin' for you."

"Shit. Okay, thanks.

She is Miss Edwards. I wonder what she wants. It can't be anything good. Since that incident with the law library she's been determined to break me. She wants to prove to me that I have no rights even though the BOP handbook says I do. She's made this her pet project; persecuting me every chance she gets.

I've been sitting in the gym watching the six o'clock evening news. I walk out and look towards the bubble, but she's not there.

"Stelman!" She's shouting my name from my tier. I go down the five stairs to the lower level. She's standing outside my cell, talking to four black guys who are playing Monopoly at a table. Two of them live on the tier across from me and the other two live on E tier. I'm pretty sure they're all Bloods.

"You called me, Miss Edwards?" I ask.

"You got a lower bunk pass?"

"Yes. It's in the computer. You can check. When I went to medical, the doctor's printer wasn't working, so he couldn't give me the paper pass, but he did note it in the computer. He told me I can get the hard copy next time I'm at medical."

"I ain't checkin' nothin'. If you don't have the paper, you got to move. I need a lower bunk for someone with a pass. Move your shit to the top bunk."

Cash, my bunky, went to the hole about two weeks ago. During a routine search the cops found a shank in his personal property. They immediately cuffed both of us, but after a few minutes of discussing the situation with the unit officer, they released me. I had no idea he had it. I was lucky because in these situations they usually take both guys to the hole and investigate after. An investigation can take up to three months. I took this as a sign that someone was watching over me.

"Miss Edwards, I have a lower bunk pass. It's not my fault his printer wasn't working. I can't go on a top bunk for legitimate medical reasons."

"Oh yeah? What reasons? You look healthy to me. What are your legitimate medical reasons?"

"Miss Edwards, with all due respect, I'm not discussing my personal medical information out here in front of everyone. It's no one's business. You can check; the bunk pass is there."

"I'm not checkin' nothin'. Are you refusing a direct order?"

The four guys sitting at the table are laughing. My sense is they see this as a black vs. white thing. I don't. Growing up in Montreal, communities were divided but only by language, as in French/English, not by race. I never experienced racism like I'm experiencing here.

I decide this is it. I need to take a stand right here, right now. If I go to the hole so be it. If I let her treat me like this now it will never end, not to mention what these guys will try to do to me after. Fuck this, it's not happening.

"Miss Edwards, I'm not moving. Call the Lieutenant please. I have a lower bunk pass. Either I stay where I am or you find me a lower bunk somewhere else on the unit."

"You think you're smart, Stelman? Move your shit right now. I won't say it again."

"No, Miss Edwards. I'm not moving. Do what you have to do."

"Give me your ID!"

"It's in my cell."

"Go get it!"

"Miss Edwards, I'm not new anymore. I've been here for three months. I'm sorry about what happened that time with the law library. I didn't know how shit worked back then. Now I do. I have a lower bunk pass, so I'm either staying where I am, or you can move me to a lower bunk somewhere else on the unit. There are other lower bunks available, I'm sure."

"Hey, you tellin', Canada! You not s'pose to tell!" one of the guys sitting at the table says. He lives on my tier, and they call him Six, probably because he lives on Sixth street, but I'm just guessing. He sleeps in a lower bunk and probably doesn't have a pass. That's why he didn't like what I said. But what I said is not "telling." I'm not in the mood for him right now, and I don't like that he's involved in what is none of his business, so I say:

"Mind your business, Six! No one's talking to you! I'm not 'telling' about anything or anyone! This doesn't concern you, so stay out of it!"

"Oh yeah?" he says. I can tell he's surprised by my reaction. Sitting with his homies, he wasn't expecting me to step up. Meanwhile, this must have impressed Miss Edwards, or maybe she decided to leave me alone to deal with Six and his boys. I'm sure she's hoping I get the shit beat out of me.

"Alright, Stelman," she says, "I'll check, but if you're lying to me and you don't have a pass, I'll be back."

With that, she walks away, and I do the same. I go back to the gym and sit back down, but I'm nervous this thing with Six isn't over. Deep down, I know it's not. The way the prevailing jail code works, he and his homies probably feel I disrespected him, and of course, he'll have to do something about it. I'm worried.

I'm right about worrying, because a few minutes later I hear loud rapping on the thick glass wall of the gym. I turn around, and Six is calling me outside. Shit, here we go. I get up fast, like I'm not worried. I know that perception is everything, and if he thinks I'm not afraid, this may not escalate. Anyway, I have no choice. I need to follow this wherever it goes. I just hope I don't get jumped by all of them. I walk out and face him, keeping a good distance between us, and I say:

"What?" like he's bothering me.

"Wanna holler at you," he says.

"So, holler,"

"Not here, in your cell."

He wants to fight. There are no cameras on the tiers, and that's why he wants to go there. Fuck! This guy's big. He's about five nine and at least two hundred and twenty pounds. The only good news is most of it is fat. He's in bad shape. I'm in good shape, and I'm sure I'm faster than him, but a cell is a confined place, so if he gets his hands on me, I have a real problem.

As I follow behind him I say: "You want to do this? No problem. I'm old enough to be your father, maybe even your grandfather, but if you want to fight, I'll fight. I'm not scared of you. Win or lose, I'm not scared of you, my man. You can't do anything to me that hasn't been done before."

I'm hoping by pointing out that I'm much older than him, a sense of right and wrong will overcome him, but that doesn't happen. Evidently, he doesn't have that sense. These guys don't give a shit about someone's age. I know I have to hit him first and surprise him. I can't take the chance that he'll change his mind or I'll get the upper hand if I don't surprise him. He'll smother me with his size.

As we reach the tier I see Aram coming out of his cell. He just woke up from a nap because he's removing his ear plugs. His bunky, another Eastern European from Estonia, named Andrei, is sitting at a table outside their cell, and Aram is about to sit down with him. I'm happy about the timing. I also notice that the other three guys aren't there anymore. They probably didn't want to be around to get implicated. Well that's good, for now anyway.

Aram looks my way just as Six enters my cell. I follow right behind him and cock my fists. When he turns around I hit him with everything I have in the side of his head. He didn't see it coming, and it knocks him back. He's stunned but not down. Shit! I move towards him and hit him again and follow with an elbow to his eye. He still doesn't go down and starts moving towards me, so I move back fast. I need to keep distance between us. I'm out of the cell and on the tier.

213

Six takes a few wild swings, but I'm far enough out of the way that he doesn't make contact. All of a sudden, Aram jumps between us.

"Enough! Stop this shit!" he yells at both of us. "What the fuck are you doing? Don't bring this shit here! You'll jack all our time! They'll lock us down."

Aram is staying neutral by saying what he said. He isn't taking my side, but he's definitely here to help me.

Six doesn't want any smoke with Aram, plus he's gasping for air. A few inmates quickly gathered at the top of the stairs at the entrance to the tier, blocking anyone's view of what's happening. A couple more move to the bubble to keep Miss Edwards occupied. She's on the computer anyway, so she doesn't have a clue what's going on. No one wants to get locked down. This is inmate business, better kept in-house.

I just caught a big break. In jail, there's an unwritten rule; never get between guys fighting because you can get hurt or implicated by either the cops or other inmates. Aram just stepped up for me.

I look at Six. He has a small cut above his eye where I elbowed him and a big mark on his cheek. He says to anyone within ear shot:

"Motherfucker sucker punched me!"

"Hey, man, you walked in my cell. I just got you first. Stop lying!"

"Fuck you, motherfucker! This ain't over! I'll see you, motherfucker!" he says as he walks into his cell. A few minutes later he comes out with a wet wash cloth on his face and walks off the tier to the main floor, headed towards the bubble.

When Miss Edwards sees him, she gets off the computer and waves him into the doorway. They talk briefly, and then they both come back to the tier. Aram, Anton and I are sitting at a table pretending to play cards. She takes everything in and then follows Six into his cell.

"I was doing burpees, and I slipped. I hit my face right here on the side of the bed" he tells her.

"Why are you doing burpees in your cell. That's what the gym's for," she says.

"I know, but there was too many people in there, so I came down here."

"Alright, just don't work out in your cell. Use the gym," she says and walks away.

Six waits a few minutes and then leaves the tier and heads to the other side of the unit to talk with some of his boys.

This situation is bad for a few reasons.

It's hard to hide the fact that there may have been a fight because of the cut on Six's face. I also have an open knuckle on my hand.

Miss Edwards may have bought his explanation and logged his injury in her watch book, which will keep him from going to the SHU for a suspected fight. If she didn't buy Six's explanation, she'll report it, and he'll be sent to medical for an evaluation and then to the SHU. They'll lock us down and do an upper body search for signs of violence. They also check hands, so I won't pass the test.

She may have figured out what happened based on the verbal exchange she witnessed between Six and me. Knowing her and how much she dislikes me, she won't report a fight, so I'm left to deal with him and his friends. Last week the Bloods beat a guy so badly for a gambling debt, he ended up in intensive care with internal bleeding and a punctured lung.

He's definitely coming back, and I'll be living with this over my head. The only time I'll be able to relax is when they lock us in at night. In the morning, when they crack the cell doors, I better be up and alert. I've seen guys get hit while they're still asleep in their beds. It's not just him I have to worry about. Any one of his boys may come.

I huddle with Aram to discuss the problem. He has a pretty good relationship with the shot-caller for the Bloods. Ice just got re-indicted for a gun case, and he's facing a three-strike sentence that will probably send him away for a very long time. He was out for one year after doing ten in Big Sandy Penitentiary, a real war zone. He's in his late thirties and he's a "serious dude" in jail and on the street.

Aram's been helping him with his legal work. Aram says he'll talk to Ice and try to quash this thing. He says the whole thing was stupid anyway and Six was just trying to bully me for no legitimate reason. He should never have gotten involved in my conversation with Miss Edwards. He says Ice will see this thing for what it was.

My only other option is to leverage my relationship with the Dominicans and see Diablito, the shot-caller for the Trinitarios. I'm pretty sure he'll help, but this will bring the problem to another level. Not a great option.

A few hours later, Aram knocks on my cell door. I'm on my rack facing the door, trying to stay awake and alert. It's not easy. I get up and nod for him to come in.

"Did you see him?" I ask.

"Yeah, I just came from there. We talked for half an hour."

I'm anxious to hear what happened, and I'm praying it went well. I'm really too old for this shit.

"He started out supporting Six, but after a while, I got him to see your side of it. He did say you shouldn't be dry snitching, and I told him you didn't."

Dry snitching is when you say something to the cops that will make them look at another inmate's business, even though you didn't point someone or something out specifically or intentionally.

"I don't think I did that Aram. All I said was there must be other bottom bunks available on the unit. Six just wanted to impress his homies by jumping on that."

"Yeah," he agrees.

"I'm not a snitch. I don't do shit like that. You and I both know what this was really about. It was about a twenty-two-year-old bully trying to make his bones in front of his people and thinking I was an easy mark."

"I know. I explained it to him, but not exactly like that. I told him you're a good dude, and you don't bother no one. He said he never heard of you being in the way. He wants a meet with you and Six. I'll be there too."

"Okay, when?" I ask.

"Right after chow. We'll meet at his house."

"You'll be there too?" I ask even though he already said he would.

"I wouldn't send you there alone." He smiles. I don't.

"How do you know they aren't going to jump us, or me?"

"No, won't happen. Just gonna talk."

After chow, Aram and I head over to see Ice who's sitting at the back of the tier at a table. Six is with him. A few Bloods are sitting at the two tables at the front of the tier, and I am immediately concerned that this may not be just a talk. Aram nods at them as we walk by and head to the back. We fist-pump Ice, sit down and get right to it.

"Canada, Six say you disrespected him," Ice says.

"Ice, I didn't. If he feels that way, I apologize. He accused me of telling, and I didn't. I don't tell. That woman was singling me out and picking on me. She had no business trying to take my rack, and she knows it. She probably knew I had a pass before she started that shit. All I said was there must be lower racks somewhere else on the unit. I didn't say she should take one from anybody. That's her job, not mine. Six and the others were sitting there listening to everything and laughing at what she was doing. Listen man, I never bother anyone or cause problems. I stay in my lane and mind my business. I show everyone respect, and I would like the same respect back. I'm not a kid, I'm fifty-three years old, and I'm not looking for problems."

"You fifty-three?" Ice asks. "You don't look no fifty-three. I don't believe you. You look maybe forty-two, forty-five max."

"Fifty-three, Ice, 1959. I have kids older than Six. What's he fucking with me for? I'm an old man."

At this point, I turn directly and address Six. I figured I know how to end this with him saving face.

"Listen Six, I knew what would happen if you got your hands on me. I mean look at you and look at me. So, I took the first shot. I don't need any trouble with you. We live on the same tier. We don't have to be friends, but we can respect each other. Edwards has some issue with me, and that's my problem. At the end of the day, she's the police, and we're inmates. She's not our friend. I just need you to understand I'm not a pussy that will be pushed around. I would do it again if I had to, but man I hope you'll let this go because I don't need you as an enemy. I'm not an idiot. I know who will win that battle. Are we cool?"

I appeal to his ego by telling him how tough he is especially in front of Ice, his shot-caller. He saves face and can feel better about the situation. By telling him he would get the best of me in a fight, he feels better about what happened. But here's the rub. He knew I didn't back down, and I told him I wouldn't back down if it happened again.

The fact that I'm even going through this is absurd, but it's everyday life in here. Everything normal goes out the window. A fifty-three-year-old man dealing with this nonsense is ridiculous, but this nonsense is my fucking life. Crazy.

"Yeah, we cool," he says with a little uncertainty in his voice, more because he wasn't expecting me to turn it around this way. I put my hand out, and he takes it. Then I turn to Ice.

"Ice, I appreciate you helping us with this. No one needs heat. We all have enough trouble in front of us. We don't need to make things worse over such stupid shit."

"That's cool. Hey, you give out the soap on supply day. That your job, right?"

"Yeah, Ice. I got you brother. You too, Six. Hey Six, I'm sorry man, really."

He feels vindicated. I've been watching these gang bangers. They come from rough, inner-city neighborhoods where they settle most beefs with a gun. Some of them like Ice, are tough dudes, and they'll do whatever they have to. Most seem to get louder and braver as their numbers grow. Six is definitely one of the latter.

As Aram and I walk back to our tier, I thank him. Truth is, if he wasn't there it wouldn't have worked out so well. Aram is my friend.

Chapter 38

A Day in the Life

I'M DOING THIS THING one hamburger at a time. They serve them for lunch every Wednesday. Somehow the weeks fly by. The time spent in pre-trial applies towards your sentence so for all the discomfort and misery, there's the smallest of silver linings. Based on information I've been able to get from speaking to other inmates, the average pre-trial wait is about a year. For some, it's much longer. Living with ninety-five men in less than ten thousand square feet is completely unnatural, yet we adapt. At what psychological cost remains to be seen.

I followed advice and establish a daily routine. They crack the cell doors at six. I pick up my breakfast tray and eat until they start yelling to return them ten minutes later. I like coffee in the morning, so I head to the kitchen area to heat up water in the microwave. There's never a wait at this hour because most guys are sleeping, and those that woke up for breakfast go right back to bed. I can't sleep anymore, so going back to bed isn't an option. After my coffee, I use the bathroom, which takes some coordinating because I have to wake my bunky and ask him to leave the cell.

I take advantage of the relative quiet the morning offers and study Spanish at a table with a book borrowed from another inmate. I learned to speak quite well, living in the Dominican Republic, but grammatically, I'm still weak, so I've decided I will use my time here to perfect my Spanish. I need to leave here with something more than I came in with, improve myself in some way. I think it's the only way I'll get through this with some semblance of sanity. I need desperately to achieve something positive.

Before I know it, it's ten thirty and everyone is waking up for lunch which is served at eleven. After lunch, I go upstairs to the second floor to check my three-day-delayed emails. The trip upstairs is an event—think going to the mall. I could do this in the morning, but I resist so that I can do it after lunch. For the rest of the day, I'll try to relieve boredom or monotony by checking again and again, even though I know there won't be any new emails until tomorrow after nine. It's just something to do and fulfills some psychological need to be constructive.

At noon, I work out with my car. Aram leads Andrei, Nick and I through a serious exercise routine. We do 100 burpees, seven sets of pull-ups and dips, 300 push-ups and 300 stomach crunches. I have trouble with the crunches because ever since that beating I took in Santo Domingo I have lower back pain. On some days, I try to squirrel out of it, but Aram doesn't let me. I argue with him about the crunches. I'm always happy once we're finished because, besides the obvious physical benefits, the exercise relieves a lot of stress.

After our work-out we sit around shooting the shit for a few minutes eating fruit we bought off the kitchen orderlies. Aram insists that muscle needs natural sugar to repair and grow after exercise. I have no idea if he knows what he's talking about, but he could be extremely stubborn and loves to argue, so I just eat it.

It's shower time which means waiting in queue again. There are sixteen guys on our tier and only one shower. By the time I'm finished it's close to three o'clock. I lie on my rack and read until they lock us in for four o'clock count. Once count clears at four thirty, they crack the doors and we run like Pavlov's dogs for our supper trays.

At five thirty the CO does mail-call, and everyone waits around the center of the unit floor, hoping they have some. Sometimes I get a piece. The rest of the evening, I spend watching the news, checking for emails I likely won't have, or playing cards.

At eight o'clock, I call home to speak to the kids. It's the highlight of my day, and it keeps me going. The calls are always rushed because the 300 minute limit lurks in the back of my mind.

It's a subtle form of torture because they're going through tremendous hardship. I want to spend time on the phone with them to try and ease their anxiety and fears, but I just can't. The possibility that something serious may happen and I'll need my minutes is always present. It's awful because I regularly cut one of the kids off mid-sentence to remind them that we've been on the phone too long. It makes them sad and insecure, and it hurts a lot.

Guys who can afford it, and who are willing to take the chance, purchase other inmate's telephone minutes. The going rate is between 75 to 100 dollars for 300 minutes. This gets settled through commissary or by depositing money to the seller's account by Western union. Both are serious violations and, if caught, they will both go to the hole, lose their commissary, telephone, and email privileges for up to six months. They will also receive a shot which could lead to a loss of good time. I would never consider such a short-sighted strategy. I mean, I did once before and look how that turned out. Anyway, from what I've seen, most get caught.

"They're packing someone out on A Tier. Do you know who?" I ask Bodie, one of the Latin Kings.

"Yeah, it's that Irish nigga from Boston, the loan shark guy. He went to the box with that nigga Juice from the Bronx who got here couple weeks ago. Stupid motherfuckers."

"Why...you know?" I ask.

"My boy Rock told me the Irish nigga was using Juice's phone. The counselor walked up on them this morning. Someone told."

"That's crazy. Why would someone tell? What do they get out of that? I don't understand it. Why the fuck would someone want to do that?"

"Niggas is jealous, Canada. They just miserable motherfuckers. They trying to jump on other people's cases 'cause they think it'll help 'em. That's why."

"How the fuck can telling on someone for using someone else's minutes help them?"

"They stupid, man. They think the counselor will tell the prosecutor how they been helped them. You need to be careful in this

221

place, hermano. Watch what you talk about. Don't talk to nobody 'bout your case."

I find out first-hand what he's talking about a few days later. Two Columbians start chatting me up one evening after chow. I spoke to both of them before, and they were surprised and impressed I spoke Spanish. They seemed like decent guys. They start asking me questions about where I live in Canada. Then they ask me to follow them upstairs to the second floor to a map of the world that hangs outside the administrative offices on the wall. Why it's even there is a mystery to me, but consistent with the no rhyme or reason ways of the BOP. Maybe it's to give us hope, who knows.

They explain they want to start a charter tour company with boats traveling from Columbia to Canada and ask me if I'd be interested in doing something with them. They say a lot of Columbians are immigrating to Canada, and they think it will be a good business. I can't believe they're trying to lure me into this conversation that I suspect will evolve into the smuggling of cocaine. I tell them I know nothing about boats or tourism, and I have no interest in doing any business with them or anyone else. I repeat it three times to be sure. I walk away and go see Aram, the only guy I trust, to any degree.

"You did the right thing. Those guys are facing serious time. They're looking to jump on someone else they can give to the government so they get a 5K-1, a cooperation agreement. Stay the fuck away from them...that's trouble."

"I see that. Man, that's incredible. The government knows I'm not a drug dealer. You mean they would let these guys lure me into a conversation out of naivety and try to make a case against me after? Is that even legal?"

"This government would do it in a New York minute. They do it all the time. They prosecute people for conspiracy on the hearsay of other criminals who are trying to get a break. I know lots of guys who are locked up because someone got them to talk about a potential illegal act that they may never have intended to do. Look at me. I'm a perfect example. Twenty-two years."

"I still can't believe it," I say.

"There are plenty of scumbags who would do anything to get time off. Last time I was here, there were these two high-level gang bangers selling bodies for five grand each. Pay them and they give you the whole low down on who got it and who did it. Then the buyer goes to the USDA and cuts a sweet deal by solving a murder and telling on people he doesn't even know. That's how the system works."

"Shit, Aram, that's crazy. No one would ever believe this shit goes on."

"You're right about that. No one believes it. They trust the government and figure if you got arrested you must have done something to deserve it. They'll always think you're lying, until it happens to them or someone they love."

"Hey, in my case I broke the law, but I've been looking at the discovery material, and they list victims and loss amounts that have nothing to do with us. There must be a million dollars in alleged victims that weren't ours. I've been leaving messages for my lawyer to tell him."

"That's important. The loss amount will affect the sentencing guidelines, so you've got to get anything that isn't yours removed from the list. That's how you help you and your wife," Aram says.

"Yeah, but I don't have faith in my lawyer listening to me. I need to get a co-defendant meeting so my wife is there with her lawyer. He'll do something about it. She's been so sick, I doubt she has the wherewithal to deal with it. I really think I need to fire my lawyer. I have a very bad feeling about him."

"Don't jump to conclusions. They're all the same. Give him a chance. I think it's a mistake to fire him right now. You need to see how he performs a bit more."

"Alright, maybe you're right, but my instincts tell me he's no good. I mean, I'm sure he could be good if he wanted to, but I feel like he doesn't give a shit about me."

"I know, but wait a bit before you do anything drastic like that."

"Okay, Aram."

"Listen, there's something else that could help. There's an Appellate Court case in the Second Circuit. It involves a telemarketer

223

who was sentenced after he pleaded guilty to one count of mail fraud based on the total amount of money brought in by all the sales people for the company he worked for.

"In his appeal, he argued that he should only be sentenced based on the loss amount he brought in. The appeals court ruled in his favor, vacated his sentence, and remanded for resentencing. From what you've told me, this ruling fits your case perfectly. You should not be held responsible for losses attributable to other people involved, that you had no hand in. I'll find it on the computer and print it for you, and we'll go over it. It's US vs. Studley, a landmark case. Your lawyer should know about it."

"Shit, that's great, Aram! I thought with these conspiracy laws, they make everyone responsible for the total amount even if you had no part in it. Are you sure about this?"

"Yes, I'm positive about the case and the Supreme Court ruling. I'm almost certain it applies to your case or should apply to your case."

"Great! Finally, some good news. I need to tell Marty."

"When are you seeing him?" Aram asks.

"Your guess is as good as mine."

Chapter 39

Cook 'n Li'l Ray

INMATES IN TRANSIT ARE also housed at MCC. Guys being sent back to their home countries through treaty transfers often fly out of New York. Inmates who are going back to court for appeals or other proceedings come through MCC while they are in transit.

It is a Thursday at six thirty in the evening when four new guys show up. They've just been released from the SHU. Two of them are placed on B tier and the other two on my tier in an empty cell. The most recent occupants are gone. One of them was caught making hooch from oranges and grapefruits he collected. They put him in the hole. The other was sentenced and sent to a prison to serve his time.

By now, my job has expanded to me handing out all sanitary supplies to inmates. Every Friday I'm given a box of toilet paper with 110 rolls in it and tasked with going cell to cell to hand them out. I keep the extra rolls locked in my prison issue, grey bin under my bed. When new inmates show up, I give them toilet paper, soap, tooth brush, tooth paste and disposable razors.

If I wanted to, I could sell the supplies on the side as a "hustle." I decide that for the few extra dollars I'd make, it's not worth the headache. Guys are jealous and someone will always be gunning for me or my job. If someone really needs something, I just give it to them, and it's usually appreciated. After a while, inmates realize that I'm not taking advantage, so I begin to garner a certain level of respect because of it.

I'm just back from B Tier where I give the new guys their supplies. I walk to the entrance of the cell on my tier where the other two are. They're both making up their bed rolls and I say:

"Hey, guys, I'm Canada. I've got supplies for you."

They're white and have braided goatees which make me think they're from somewhere down South. They give me a nod. The one on the bottom rack is big; six feet two and at least two hundred and thirty pounds. He looks chiseled out of stone. Both arms are covered in tattoos, and I have no doubt there are more under his T-shirt. His hair is light red, blond and curly. The other guy is also big; about five-ten, 200 pounds. His face is pock-marked from acne, and he looks as mean as a junk-yard dog. He's completely bald with some numbers tattooed on the back of his head above his neck.

The bigger one says: "I'm Cook, and this here's my kin, Li'l Ray."

"Cook, Li'l Ray, nice to meet you." I put my fist out to pump theirs. "I got a roll of toilet paper, toothbrush, tooth paste, soap and some razors for you."

"Thanks, Canada," Cook says. "Sure do 'preciate it. Hey, there a store guy I can talk to? I'm hungry as a motherfucker."

Some inmates stock up on commissary items and sell them to other inmates at 30 percent markup. It's a good business if you can deal with the risks, which include guys who owe you money going to the hole, guys not paying when they promise to, or the cops busting your store and taking everything for having more commissary than you're allowed to have. Most store debts are settled on commissary day so, if I take a honey bun that's worth one dollar from a store guy, I'll have to pay him back a honey bun and a postage stamp.

"Yeah, sure…upstairs, guy called Biker. He's in the first cell on the right. He'll fix you up. He's a good dude," I say.

"So, where you guys from?"

"We're from Georgia, but we're doing our time in the pen at Coleman, Florida. We're on our way back. We was on a writ for a State case in West Virginia. Motherfuckers sent us half-way cross country. We was at Oklahoma, then Canaan, now here."

"Yeah, from what I've seen, they wouldn't make it in the travel agency business. So, you guys are experienced with the system," I say, smiling.

"Yeah, we been down some," Cook says.

"You said you're family? Is that what you mean by kin? We don't use that term in Canada," I say, half joking.

"Yeah, Li'l Ray's my nephew... sister's boy," Cook tells me.

"How's this spot?" Li'l Ray asks.

"It's okay, I guess, although I don't really know the difference. It's the only place I've ever been, aside from the jails and the prison in the Dominican Republic where I was arrested. I was extradited here. It's pretty buttoned down, no movement really."

"That's how all detention centers are, but this one is real tight. Food any good?" Cook asks.

"Terrible...and very little of it," I say.

"When's commissary?" Ray asks.

"It's on Wednesday. They pass out the forms on Tuesday night. I got a couple in my cell. I'll get them so you guys can take a look."

"'Preciate it. Where are the computers?"

"Upstairs, second floor...so are the counselor and case manager's offices. Hopefully you don't need them, because they're both completely useless."

"No man, we don't fuck with cops...don't need nothing from 'em. Think the email's working yet?" Cook asks.

"No, you'll have to wait twenty-four hours."

"Usually how it is," Cook says.

"Canada, how do we get clothes?" Li'l Ray asks.

"There's a form you fill out which the counselor takes to laundry. It's supposed to take a day or two, but with her you never know. I've seen guys wait over a week. The guy who does the job filling out the forms is Ant. I'll find him for you and ask him to come here, and you can fill them out if he has any. This way he can slide them under her door and hopefully that will save some time."

"Maybe she won't take too long for us," Cook says.

I'm not sure what he meant, but it sounded ominous, like she wouldn't want to piss them off. Personally, I don't think she gives a shit.

Just then Aram and Nick stick their heads in and greet both of them.

"I got a pair of shower shoes. I only have the one, but I'll try and find another pair. I also have a few soups, a bowl, and spoons. Let me know if you need anything else," Aram tells them.

"I got an extra pair of shower shoes. I'll go get them," Nick says.

They thank them and Aram stays to talk. Aram tells them he's doing his time at the medium in Victorville, California, and they go over their prison resume with him.

"I been locked up since I'm seventeen," Cook explains. "My first bid was four years in the State, and then I was on the street for a year when I caught my first Fed case. I did five on that one. Now I got eight in on this one and ten to go. I'll be forty-five when I'm done this motherfucker."

"Drugs?" Aram asks.

"Yeah, crystal meth. Manufacturing and distribution, but I got violence too."

"What about you, Li'l Ray?" Aram asks.

"Crystal and guns. Been in Coleman for the past two years, but I was in USP Atlanta for three before that. Started out in USP McCreary. Did three there. Got eight in and four more to go. Lost all my good time in a riot in McCreary. That place was a war zone. I was lucky I didn't get more time for that one. They charged a lot of motherfuckers."

At this point I've heard enough to know these guys are the real deal. I tell them I'll see them later and mention that I'm two cells down if they need anything. Aram stays and keeps talking to them.

In prison, people look out for "their own kind." Even though Aram is Armenian from the former Soviet Union, he's white so he immediately opened the door to Cook and Li'l Ray. Nick is Albanian but also white. That's the way it works. Personally, I think it's ridiculous.

The next morning when they pop-the cell doors for breakfast we all lined up to get our trays. Cook and Li'l Ray are in front of me. When they reach-the serving line they take their trays and wait on the side for everyone to go through. Once the inmate orderlies finished serving everyone, Li'l Ray asks the head orderly for extra milk.

The head orderly, a Puerto Rican from the Bronx called Chill, has been here for over three years. He says it's because his case is complicated, but who knows. Chill tells them that there aren't any seconds, but if they want any extra fruit or milk to come see him on 2 Tier, and he'll sell them some.

After every meal, Chill's bunky, T, brings the garbage can from their cell to the kitchen and they load it with the extra food. Chill must feel entitled because he sells the extra food. I always felt he should be giving out seconds, but I'm not about to rock the boat.

Back on the tier, Aram, Li'l Ray, Cook and I are sitting at a table eating breakfast when Cook asks: "What's up with that Mexican who works the kitchen, the one stealing everything?"

"He's Puerto Rican," I say.

"Same fuckin' thing, wet-back motherfucker," Li'l Ray says.

"I don't know him too well, but he's been doing that since I got here. He ran a few blocks in the Bronx. New York guys don't challenge him. I know he's making a lot of money because he charges a fish for milk and fruit." I say.

"Yeah, he gets away with it," Aram adds." I respect a hustle, but that's our food he's selling."

"Somebody outta check that motherfucker," Cook says. "I ain't paying him nothin'!"

The next morning, when I get up for breakfast, Li'l Ray and Cook are already on the tier. I don't know what it is, but they seem preoccupied. They are both pacing back and forth and every few minutes they talk in whispers.

"Something's up," Aram says to me in a very low voice. "I've seen it a million times before. I can feel the tension."

"What do you mean? Cook and Li'l Ray? Yeah, I feel it too."

"Yeah, keep your eyes open, something's gonna pop."

I just look at him and wonder what can be going on.

When they call our tier to chow, Cook and Li'l Ray make their way to the front of the line. I'm about eight back with Aram when I hear Cook say to Chill:

"Amigo, if you got extra milk I want one."

"Yeah, sure, come see me after. I got you," Chill answers.

"No, I mean now. I want one now, and I don't wanna buy it. I want you to give me one."

"It don't work like that, brother. I told you how it works, see me after."

"Okay, man. I'll see you after," he says, and they both walk off to the tier.

Aram and I follow and, when we get downstairs, we see Cook and Li'l Ray emptying all the food from their trays on the table. Then they slide the hard-plastic lids back on them. I think I see Cook tuck something into his overalls, but I'm not sure. Then Li'l Ray goes to the stairs to watch.

A few minutes later, Chill's bunky, T, comes down the stairs from 2 Tier, garbage can in hand. Suddenly, Cook and Li'l Ray shoot up the stairs, trays in hand, and Li'l Ray says: "Hey, my man, I got a question for you." T stops in the middle of the floor.

"Whasup?"

They're two feet away from him, and with all their strength, they take the trays and smash them across T's face in one of the most violent outbursts I have ever witnessed. Blood starts spurting from the bridge of his nose and head, and he falls to the floor—but not before Li'l Ray grabs him by the hair and starts punching him wildly in the face.

A second later, Cook runs to the kitchen where Chill and the other orderly are cleaning up, and with ridiculous force, he smashes Chill across the forehead with a combination lock that he has in a sock. Chill's head opens up, and he falls back across the kitchen counter. Cook doesn't lose a second, pounding him with the lock, using his right hand, while he steadies him with his left. I think he's going to kill him.

"You wanna sell food you supposed to give us? Fuck you, motherfucker! Who the fuck you think I am? You think I'm gonna pay you?....slimy motherfucker. I'll kill you!" The other orderly runs out of the kitchen, and Cook continues beating Chill until his entire face is a blood covered mass.

Everything is happening so fast that the CO just catches the tail end of it. He recognizes how dangerous the situation is so he stays in his bubble and hits his body alarm.

Less than a minute later, enough time for Cook and Li'l Ray to unleash their fury, both the main and emergency doors come blasting open and twelve COs storm the unit, yelling at everyone to get down on the floor, face down. They tackle Cook and Li'l Ray, hold them down and pepper-spray them. Both quickly succumb, and the COs turn them on their stomachs and handcuff them. They lift them up violently and haul them out of the unit. We know we won't see them again.

In the meantime, they turn their attention to Chill and T, who are both in bad shape, and yell at them to stay on the floor, face down and cuff them. Chill is unconscious.

Five minutes later, medical staff arrives, dressed in protective suits. They lift T to his feet and walk him off the unit and place Chill on a stretcher and carry him away.

Just like that it's over. For the next forty-eight hours we're locked down. On the third day they open up the unit at six in the morning, and for the next few hours, everyone talks in whispers about what happened. Most guys are happy justice was served.

The counselor appointed new kitchen orderlies, and they were instructed to distribute seconds with the extra food. A second line forms on a first-come-first-serve basis. Of course, this opens the door to bullies pushing their way ahead in line. I figure it will just be a matter of time until someone deals with that.

Chapter 40

Baby Girl

"MY DAUGHTER TOLD ME you'd be coming this week. Thanks for giving her a heads up. It gave me a chance to prepare," I tell Marty.

We're in one of the legal meeting rooms. I've been here at MCC for almost six months, and I still don't see any light at the end of the tunnel. Our case hasn't advanced because of Lana's health issues which cause postponements and delays. She's been in and out of hospital with serious complications. Aside from the toll it's exacting on her, the kids and I are worried sick all the time. Not being able to get information about her condition is frustrating. It's hard not to think the worst even though we try not to. On the other hand, I keep thinking it may not be a bad thing where Lana is concerned when it comes to her sentencing. Her health issues may lead to Stolberg giving her a lenient sentence. I mean how much does she have to suffer?

"Well I finally had a break from court so I came right away," Marty says.

"I certainly appreciate that, Marty. I feel like we're not doing enough at this point. Will you have more time now to dedicate to my case?"

"I've been busy with a murder case for the past few weeks, so it's been hard to find time to come and see you. Plus, my daughter just gave birth to our sixth grandchild, a little girl. We were in Colorado visiting them for a week."

"That's wonderful...about your granddaughter, mazel tov to you and your family!"

"Thank you," Marty says, proudly.

"So, is this the same murder case you were working on last time we met?" I ask.

"No, no. That one's over. This is a different one."

"Oh, okay. How did the last one turn out?"

"Not so good. I never expected it to turn out good. He was found guilty at trial. I told him to take a plea, but he wouldn't listen. Now we're waiting on sentencing. Some of these guys are not too smart."

"I see...did he do it?"

"Of course he did. City cameras caught the whole thing on video. When they arrested him, he was still wearing the same baseball cap he was wearing when he committed the murder. They even had DNA evidence. Impossible to defend. I told him to take a plea."

"Yeah, I guess he should have, considering all that. What were they offering?"

"Thirty to life. Now he'll get life for sure."

"Wow, young guy?"

"Gang kid...twenty-four years old. Three brothers... all in prison too."

"Family business, I guess. Anyway, Marty, hope you have better luck with the new murder case."

"Thanks, but I doubt it. They have two witnesses who saw the whole thing," he says, sounding defeated.

"I imagine you advised him to take a plea deal also?"

"Won't do much good. It's his third strike and a history of violence. He might as well take his chance at trial. Maybe he'll beat it on a technicality, but I doubt it. Too bad, he'll never get out."

I almost feel lucky the government only wants to give me a decade, give or take some. I start wondering how much of this is true or just Marty's pitch to get me to be more flexible. Either way, it doesn't matter, because I'm not going down without a fight.

"So, talk to me, Marty. Do you have any news for me?"

"Well, we finally had a conversation with the AUSA. She's tough. She's adamant about the loss amount, and she won't budge on the guideline level. If you go to trial and lose, she's going to ask for the statutory maximum. If you take a plea, she'll recommend twelve years," he tells me.

"The statutory maximum? Marty, that's forty years. You mean to tell me she would actually want to put me away for the rest of my life and maybe more, in other words, a life sentence for allegedly stealing less than a million dollars of which I stole a fraction? Are you being serious, or are you trying to scare me more than necessary?"

"It's what they do. This judge is capable. He's a tough judge, I told you that."

It's funny, but I'm starting to get used to the idea of spending twelve years behind bars. I've spent hours imagining what life would be like when I get out. How old my kids will be, what I'll do, and how much I will have changed. The time this government doles out is so outrageous, by any civilized country's standards. Somehow, a sentence of five to ten years seems like a slap on the wrist.

"No way, Marty. It seems to me they would need to prove the losses they provided in the discovery are attributable to us. They can't. I went over every single amount with a fine-tooth comb. Are you aware that there are even adding mistakes? I checked the totals they listed, and they have 230 thousand dollars more than they provided details for."

"Are you sure?"

"About the addition mistakes? Yes, of course I'm sure."

"Secondly, there's approximately 700 thousand that has nothing to do with us or our case. I don't understand why it's there. They can never prove that it is related to our case. Lastly, all they can attribute to me is under 200 thousand dollars. Based on that, they aren't anywhere close to twelve years. The way I see it, with the loss amount I'm responsible for, I should be looking at twenty-seven months."

"That's not how it works. In conspiracy cases you're liable for the total loss."

"I think you may be wrong about that, Marty. Have you ever heard of US vs. Studley?"

"No, why?"

"It's a landmark appellate court case from the Second Circuit in 1995. It was brought by a telemarketer in a conspiracy to appeal his sentence based on his guideline range. He argued that it should only be based on the loss amount attributable to him. The court ruled in his favor and said he was only responsible for the losses he caused. His sentence was vacated, and remanded for resentencing. You need to read the case, Marty," I say.

"Okay, I'll look at it, but I'm not so sure about that."

"Sure, about what?"

"That you're not responsible for the total loss."

"Marty, the case is blatantly clear, please read it and ask Stewart to as well. I'm pretty sure I'm right about this."

"Alright, I'll look at it then we'll talk again."

"Will you remember the name of the case, Marty?"

"Yes."

"You don't think you should write it down, just in case you get a new murder case, and you can't remember the name?"

"Very funny," he says. "You said Studley, right?"

"Yes, Studley. US vs. Studley. s.t.u.d.l.e.y." I spell it out for him as he writes.

"Okay, I'll have my office pull it, and I'll look at it," he says.

"Have Stewart do the same to help Lana. Then we'll have a co-d meeting to discuss it. If I'm right then we'll need to discuss a strategy to deal with the worst prosecutor in the Southern District. Can we meet next week? Lana is back downstairs, and I hope she stays here, but it's unpredictable. Let's try and take advantage of her being here."

"I can, but I can't speak for Stewart."

"Obviously, but please speak to him and emphasize the importance of this meeting and the Studley case. You can let my daughter know when you'll be coming exactly."

"Yes, of course. I'll call him today."

"Thanks, Marty. Marty, still no luck with the CorrLinks?"

"What's that?" he asks.

I can't believe he's asking me what it is. "It's the BOP's email program. You still haven't accepted me. Why not? You promised you would. And what about that ridiculous separation we have. You need to fix that. It's been six months, and I still can't use the library."

"Shit, I forgot. I'll write a letter to the prosecutor today, and I'll tell Stewart to do the same if he hasn't already. It's just that I've been so busy with these murder trials and my granddaughter's birth," he says looking for understanding.

"And CorrLinks, Marty? What about the CorrLinks?" I ask again.

"Yes."

"What yes? You'll accept me?"

"Yes."

"Today?"

"Yes, today. I already told you I will."

"Marty, you need to appreciate what this is like. To be so helpless and to depend entirely on someone who isn't doing what they say they will do is so disappointing. Please, Marty, please keep your word."

"I understand. I promise."

"Okay, Marty, thank you. Now, Marty, on the strength of the Studley case, if the government doesn't agree to a reduction in the loss amount, I understand we can ask for a Fatico hearing. Is that right?" I ask.

"Fatico was the name of the defendant in the case. It's referred to as Fatico, but it's actually an evidentiary hearing. And yes, we can request one from the judge. If he feels there are grounds, he'll grant it," he explains.

"Alright, so if the government won't budge, we can request one then?"

"Yes, we can."

"Alright, Marty. Then the things you will do for me, in this order are: You will read the Studley case and have Stewart do so as well. You will write the letter about the seps, accept me on CorrLinks and arrange a co-defendant meeting for next week. We agree on this?"

I can tell I'm beginning to make him sick. The nerve—a client demanding so much, especially when the government is paying him so little. Nonetheless, he answers like the professional he is.

"I said I would, and I will!"

"I apologize for being so pushy. It's just that it's not the first time you promised to do something you didn't do," I reiterate. I'm beginning to make myself sick.

"I know, I know. I was busy. I'll do it!" he says.

"So, what's her name?" I ask.

"Who?"

"Your granddaughter. What's her name?"

"Oh." A smile appears on his face. "Her name's Rachel," he says proudly.

"What a beautiful name. I'm very happy for you, Marty. You're very fortunate."

Chapter 41

Good News

HE ACTUALLY KEEPS HIS word, sort of. Two days later I hear my name being called from the second floor, so I climb the stairs and head to the counselor's office.

"You called me, Miss?" I ask.

"Yeah, legal mail. Sign here." She points to an entry in a log book.

I sign my name, and she takes the envelope, opens it, removes the contents and examines it.

"Is that standard procedure?" I ask.

"Is what standard procedure?"

"Checking legal mail," I say.

"Yeah, checking for contraband."

"Does it ever happen?"

"Does what ever happen?"

I don't know why she's making me repeat every question. Maybe she's stalling to make sure she has time to think of the right answer, or maybe, in keeping with company policy, she's just trying to make every little thing difficult.

"That a lawyer sends contraband in a legal letter to an inmate on pre-trial, knowing the mail will be opened. Seems like a sure-fire way to lose their law license, not to mention go to jail," I say.

"Never seen it, but it could happen," she says.

"I guess there's always someone stupid or daring enough to try anything. You can never be too careful," I say.

I don't wait for a response. I take my mail and head back to the quiet of my rack to read it. I'm ecstatic to see that it's a copy of a letter that Marty sent to the AUSA requesting that she remove the separation. Okay, so far so good. I hope it works.

He must have landed a new murder case because he didn't accept me on CorrLinks that day or the days following our meeting. I'm fighting mad at him and left an angry message with his secretary demanding that he do it right away like he promised. Evidently, she never relayed my message because he didn't accept me after that either.

My anger is diminished somewhat a few days later when I'm called to the case manager's office.

"Yes, Miss Sands, you called me?" I ask.

"Stelman, your separation has been removed," she informs me.

"Oh shit! That's great! Thanks, Miss Sands!"

I'm so happy and feel so uplifted. It's like I won a lottery. That's what losing your freedom does to you. It makes you appreciate, cherish and be eternally grateful for the smallest of liberties. Now I can go downstairs to the library for two hours once a week and work on my case or select up to three books to take with me. Until now, I've been reading whatever I can find on the unit.

On library day, I make sure to be the first one in line at the door when Miss Edwards calls it. I stand there like a little kid waiting for the ice-cream truck to come around the corner. Miss Edwards sees my excitement. It's impossible to hide. About twenty minutes later, with a line of about fifteen guys formed behind me, she comes out of the bubble and yells:

"Lock it down! Lock it down!"

She looks my way and gives me a sly little smile.

"Hurry up! Lock it down! Move!" she orders, while looking straight at me.

Motherfucker! I think to myself. I'm finally allowed to go to the library, and it's cancelled. I can't take this shit!

Lockdowns aren't fun. It's like living in the SHU except with the creature comforts of your own cell which offer little more than the SHU. You're fed through the slot. On a normal day, we're only locked down during stand-up count and then again for the night. Lockdowns are twenty-four hours. They can last days or weeks depending on the reason for it. During hurricane Sandy, we were locked down for two straight weeks as lower Manhattan had no electricity and no hot water.

We only showered every three days in freezing cold water. Using the toilet with another man in your cell isn't comfortable either. Some guys run a laundry-bag cord across the center of the cell like a clothes line and hang a sheet over it to create privacy, but most just ask their bunky to turn around and face the wall when they have to go. It's proper prison etiquette to continuously flush so as to ensure there's no bad odor.

Thankfully, this lockdown only lasted ninety minutes. We learned from cadre workers, inmates who are at the end of their sentence and who do building maintenance and enjoy much more freedom that they locked us down because they were bringing a high-profile prisoner to Ten South, the most secure SHU on earth. For this type of controlled move, the lockdown measures extend to outside the building for several city blocks.

America takes their job as world's premier jailer very seriously. Juaquin Guzman (El Chapo) is there now along with some other infamous terrorists. I think if it was up to Anna Gabro, the AUSA, I'd be there too.

Chapter 42

Upward Trajectory

"THANKS FOR ARRANGING THIS meeting," I say to Marty after we've dispensed with the greetings.

It's been two weeks since I last saw him, and as agreed, he spoke with Stewart. This is the result; Lana is here and Stewart brought Joseph, as usual.

"So, did you guys take a look at Studley?" I ask.

"Yes, I did," Marty announces, looking at Stewart. "I also had a few other lawyers in my office review it, and the general opinion is you're right. This case is perfect for us."

"We looked at it as well and were quite surprised by it. We agree," says Stewart.

"At the very least the case gives us leverage to negotiate a better plea deal with the government. They won't be able to ignore the appellate court's ruling. Well, they actually can, they can do whatever they want and leave it to the judge, who can also do whatever he wants, but hopefully they will be more reasonable than they've been up to this point," Stewart adds.

"That's great. I'm happy you guys agree that there's something real here." I turn to Lana.

"Lana, do you understand what this is about?"

"Sort of, a bit, but not really."

"Whatever Ross brought in can't be applied to you or me. Whatever I brought in can't be applied to you and Ross and whatever you brought in can't be applied to me or Ross. Ross was the bulk of the losses, so it will significantly change the loss amounts relative to the sentencing guidelines and the point level they can use to determine our sentences. There's no way we're looking at twelve years. It will be much less than that," I say, feeling like Perry Mason. "Do you understand what I just explained?"

"Yes," she answers.

"Great. Stewart, can Lana get a copy of the case and the Appellate court's decision so she can read it over?"

"Absolutely. Joseph?"

"I'll mail her a copy today," Joseph says.

"Okay, good. Lana please read it carefully and make sure you understand it. I think you will," I tell her. "Marty, Stewart, what are next steps given our consensus on this case?"

"Well, we need to have a very serious conversation with the AUSA. As I said, she can ignore the facts of the case entirely and do what she wants. Stolberg can also do what he wants at sentencing. Then you would have to appeal. Obviously, that's not what we want to see happen. We want her to take Studley into account and be more reasonable with the guideline range to reach a satisfactory plea agreement," Stewart says.

We all agree and then I ask, "Stewart, what about Lana? Her situation's been very difficult. Won't they consider that and be more lenient with her?"

"Not this prosecutor and certainly not for a plea agreement. That's something I'll deal with at sentencing. I'm really hoping the Judge will be sympathetic. I'm going to try hard to get Lana as little time as possible given her medical history and current health. She's suffered enough. She should be home with her children."

With that Lana begins to sob. We all wait for her to compose herself. Once she does I say:

"Okay, what about the adding mistakes in the discovery. Like I said, there's 230 thousand dollars added on incorrectly. I don't understand how they can make such a stupid mistake unless it's intentional and they're hoping you guys aren't smart enough to catch it."

They are smart enough, well, Stewart is, but they might miss it. By saying it this way, I hope to make them really drill down on the numbers. I've learned that if you don't work hard on your own defense you're putting yourself at the mercy of a government that will do anything to lock you up for as long as they can. That's been my observation since I've been here. It's sad, unbelievable for the average person, but true.

"I didn't check that. Can you show us right now?" Marty asks.

"Of course. There's also an additional 706 thousand dollars that has nothing to do with us. It's just not from our case...it doesn't belong in our discovery. It may be from some other case, but it has nothing to do with us. It shouldn't be there. It makes a huge difference in the loss amount. It brings the totals to under one million."

"Interesting. You're sure about this, Warren?" Stewart asks.

"Positive. I highlighted everything and made footnotes. I was able to make photocopies in the library." I pass the copies to both of them. Suddenly, everyone is taking me seriously. Evidently, bringing Studley has elevated their opinion of me and impressed them enough that they're listening. I thank Aram again in my mind.

After spending ten minutes reviewing what I prepared and some conversation between them, Stewart says;

"Obviously this change in the loss amount will impact the guideline range for any plea deal."

"Exactly. That's what I've been telling Marty. We really have leverage now. Between the Studley ruling and these mistakes, we're in much better shape. Don't you agree?" I ask, looking at Marty.

Stewart doesn't wait for Marty's answer and he offers: "Yes, I definitely think so." Joseph nods his head in agreement and Marty stands up and declares, "Yes this will help a lot. I'm happy we found this case and these irregularities in the discovery."

Wow...this guy's too much. He just took ownership of something he had nothing to do with. Left up to him, I would probably get two life sentences plus fifty years. Unbelievable!

I look towards Lana and say, "We're going to be okay, Lana. You have a great lawyer representing you, and he's going to work hard to get you home as soon as possible. You just need to keep fighting, okay?"

"I will, Warren. I want to be home with the kids. I want you to come home so we can be a family again. I love you," she says, tears welling up.

"I love you too, Lana. Let's be strong and get through this shit. Listen, you'll be home before me, I think, but you need to concentrate on getting healthy. I'll be fine whatever happens. If I can survive the jails in Santo Domingo, I'll survive this."

"What do you mean? Were they bad? You didn't tell me last time."

"It doesn't matter now. I'll tell you about it another time. I'm here, and I'm fine, and do not say anything to the kids about that," I tell her gently.

"Okay, so when does this conversation with the government take place?" I ask, looking to Marty and then Stewart.

"As soon as possible. We'll take a day or two to review everything and prepare a concise argument. Then we'll send her an email on our position. Marty, we'll talk before the email goes out," Stewart says.

"You won't actually meet with her?" I ask.

"We told you what she's like. She probably won't meet us," Marty says.

"What about the other guy who works with her, Peter Demore? Maybe he'll meet with you," I suggest.

"Yes, I suppose we can try and meet with him. If he won't, then we'll just send the email. Let me review everything, and we'll prepare our argument. Should take a day or two, then we'll reach out to him," Stewart says.

Everyone looks around at each other. It's feels like the close of a successful board meeting. Too bad we weren't distributing stock options. With that, Marty has to leave and Lana and I, accompanied by Joseph, stay together for the next half hour.

I am grateful.

Chapter 43

On a Mission

LANA'S BACK IN THE hospital. I found out when I called home last night. The kids hadn't heard from her in days, and we assumed she was there, but we didn't know for sure. I asked one of the female nurses who comes to the unit every day to administer pills if she could tell me anything. All she would say is Lana's alright and not to worry. This was a lot more than I used to get. Then Stewart received a call from the BOP's lawyer at MCC to advise that she was in hospital. He called the kids, and they told me.

I sent a letter to Rabbi Mintzer asking if he can visit her in the hospital in the capacity of clergy. I don't know if it's allowed, but if anyone can pull it off, he can. That's how we measure success now. Not by how much money we make or the things we have but by arranging for someone to visit her to keep her spirits up. This experience is changing us all. In the meantime, life on the unit goes on.

"Who's the new guy?" Frank asks one morning before lunch. Frank got here a couple of weeks ago. He's looking at ten years for marijuana trafficking. It's not his first time. He's half Irish, half Italian. He's a really nice guy and more intelligent than most here. We've all hit it off, and he fell into our car pretty easily. Aram, Nick, Frank and I are sitting around the table on the tier.

"I don't know, but he's acting real strange. He's been doing pull-ups and push-ups non-stop all morning and pacing back and forth. He's all cranked up. I haven't spoken to him, has anyone?" I ask.

"Not me...no reason," Aram says.

"Maybe I will after lunch. He definitely looks nervous though," Nick adds.

He got here last night. They put him on our tier in the first cell near the stairs. He's black, about five eight, 185 pounds...late twenties, early thirties at most. He looks like a hard street thug. He has a scar under his right eye that goes down his cheek and follows the line of his chin.

I've seen this type of scar before on other inmates. Someone told me it's what they do on Rikers Island when they cut you. They call it a buck fifty because it takes 150 stitches to close it up. Everything tells me he's trouble, so I'm staying away from him; best to find out what he's about first.

After lunch I go upstairs to do my job. I've advanced to the position of counselor's orderly, a coveted job on the unit. It gives me some privileges that include being let out of my cell immediately following count, with the kitchen workers who set up for chow. This lets me get to the telephones and computers before anyone else. I also get a second tray for most meals after everyone is served. I already had access to the supplies, but now I'm able to get extra clothes from laundry. More importantly I have the counselor's ear, and she listens to me.

I still never charge for anything I have access to. Again, this would only bring problems. Instead, I work hard to resolve other inmates' issues. I get the counselor to approve inmates' visitor requests quickly. It requires a background security check on all potential visitors through a Federal database. When I first arrived, it took her almost two months to give me my approved visitor list. She would just let the forms pile up, leaving inmates frustrated and angry.

I also make sure she gets the laundry orders filled quickly. I've convinced her to let me handle bed move requests. It's important because when two men live with each other in a tiny cell, bad arguments can erupt that could lead to much worse. Managing bed moves helps keep the peace on the unit. Inmates come to me with their issues, and I arrange better alternatives, which I present to her for approval. She always approves my recommendations.

Between studying Spanish, working out, and my job, the days go by quickly.

The new guy is still acting strange into the afternoon and evening. He is increasingly edgy. Nick hasn't spoken to him yet nor has anyone else.

Every night at around eight fifteen after I speak to the kids I make myself a cup of tea and eat a honey bun. Even though I get an extra tray, I'm always hungry because of the amount of exercise Aram has us doing. It's my treat each night, and I look forward to it.

I am heating water in the microwave and the new guy is waiting behind me with a mug of water in his hand. When I finish, I walk back to the tier and sit down at one of the tables to sip my tea and enjoy my honey bun. Aram and Andrei are playing chess at another table and arguing in Russian about a move. Most guys are out on the unit floor, watching television or reading on their racks. The new guy comes down the stairs, mug in hand, and goes to his cell.

Several minutes later my old friend Six walks down the stairs heading to his cell when the new guy comes out and calls to him. He is still holding his mug.

"Yo, my nigga, lemme holler at you fo' a minute," he says to Six.

Six turns and replies, "Yeah, wassup, my nigga?" and starts towards him, probably thinking he has a question about something.

Suddenly, the guy takes the mug and throws its contents in Six's face. Then he reaches into his overalls, pulls out a shank and starts slashing at him. Six is screaming, and his face is blood red. I realize he's burnt badly from the scalding liquid.

The CO hears the screaming and hits his body alarm. By the time the cavalry arrives, Six is on the floor, his face a scorching, red mass, and he's bleeding from the side of his neck and arm. He's in bad shape.

The guy moves away when the cops approach and immediately lies down on the ground with his hands behind his head, waiting to be cuffed. They yell at everyone to hit the floor and cuff him. They also cuff Six while they wait for medical to arrive.

By now, there are twenty COs on the unit running from tier to tier yelling at everyone to get in their cells and "lock it down." If anyone takes too long to move, they throw them to the floor roughly and cuff them. These guys aren't playing. In situations like this, when they don't know what's going on, they fear for their own safety, so their adrenaline takes over, and they get extremely aggressive.

About fifteen minutes later they take the new guy away and send Six to medical. All the cops leave except for four, and we're left on lockdown. We know they're going to start a body search very soon and also realize this lockdown won't be short. I call to Aram through the cell doors.

"Man, did you see that? He doused him with boiling water. It looked like his face just melted."

"That wasn't water. It was a mug of boiling Muslim prayer oil from commissary. That's why the dude was acting so strange. He was planning it all day. He either came here for that or decided to do it for some reason when he got here. He must know Six, but it didn't seem like Six knew who he was."

We stay locked down for four days. During the lockdown SIS comes and takes a few guys off the unit presumably to question them to try and find out why it happened. Late on the fourth day they lift the lockdown and everything goes back to normal. Everybody is talking about what happened but nobody has any answers. Most of the guys SIS pulled out are back and they deny knowing anything. I can't wait for the counselor to come in because she is confiding in me and will sometimes give me information on different things. I am expecting to learn something from her.

"He's in the SHU. He won't be coming out, and he'll be charged for the attack," she tells me.

"What about Six?" I ask.

"He's in the hospital. He suffered serious burns and seven stab wounds. He'll live, but he won't be so pretty anymore."

"What's going to happen to him after they discharge him?"

"He's not coming back here. He'll probably be sent to Queens," she tells me, whispering.

"Queens? Isn't that a cheese factory?" I ask.

A cheese factory is where they send very high-risk informants whose lives are in danger. It's a jail or prison that houses rats.

She looks at me and raises an eyebrow as if to say: What do you think Six is?

"I don't believe it! He once accused me of dry snitching. He's a rat? Unbelievable. I guess someone doesn't like him and wanted to do something about it."

She just shrugs. I assume she won't offer anymore but then says:

"The guy was in the building for sixteen months, and this was his fourth incident. He kept getting into fights on different units and going to the SHU knowing when he got out he'd be moved to a different unit. He finally made it here. Probably what he was trying to do all along."

A few days later, word gets around about what really went down. Six was testifying against a couple of high ranking Bloods on a murder indictment. Somehow, they found out Six was the government's witness, so he was sent to deal with it.

I learned something. It's the guys who talk about other people "telling" that are most likely rats. They do it to deflect attention from themselves. I've seen it so many times since. I make it a point to stay away from anyone who talks like that.

Chapter 44

Lies

"IT'S THEIR BEST DEAL. They won't budge. They've agreed to reduce the loss amount to less than one million, which reduces the guideline range. The net offense level is twenty-six points after acceptance of responsibility. You're looking at a sentencing range of sixty-three to seventy-eight months. Take it," Marty tells us.

We're here again, same cast of characters. We have a revised plea agreement. Marty and Stewart presented it to us. It's only open for acceptance until tomorrow afternoon at five. It appears the government has no qualms pressuring criminals into signing important documents under extreme duress.

We don't say a word. Lana and I just look at each other. After a moment of silence, Marty tells us how great this offer is.

"Their last offer was 97 to 121 months. This is 30 percent better. We worked hard to get them to reduce the guideline range. I strongly advise you accept this."

"With all due respect, Marty, I'm the one who brought Studley to the table. You had no idea it even existed. I also found the grade three math adding mistakes, so please don't take credit for hard work on this case. Without Studley, you would strongly be advising me to take 97 to 121 months," I say, annoyed.

"With all due respect to you, Warren," Stewart interjects, "that's only part of it. We worked hard to get the government to entertain the argument we made. They didn't have to budge at all. They don't want to go to trial, but they know that if you do and you lose, you'll get a very long sentence. Based on that position, it's not easy to get them to negotiate. It never is. Plus, they wanted to enhance Lana with a leadership role for bringing you into the conspiracy. An enhancement is an increase in the point score used to determine your sentencing guideline range based on additional conduct associated with your crime. That would be another four points and at least two additional years for her. I had the government agree to drop that."

"Well, there is that," I say. "You did a great job of that. But, you know, neither Lana or I were ever leaders, organizers, or managers of anything. You know that, and I assume the government does also."

"It doesn't matter. The law says that by recruiting you, she had a leadership role. That's enough to get the enhancement," Stewart says.

"Marty, Stewart, we're happy they reduced the loss amount to below one million, but it's still not enough. The Studley case is clear. Based on our actual loss amounts, it should be below 400 thousand, which will bring the points down an additional level. Most of the money was brought in by Ross, not us. The guideline range should be fifty-one to sixty-three months. With the good time deduction and assuming the judge sentences us to the low end of the guidelines, we'd be looking at forty-four months. That's a huge difference. For that reason, we're not accepting this," I say as I look to Lana for support.

"You're making a huge mistake!" Marty says. "You don't know what you're doing! You're going to piss them off, and they will really try to screw you! Believe me!"

Stewart looks at Lana and says:

"Lana, I'm strongly advising you to accept this plea deal. It's the best they're going to offer."

"Warren? What do you think? Maybe we should. I'm scared of what they might do if we don't," Lana says.

"No! We can't accept it. It's not right! It's more time than the law says we deserve! I'm not signing it. Let's ask for an evidentiary hearing so we can call this stuff out and demonstrate what's real and what's not," I say.

Marty stands up, practically knocking his chair over in the process. With a raised voice he looks directly at me and says:

"You want an evidentiary hearing? You think that's the way to go? Let me tell you what's going to happen at an evidentiary hearing. You'll present your case to the judge who will listen to everything. Then he'll call the government to present theirs. They'll call an FBI agent to the stand to testify, and that FBI agent will lie through his teeth about everything. By the time he's done, you'll wish you listened to us. The judge will make a ruling, and it won't be in your favor, I promise. You'll be begging to get this offer back, only it will be too late. You'll end up getting screwed and doing a lot more time. That's what will happen, believe me! Tell them Stewart," Marty says.

"It's true. Take the deal. Don't play around. You'll be very sorry if you don't. I'll work hard to get Lana a downward variance from the guideline range. It's only that, a guideline range. It's advisory. The judge doesn't have to follow it. He can sentence below the range. That's what I'm hoping for in Lana's case," Stewart says. "Besides, Studley is relevant to sentencing, not to the total dollar amount of the conspiracy. The amount constitutes the total losses of the conspiracy. You'll be able to argue Studley at sentencing. If you try to do it now, it'll backfire."

"What do you mean they'll lie? That's crazy. The government will actually lie? Why would they? I mean we're guilty, and we're going to prison, so why would they lie to send us away for longer? Are you serious?" I ask incredulously.

"They do it all the time!" Marty says.

A deafening silence overtakes the room. I can't believe what they just told us. The FBI will lie? The prosecutor will orchestrate the lie with the FBI? I'm not even sure if Marty and Stewart are lying to us right now to get us to accept the offer, but my gut tells me they aren't.

I look at Lana and see that she's scared and confused. I know she doesn't want to go against me, but she wants to follow Stewart's advice. I can bluff and tell them I'm ready to take my chances and hope that the government will come back with a better offer, but what if they don't? Maybe pushing too hard will piss them off and, even if I end up being right, I'll be wrong. Damn this. I need to think about it. I need to talk to Aram. He'll help me figure out what to do.

"When you say we can argue Studley at sentencing, what do you mean? How do we do that?" I ask both of them.

"When you go for sentencing, we prepare a sentencing memorandum for the judge. We can present the Studley argument in that memorandum. If he agrees with the argument, then he can give you a sentence below the guideline range you agreed to in the plea," Stewart explains.

"Okay, I understand. But if he doesn't accept the argument, we have no right to appeal the sentence because we waive our right to an appeal once we sign the plea agreement. Is that the case?"

"Yes. Look, this is not an easy situation, but you need to trust us because we know what we're doing. This is your best course. If you piss the government off, they will come at you very hard," Stewart says.

"Listen, I need to think about this. I need a couple of days," I say.

"You don't have a couple of days. It expires tomorrow at five o'clock," Marty reminds me.

"I don't care! Let them extend it! How can we be expected to sign something as important as this under such duress? I'm not signing anything right now! Lana, you have to agree! We should have the right to think about it for a couple of days. This is a serious decision," I tell her. "We didn't even get to read it properly." I look directly at Stewart and Marty.

"Would you sign something without reading it and making sure you understand it first?"

"Warren's right. We need some time," Lana says.

Stewart and Marty can't seem to mount a credible objection to this, so they agree to ask Anna Garbo for a forty-eight-hour extension. Stewart turns to Joseph and asks him to leave the room and make the request.

"I have another important question," I say looking at both of them.

"What is it?" Marty asks impatiently.

"The government froze all of our bank accounts and seized all of our personal property, including vehicles. The majority of the money they froze in our bank accounts has nothing to do with ill-gotten gains. We had a lending business for a considerable time, and that money was earned legitimately. Can they keep that money too?" I ask.

"Stewart?" Marty asks.

"It's a difficult situation. The simple answer is yes. They expect you to forfeit money that equals 996 thousand dollars," Stewart explains. "You'll have to sign a forfeiture order for this amount, and it will be applied against anything they seize. In addition, they are demanding that you sign a restitution order for the same amount, which you are obligated to pay jointly and severally. They can seize assets."

"I'm not sure I understand. Are you saying that they can ask for the same amount twice?" Is that what you just said?" I ask.

"Um.... technically, yes. That's what it means," Stewart says.

"So, we're obligated to pay double the loss amount plus go to prison? How does that make any sense? How can that even be legal? You must be mistaken," I say.

"No, I'm not. That's how it works," Stewart says.

"Marty, is Stewart right?" I ask.

"I'm not sure, but Stewart knows what he's talking about," Marty says.

"You never had a situation like this before?" I ask.

"Maybe, I don't remember. I would need to check. But I'm sure if Stewart says it's that way, then it is," Marty repeats.

"In our case we made the money after the crime was committed not before. It was earned legally and had nothing to do with the crime and didn't involve any moneys from the crime," I say. "Are you sure they can seize anything?"

"That's what they do," Stewart says.

"Can you prove the money was not proceeds of the crime?" Marty asks.

"Well, we have an attorney that has all the paperwork and contracts for the business in his office. He visited me in the Dominican prison, and he told me he has everything. We also had all the bank statements in our office. From what I understand, everything in the office was seized by Interpol. If we can get everything then we can prove it."

"Now, you're talking about a foreign country and a foreign government. We don't know anything about that. That's more than we are able to do in our capacity. You'll need to find another way. We can't help with that," Stewart says.

This is crazy, I think to myself. Hog-tied again. What a system. I need to call that woman lawyer I gave the mandate to. I haven't even thought about that since then. Frankly it just wasn't top of mind with all the other problems we have, but now I wonder what's going on with that. I need to try and reach her somehow and find out. I decide to say nothing to Marty or Stewart. If we're going to prison, having that money will be a big help for our kids.

"Marty, one more thing. Stewart said he will argue for a downward variance for Lana because of her health. Are you going to fight to get me a downward variance based on Studley and the loss amount attributable to me if I sign the plea?" I ask.

"Of course. I'll try to get you the least amount of time possible, but that's up to the judge and, as you know, he's tough," he explains.

"Yeah, I know. But will you fight hard? That's my question."

"Yes, I will."

"We've got a lot to think about. We need at least two days. Lana, I suggest you take the time to read this agreement carefully," I say.

Just then Joseph enters the room and announces that he called his office and had his secretary text the prosecutor who agreed to a seventy-two-hour extension.

"That's even better. Today is Monday. Let's meet again on Wednesday morning," Stewart suggests. "Marty, is that okay for you?"

"Let me check," he says as he takes out his day planner. "Yes, Wednesday morning is fine. I hope we won't have trouble getting in early. Can we be here for eight o'clock Stewart?"

"I'll be here at seven thirty," Stewart answers.

"Unfortunately, we'll be here whenever you need us," I say.

Chapter 45

Deal Done

"SO, WHAT DO YOU think?" I ask Aram.

"Look, I said right from the beginning you were looking at five years. That's the range. As for an evidentiary hearing, they could be right. There's risk. If an FBI agent gets up on the stand and testifies that you guys worked in tandem in any way to advance the scheme, you're fucked. If they show that even one victim spoke to more than one of you, Studley's out the window. Considering your judge, I wouldn't try. I looked at a bunch of his cases; he's a tough sentencing judge. Your lawyers aren't exaggerating about him. He likes to give long sentences."

"That's great news, Aram, just what I needed to hear. But don't you think that asking for an evidentiary hearing may push the government to come back with a better plea deal?"

"Who knows? I mean, it's possible, but you've got to realize, these people know their business. They do this every day, and from the sound of it, your prosecutor isn't too merciful."

"No, our lawyers say she's terrible."

"Listen, if Lana's lawyer can get her time served or a significantly reduced sentence, that's a big win. She's too sick to be in prison. Too many things can go wrong in these places when you're sick. As far as you're concerned, I think you'll get sixty-three months, the low end of the guideline range. After the good time deduction, you'll have about fifty-three months left. By the time you get sentenced and designated, you'll have done at least twelve months, so it will leave about forty-one months. That will fly by. You'll be home before you know it. On top of that, maybe you can get the treaty transfer to Canada. If you do, by then you'll have completed two thirds of your sentence, and Canada will release you," Aram says.

"Forty-one months is still a long time. It's three and a half years," I say.

"No. Twenty-two years is a long time, forty-one months is a vacation from life," Aram corrects me.

"I'm sorry, Aram, I didn't mean to sound insensitive."

"No, that's alright. Look, you'll be in a real prison, not this shit hole, and you'll get into great shape. Before you know it, they'll be calling you to R&D to release you. You'll make up the lost time and more on the back end by taking care of yourself and extending your life. It's not so bad, Warren, trust me."

"Aram, again I apologize if I sound insensitive, it's just that you really minimize this thing."

"You have to approach it properly, or you'll go crazy. I've seen a lot of dudes burn out with less time than you're looking at. They spend their whole bid on psych drugs, sleeping away their time. They end up seriously fucked up. If your attitude is right, it'll be easy time, and like I said, you'll win on the back end. So, just man up, motherfucker!" he says with a smile.

"I hear you, Aram, but I think I'd be remiss if I didn't try to squeeze a little bit more out of this. I still think there may be some wiggle room. I've got to try."

"Can I give you some advice?" he asks.

"Of course, you can. I hope you will. What is it?"

"Do not fuck with these people! They don't play games! Once the train leaves the station, there's no stopping it. Don't be arrogant. I know you have a lot of business experience, and you think you can apply the same negotiating principals here, but you can't. I've seen a lot of dudes come back from court freaked out. I was one of them. Five years is really manageable, so don't fuck with this. You won't win. They don't like you. Don't give them a reason to make an example out of you. They can, and they will. Believe me."

I stare at Aram for the next minute, saying nothing. I'm processing what he just told me, and then I say:

"I learned a long time ago not to try and reinvent the wheel. I know you've seen a lot. I'm going to listen and heed your advice. You're a smart man, and I'd be a fool to try and second-guess you. I appreciate it. Thank you, Aram."

So, we signed the plea agreement, and we're waiting to be sentenced. In many ways, it's a relief. Now we can get on with our lives. Sitting in MCC New York is no way to live. It's incredible that I'm looking forward to going to prison so that I can get out of this place and have a better quality of life. If anyone ever told me I would wish for something like this, I wouldn't even understand it. Right now, prison promises to bring the beginning of the end.

After I made the decision to accept the plea, I saw a number of things happen, which reinforced my decision. One gang member from New York was offered twelve years on a plea deal. He refused and went to trial, believing the government didn't have enough evidence to convict him. He was wrong. He got thirty-four years.

Another guy is here for a bank robbery, which he swears he didn't do. He was offered fifteen years but refused, leaving it instead to God. He's become extremely religious and leads bible class daily. He had two prior convictions for bank robbery where he brandished a gun, but never hurt anyone. A gun was involved in this robbery too, so he's being classified as a career and violent offender. Trusting in God, he went to trial and lost; here they refer to it as "blowing trial." The judge gave him forty-five years. He's forty years old now so in all likelihood he'll die in prison.

The one that really made me feel comfortable with my decision was a fraud case. The guy refused the plea offer the government made. He was looking at twenty-seven months but used the threat of going to trial as leverage to get a better deal similar to what I was thinking. Three days before trial, the government still hadn't made a better offer, and it became clear they had no intention of doing so. He asked for the original plea deal back, but they refused. In the end, his lawyer was able to get him a new deal: fifty-seven months.

So now the only thing left to do is work to get Stolberg to go easy on me. I think there may be a good chance for that once he hears my story and understands the mess I was in. Given my age, the fact that it is my first time, my family background, the non-violent nature of the crime (they really hate violence for obvious reasons), the circumstances that led me to commit the crime and the influence of alcohol, Stolberg may show some mercy.

On sentencing, you can submit letters to the judge from family, friends, business associates, for character references and support. You can also write a letter on your own behalf, which is what I begin to do, to let Stolberg know how sorry I am and why I did what I did. I write and re-write it many times, until I think it is perfect. I let a few other inmates read it and everyone to a man tells me the letter will definitely impact the judge. A couple of them even started to tear up. If it could have that effect on hardened criminals, surely it will move the judge... I'm gaining more confidence with each expert opinion.

The last hurdle will be the Pre-Sentence Report (PSR), which is prepared by the probation office and submitted to the judge. I'm waiting to be interviewed, and I'm hoping that we can get them to write a favorable report. Marty will be with me when I meet them. From what I hear, most PSRs are very negative. I hope I don't end up with the worst probation officer in the Southern District as well.

Chapter 46

Dr. C

"ARE YOU STILL HAVING dizzy spells?" Dr. C asks me.

I'm at medical. I was on the call-out this morning to see Dr. C. Guys complain about the medical here, but so far, my experience has been okay. This is my second time seeing the good doctor in ten months, and I've seen a Physician's Assistant a couple of times.

"Well, as you know, I had the one a couple of weeks ago, and I do get them from time to time. I've had problems with vertigo most of my life, at least as far back as I can remember. I think it may have something to do with all the inner ear infections I had when I was a kid," I say, trying to sound pitiful. "Back then, doctor's still made house calls in Canada, and I remember our family doctor coming to the house all the time. He was a nice man. I even remember his name. Dr. Avalin."

"That's nice," Dr. C. says, probably hoping I'll shut up. He has ten other guys waiting outside his office, and he's listening to my useless babble. "Do you still get ear infections?"

"From time to time, not that often. But I do suffer from terrible sinus infections. I don't know if that's related."

I'm trying to cloud the issue. The fictitious bouts of vertigo, which cause my fictitious dizzy spells, which lead to my loss of balance and falling down, are what got me my bottom bunk pass and how I hope to keep it. The BOP won't risk a lawsuit if I fall off the top bunk with a documented medical condition when it could have been avoided.

I had an attack two weeks ago when we were lining up to get our lunch trays. It was staged, of course. I had Aram and Frank catch me as I fell backwards. It caused some commotion when they lay me down on the floor. I tried to get up, but the pretend-dizziness made me lose my balance and fall back down. By then, the CO was there, yelling at me to stay down and not move while he called medical. Two hours later, I was back on the unit after a thorough check-up and an hour of observation by the nurse and PA on duty. Everything was documented, and they scheduled this appointment to see Dr. C.

Now, I'm here. It's a lot to go through for a lower bunk pass, but I figure it's a worthwhile investment, as I expect to have quite some time to serve when the honorable judge gets through with me. Once all this history is documented, it should be a no brainer to keep my lower pass when I get designated. It's my last fraudulent act. I promise.

"How do you feel today?' he asks.

"I feel fine, pretty good in fact, considering." He doesn't know what we should be considering, but that's good because neither do I. "That's how it happens, Dr. C., out of the blue, without warning, I just get these attacks. It's crazy. I get dizzy and lose my balance. The room actually starts spinning."

"So, it's happened a lot in the past?"

"I don't know what you consider a lot, but a few times a year. It used to happen when I flew on airplanes. Maybe the change in pressure caused it, who knows? When I got up to de-board the plane, I would get an attack and literally fall back down into the seat. One time I stayed on the plane ten minutes after everyone else got off because I couldn't stand up. Do you think it was the pressure, Dr. C?"

"No way to know for sure. Maybe."

"Yeah, that's what I thought." I'm sure I'm making him sick at this point.

"Do you think it could be related to lack of sleep?"

I have no idea what I'm talking about, really, but I'm going somewhere with this. At the very least, I'm complicating the diagnosis for him. He's writing, so that's good.

"Maybe. You never know with these things. Why? You're not sleeping?" he asks.

"Not really, Dr. C. Obviously I'm worried about my wife, given her situation. Then there's the kids, we have four, you know. Also, my parents are quite old, and I worry about seeing them again. All that aside, it's almost impossible to get any real rest because of the mattress. I sleep on my side, and after twenty minutes, I wake up from the pain in my shoulder and hip. Is there a better mattress or a medical mattress I can get Dr. C?"

"No. Unfortunately we don't have any special mattresses. We used to, but not anymore. Everyone complains. They keep saying they're getting new mattresses, but nobody knows when. I know sleeping on them is tough, sorry."

"I understand, Dr. C. Thanks anyway."

"I see you have colon cancer in your family," he says.

"Yes, unfortunately," I answer.

"Have you ever had a colonoscopy?"

"Yes, but not in the last five years. I should have had one, but I was putting it off. I was about to schedule one when all this happened," I say.

"Do you want one?" he asks.

"Why? Do you do them here?"

"No, not here. We send you out to the hospital. Do you want me to schedule one? I think you should have it."

"Yes, Dr. C. I think that would be smart, don't you?"

"Yes, that's why I'm asking," he says.

"You're very thorough, Dr. C., thank you. Please schedule one for me."

"Okay. You'll have to spend a night in the SHU to take the prep, and you'll go out the next day. You're alright with that?" he asks.

"Yes, that's fine. That's a good idea actually. It would be hard to take that prep and spend the night in a cell with my bunky. I'll be alone in the SHU, right?"

"Yes, you'll be alone."

"Good, thank you."

"Alright, Stelman, I'll schedule that. I guess that's it for now. You have a lower bunk pass, so I'll extend it another 180 days. If you're sent to another institution, it will be in your file at intake." Jackpot!

"Oh, shit Dr. C. I didn't even think of that. That's good. I appreciate it. I'm sure that'll make it easier on the medical staff in the prison I'm sent to. Thanks," I say.

Mission accomplished!

"Okay, Stelman, that's it...you can go now," he says, guiding me out the door.

"Okay, Dr. C. Good to see you again, thanks."

Dr. C. is a good man. He gives me hope.

Chapter 47

The Greatest SHU on Earth

IT IS TWO WEEKS later on a Wednesday morning when a CO comes for me. I ask where I'm going, but he doesn't answer.

When we get into the elevator, he turns his key and presses the button for the tenth floor. Wait a second, tenth floor? What's this about? The only thing on the tenth floor is Ten South, the mother of all SHUs. It's where they keep the worst criminals on earth. These guys are too dangerous or evil for the regular SHU.

"Hey, CO, why am I going here? What's up? Can you tell me?"

"You're going out to the hospital, but first you need to spend some time in the SHU," he says.

"This isn't the SHU, at least not the regular SHU. Why am I here?"

"There's no room in the regular SHU, so you're staying here," he explains.

"Oh, okay, so I'm not in trouble."

"Why? Did you do something wrong?" he asks.

Serves me right for opening my mouth. I'm learning the less you say, the better. I have to stop making idle conversation.

"No, CO, I never do anything wrong. I'm a model inmate."

"Of course you are, Stelman," he replies.

When we arrive at the door to Ten South, he radios Control. "One for Ten South at the door."

"Roger. Control releasing main, Ten South," I hear over the radio. The door buzzes, and the lock pops. We enter a small vestibule, and the CO closes the door behind us. There's a camera in the corner of the ceiling staring straight at me, and a few seconds later, the door releases and opens. Another CO is waiting at the entrance to the mother of all SHUs. He's huge, about six feet four inches tall, and he must weigh 275 pounds. He reminds me of Arnold Schwarzenegger in Terminator, only bigger. He doesn't look friendly at all, and he looks at me with total disdain.

"This him?" he asks.

"Yup. Stelman. Take good care of him," he says with a smile on his face like something's funny. I'm starting to feel very uncomfortable.

"Turn around and face the wall. Spread 'em, and don't talk!" Terminator says. Fuck, I think to myself. I do as he says, and I hear him reaching for the tools of his trade. He pats me down roughly and says:

"Turn around, and put your hands in front of you!"

Again, I do as he says. He wraps a chain around my waist and slaps a black metal box on my wrists and cuffs my hands. He threads through to my feet. Then he orders me to sit down in a chair, and he shackles my legs. My hands and feet are joined by way of the chain. He must be confusing me for Hannibal Lecter. I'm trying to figure out why all the hardware.

"Walk that way!" he barks, even though it's the only way to walk, unless we're leaving. We reach another door, which he unlocks, and I see that we're on a tier with eight cells. "Keep moving! Last one on the left!" Still barking.

I do as he says, and I keep my eyes forward as we pass the other cells. I want to look, but I don't want to give this prick any reason to mess with me. I can tell he's just waiting for one. He's treating me like a mass murderer even though I'm only here to prep for a colonoscopy. When we arrive at the last cell on the left, he unlocks it and orders me inside. Then he proceeds to remove the hardware. I can't fucken believe we went through all this stupidity to walk twenty yards.

"CO, do you know how it works for the colonoscopy prep?" I ask.

"No. Medical will be here to see you...make sure we don't have to wake you for count!" he says.

"Count? There's no count now...it's seven in the morning," I say.

"When we count at four o'clock, make sure you're awake," he says, loudly.

"Oh, okay, CO. I'll make sure," I answer. There goes that mindset again. Looking for things I'm going to do wrong before I even do them. Lord get me out of here, please.

At around nine a nurse appears at my door. Terminator is standing behind her. I know her, and I'm happy to see her. She's really nice.

"Stelman, I have your prep. You need to drink this whole thing down. I brought some orange juice to mix it with. It doesn't taste too good. Have you ever done this before?" she asks.

"Yes, I've had colonoscopies before, so I'm familiar with the process," I answer.

"Ms. Washington, can I get some extra toilet paper please? I'm sure I'm going to need it."

Terminator looks pissed off. I would have asked him, but I felt he wouldn't give me any. Judging from the look on his face, I'm not wrong.

"Sure, let me go and get you a couple of rolls," she answers. I decide that it's now or never, so, as she's walking away, I yell, "Ms. Washington, I also need another blanket please."

Terminator looks at me like he wants to kill me. I'm getting what I need, and that's all I care about. I remember the last time I was in this situation.

She comes back, and he takes everything from her. He unlocks the cell door and asks her to stand back. He throws the blanket and toilet paper on the floor. Asshole, I think. Ms. Washington looks at me and rolls her eyes,

"Okay, Stelman, drink the prep, and we'll get you when it's time," she tells me.

"Ms. Washington, when will I be going? Will it be today?" I ask.

"I can't tell you that, security reasons."

"What can I possibly do to breach security? I'm locked in the most secure SHU on earth," I say. "I just want to know how much time I have to drink the prep."

"You need to drink it as soon as you can. Okay, I have to go...see you later."

I decide to get it out of the way fast in case they come for me later in the day, so I drink the whole jug within thirty minutes. For the next two hours I do my business, and when I feel completely empty with no risk of accident, I make a pillow out of my orange overalls, lie down on the rack and fall sleep until my body clock automatically wakes me up for four o'clock count.

Terminator must have left for the day because there's another CO doing count with a Lieutenant. Once they pass my cell, I see the guy in the cell across from me for the first time. He has his face to the small glass window, and he smiles and nods my way. I know that guy, I think to myself. How do I know him? Have I met him in the building? No, I don't think so.

Suddenly it comes to me. Abu Anas al-Libi, the guy accused of the US embassy bombings in Kenya and Tanzania. This is surreal. I can't believe I'm locked up in the same place as this guy. I've seen his picture on the news and in newspapers. I'm pretty sure the American government said he's at Guantanamo Bay, but obviously he's not. This is one very bad dude.

I imagine he'll be living like this for the rest of his life unless he gets the death penalty. Well, I suppose he deserves what he gets. Then I get to thinking about it. I was in the SHU for one week, and it was maddening, mostly because I didn't know when it would end. I'll be here for a day or two now, and it's hard. This guy will spend the rest of his life locked down in solitary confinement for twenty-three hours a day. His only way out: death.

The strength of the human spirit and natural instinct for survival, notwithstanding, I'm pretty sure I'd rather be dead. I suppose there's always the distant hope that one day they'll let him live in general population, but given the heinous atrocity he committed, I doubt it. Most people, including myself, would say he's getting exactly what he deserves for killing so many innocent people, but they haven't spent any time in the SHU. I could take months or even years of SHU time if I knew there was light at the end of the tunnel. It would have a tremendous psychological impact, but at least I would be living with hope. Without hope, I can't fathom it. I realize that for me, death, as terrifying as that prospect may sound, is the more humane option. If I had to live like this for the rest of my life, I would not want to live—this coming from someone who could never understand how someone could take their life over things like financial ruin or divorce. I always viewed it as the ultimate selfish and cowardly act, leaving the people who loved you, broken. But, in this situation, I would make my family understand it's the only option.

Thankfully, I don't need to do more than think about this fleetingly because I'm here to prep for a colonoscopy and nothing else. More than ever, I really appreciate the saying "it could always be worse."

Through the course of the day, I learn there is another Arab terrorist and two Americans on the tier. One of the Americans is the infamous cannibal cop, Gilberto Valle, a disgraced New York City police officer convicted of plotting to kidnap, kill and cook a laundry list of women. Nice...

They don't come for me that day or the next. By Thursday morning, I am suffering with a migraine headache from not eating and caffeine withdrawal. Finally, on Friday, at around one in the afternoon, they come. Why I've had to be in the SHU since Wednesday morning at six is a mystery to me. "Stelman! Get ready...five minutes!" the CO yells from down the tier.

C'mon, are you serious? Now you're gonna start with this bullshit again....

Chapter 48

Lost in Transfer

"CANADA, CO'S CALLING YOU."

"Oh, yeah? Thanks, Angel."

I'm upstairs on the computer checking for new email. There aren't any. I received two earlier from my wife. She sent them four days ago.

"CO, you called me?" I ask.

"Oh, there you are, Stelman. You need to go downstairs, get dressed."

"Okay, give me a few."

I don't ask if he knows why or where I'm going, both fair questions in the real world. Here they go unanswered, so I don't bother.

The elevator doors open at the basement level, and the CO directs me to R&D. I'm placed in a small holding cell and told to wait there. He leaves the door open, which has never happened before. It makes me happy.

About fifteen minutes later, a CO named Shea calls my name and takes me to the changing room and tells me to change from brown to blue. I'm going somewhere, but where? It could be court, but I doubt it because I would probably know about it. Once I'm dressed, he directs me to the main service desk where we're joined by another CO named Smith.

"Stelman, we're taking a trip. You need to sign here," Shea points to a piece of paper on a clipboard. I went through this same drill a couple of weeks ago.

"A trip? Where're we going?" I ask.

"Just sign here," Shea repeats.

"What am I signing? Can I read it?"

"It's standard shit...rules about going on an escorted trip. Basically, says that if you try to run we can shoot you in the back. That sort of thing."

"Nice," I say. "It's hard to run with shackles on your feet though. I'll wait for a better opportunity." There I go again with my stupid mouth.

"You'll never have one," Smith says.

"I know Smith, I'm just kidding. Where's your sense of humor?"

"Very funny," Smith says. "You're a riot."

"Really, though, where we going?"

To my utter disbelief, Shea answers. "Hospital."

"Hospital? What for? Do you know?"

"No. Just sign the fucken paper, Stelman."

For the first time I look at the paperwork. Like he said, there's a list of rules and disclaimers regarding the escorted trip, so I take the pen and sign at the bottom. Shea flips the page to a second form.

"Here too," he points.

I take a quick glance at the paper and see the word colonoscopy...can't be, not again. It's been about ten days since my colonoscopy. They took me to New York Downtown Hospital, and the procedure went well. The Doctor told me everything looked great and I wouldn't need another one for at least five years. While he was at it, he asked if I wanted an upper GI scope, so I said yes. Healthy as can be.

"I think this is a mistake, fellows. I just had a colonoscopy. I don't need another one."

"It's not for that. Just sign it," Shea says.

"That's what the paper says. I'm telling you, this is a mistake. We're going for nothing. I just had a colonoscopy ten days ago. You can check with medical."

"Medical ordered the trip. It's for something else," Smith says.

"Then why does it say colonoscopy if it's for something else? I don't want or need anything else."

"Stelman, sign the fucken paper, or you'll get a shot for disobeying a direct order."

"Can you even do that? I mean, can you force me to sign something I don't want to sign? I don't need another colonoscopy."

"Asshole, sign the fucken paper!" Smith orders in a menacing tone. I know him from working our unit, and he's a real shithead. I don't need to be on his bad side. I decide that if they insist on taking me to the hospital after I repeatedly told them I don't need to go, it's on them. I'll absolutely refuse if it's for a colonoscopy once I get there. But before I concede, I try one last time to reason with them.

"Smith, Shea, I mean no disrespect to either of you. I know you're just doing your jobs, but I'm trying to tell you this is a mistake. We're going for nothing."

"And we told you, it's not for that," Shea says.

"Then why does it say that?"

Smith steps towards me and, in a quiet voice, says, "Listen, motherfucker, sign the paper now."

He looks like he wants to kick the shit out of me. The problem is if these people want to, they can make your life miserable. They can shake down your cell every day or put you in the hole under investigation for countless fabricated reasons. Because it's an old boys' club, they'll tell their colleagues to take up the cause as well. I see it happen all the time when they want to retaliate against an inmate, so I sign.

After outfitting me with travel gear and navigating the intense security procedures, they put me in the back of a BOP van. Shea fastens my seat belt, and we drive away. Once we pass the security check-point a block away, Smith turns towards Brooklyn. This isn't the way, I think to myself.

"Hey, Shea, this isn't the way to Downtown Hospital," I say.

"We're not going there, we're going to another hospital," he says.

"Oh...okay... Brooklyn? It's in Brooklyn?" I ask.

"Don't worry about it, Stelman. Just sit back and enjoy the ride. You can look at all the pretty girls. It may be your last chance for a long time," he says with a snicker.

Funny guy, I think to myself. I take his advice and sit back, watching the scenery as we enter Brooklyn. It's been years since I've been here, and I don't remember it very well, but it sure looks a lot nicer than it was.

"So, I was on my way out the door when Menendez called and asked me to do this one. Bartell and Collins were supposed to, but they're working the SHU because of that fight on 9 North. They brought twelve guys in. I was happy he called. I love the overtime," Shea tells Smith.

"Yeah, me too. I was on my way home when he called, so I turned around. This is my third OT shift this week. I made an extra twenty-seven thousand last year...put two kids through college with the overtime in the last ten years. Younger one graduates this year...can't wait, then me and the wife can start enjoying life a bit," Smith says.

"We're already doing that. We're going on vacation in two weeks. We booked an all-inclusive trip to Punta Cana in the Dominican Republic. My brother and his wife were there last year, and they had a great time. I can't wait to lie on the beach and get drunk," Shea says.

"Hey, Shea, I lived there for a few years. That's where I was arrested. They extradited me here. I know Punta Cana really well. I can give you some places to go and things to do if you want," I say.

"Oh, yeah? You lived in Punta Cana?"

"No, I lived in the capital, Santo Domingo, but I rented a house in Punta Cana on the beach for a year, so I know the area really well. What hotel are you staying at?"

"It's called Dreams, you know it?"

"Sure, I know it. I used to go there. I know the manager. Mention my name. I'll give you his. You'll like it, lots of Americans. The beach is gorgeous," I tell him, trying to deliver good news.

"Oh, yeah? Good. I'll tell my wife. How big is Santo Mingo?"

"Santo Domingo," I correct him. "It's a big city, three and a half million people. Not as big as New York, but most cities aren't."

"Shit, I never knew that," Shea says.

For the next fifteen minutes Shea and I talk about his upcoming vacation. I give him the names of some good restaurants and shopping outside of the hotel and a crash course on tourist money grabs from the locals. Even Smith starts warming up to me and jumps in the conversation.

When we pull up to the hospital, Shea takes me out of the back seat. We wait while Smith goes to park the van. There I am, standing at the entrance in cuffs and shackles while normal people go in and out. Everyone gasps when they see the criminal. Mothers put their arms around their children's shoulders and clutch them tightly to protect them. I am literally sick to my stomach. I want to scream:

"You don't understand...I'm no threat...I wouldn't hurt anyone...I have children too!"

How can they not react this way? I'm restrained like a dangerous, violent criminal. Smith joins us and grabs the back of my pants at the waist and starts to walk me into the building. We proceed down a hallway and turn left where a big sign reads: Gastroenterology and Colo-Rectal Surgery Department.

Now I know for sure this is a mistake. I say to Shea who's walking a few feet behind us:

"Shea, you said it's not for a colonoscopy. Why are we going to gastroenterology then? I told you right from the beginning, this was a mistake."

"Stelman, please just walk," he says.

Did he say please? Wow! I think that may be the first time I've had anyone from law enforcement say please since I've been locked up. How can I do anything but comply? Imagine living in conditions where someone using a nicety like the word please has such resonating impact.

"Okay, Shea," I say.

We make our way through two large glass double-doors that open electronically, and we're greeted by a very cute receptionist. There are about seven or eight people sitting in a waiting area, and they are all aghast when they see me. Discomfort fills the room, yet I can tell my presence unleashes a morbid curiosity. They can't stop staring.

Cutey directs us to a small examining room away from the regular civilians. It's good for business having a contract with the BOP, but bad for business having dangerous inmates in the common waiting area. While we wait, Shea asks me a few more questions, and I'm happy to answer.

About ten minutes later, the door opens and a very distinguished fifty-something gentlemen walks in and introduces himself.

"Good afternoon, Mr. Stelman. I'm Doctor Goldman. I'm a gastroenterologist."

"Hello, Dr. Goldman. I don't want a colonoscopy," I say.

He looks at me puzzled, and then at the two officers. Before he can ask. I decide to help him out:

"I just had one ten days ago. I told these officers this is a mistake. I don't need another colonoscopy. I told them we're coming for nothing."

"You just had one? Are you sure what you had was a colonoscopy?" he asks.

"Yes, Dr. Goldman, I'm quite sure. It wasn't my first, and I recognized the procedure. For added assurance, the doctor who did it told me he was doing a colonoscopy. I have no doubt. He also did an upper GI."

He looks confused by the news and starts flipping through his paperwork. He announces that he'll be back in a few minutes and leaves the room.

So, we wait, and I get to listen to Shea and Smith talk about their recent firearms training. Apparently, Smith is one of the best sharp shooters in MCC. I need to remember that. Fifteen minutes later, Dr. Goldman returns with paperwork in hand and says:

"Okay, Mr. Stelman, it looks like you're right. I called MCC to verify, and they checked with medical records. I just received a fax detailing your colonoscopy results. I guess this is a mix-up after all. We just started providing service to MCC, and it appears that your case got crossed in the transfer of files. We're sorry for this," he says, and I assume it's on behalf of the hospital and the United States government.

"That's very understandable, Doctor," I say. "I see how that can happen, and I'm not holding anyone responsible. I'm sorry for all the trouble this may have caused you, but as I said, I knew it was a mistake."

"No, no, it's not your fault at all, Mr. Stelman. Just a mix-up," he says.

My fault? What the fuck is he talking about? He must have gone to CO school after he graduated medical school.

"Mr. Stelman, looking at the results of the colonoscopy you just had, it wasn't 100 percent conclusive. The doctor noted that you weren't perfectly cleaned out. There was some stool in the bowel, so he didn't see everything."

"That's funny, Doctor, because he came to see me after the procedure, and I distinctly remember him saying I was totally clean. Maybe I misunderstood because of the medication I was on, but I don't think so," I tell him.

"That's fine. We can do it again. Would you like me to do another colonoscopy to be sure? I see you have colon cancer in your family. Better safe than sorry," he warns.

He's trying to scare me in to agreeing. He doesn't know who he's talking to. What a weak pitch.

"Dr. Goldman, I really appreciate your concern and professionalism, but I don't think it will be necessary. I feel quite confident that I'm okay. I apologize again for the inconvenience. I know you must be very busy. These officers were just doing their job by bringing me here, but no, I don't want another colonoscopy, thank you," I say.

"Are you sure, Mr. Stelman?" he asks.

"Yes, Doctor, quite sure, thank you."

"Like he said…better safe than sorry," Smith offers.

"Thank you, Smith, but I'm fine. I appreciate your concern as well," I say.

"Doctor, I do have a question though, if you don't mind."

"Of course, Mr. Stelman, what is it?"

"When would you do this colonoscopy if I had wanted it?"

"We would do it this morning, Mr. Stelman. The room is scheduled," he says.

"I see, Doctor. Well, like I said, I won't need it, but Doctor, do you understand that I wasn't prepped at all for a colonoscopy? I was just called down from my unit to come directly here. There's no way you could have done one anyway, so all's well that ends well, I guess."

"You weren't? I thought you were ready for the procedure. You were supposed to be. That's strange, let me try and find out why. I will..."

"No, no. Doctor, no need to waste any more of your valuable time on this. I'm sure you're very busy. It was just a total mix-up. Like you said, paperwork was improperly handled in the transfer. That sort of thing happens all the time," I say.

"Yes, it does. Okay then, Mr. Stelman, it was nice to meet you. Take care of yourself," he says as he opens the door to leave.

"Likewise, Doctor."

Everybody's looking for their end. The Doctor wants to bill the Federal government for an unnecessary procedure and Smith and Shea took me out against my objections because they wanted overtime pay. They even wanted me to do the procedure again, even if it was unnecessary just to collect more money.

I think about the money pilfered by the BOP every day because of mismanagement, incompetence, indifference and overall inefficiency. Add to that all the other government agencies, and it's no wonder the US debt is what it is.

Chapter 49

Just Try Us

IT'S LATE JUNE 2013, and I reach out to the lawyer in the Dominican Republic. She was meeting with another inmate on my unit, and we started talking. Manon said she could get our bank accounts unfrozen. The Dominican authorities froze them under direction from Interpol and the US government even though most of the money in the accounts had nothing to do with our crime. Whatever money we made from the crime was long spent. Just before I left for New York, she drafted documents giving her authority to represent us. She was the best and only chance we had. It also helped that I trusted her much more than any other Dominican defense lawyer I met in jail. That was the last time I spoke to her, and lately, I've been wondering, so I'm going to call.

Obviously, it would be better if I didn't call from here. The better option would be to explain everything to Stephanie on a visit and have her call Manon. But last time they visited they had a terrible experience, and I don't want them to have to go through that again.

The COs working the visiting room and the visitor entrance treated Andie and Paige terribly. They were crying and distraught when I saw them. Apparently, the Justice Department encourages the BOP to treat the families of criminals as bad as the criminals themselves. I don't want that to happen again. I don't want to subject them to the intimidation and humiliation. Plus, it's a major expense for the kids to drive to Manhattan and stay in a downtown hotel for the weekend even though they want to come. I told them it's not necessary right now and urged them to put off the trip for our sentencing.

I have Manon on my approved contacts, so I dial her cell phone number.

"Hello," she answers.

"Hello, Manon. It's Warren Stelman speaking. We know each other from Najayo. Do you remember me?"

"Warren, of course I remember you. Did you get my message? I sent your daughter an email. I have good news for you."

"Good news? No, I didn't get the message. What good news?"

"You won the case. The government is going to unfreeze the accounts!"

"What? Are you serious? That's fantastic! Are you sure?"

"The government is releasing the money. I had several meetings with the Fiscal and the Money Laundering Department, and they've agreed to release your accounts. I'm just waiting for it in writing. It could happen any day now."

"Oh, wow! That's great news, Manon. I can't believe it. Finally, some good news."

"I sent your daughter an email last month, but she never replied, so I wasn't sure what was going on."

"That's strange. Stephanie's always on top of things. I wonder if she got the email. Maybe it went to her junk mail. I'll check with her when I speak to her. So now the accounts will be unfrozen, that's great."

"Yes, and I can have the money transferred wherever you want if you give me written instructions."

"Okay, let me think about that. Manon, is there any reason you can think of that we should be afraid to leave it in the accounts?"

"No, I don't believe so. Now that this is resolved, they'll never freeze it again. You don't owe any taxes to the Dominican government, do you?" she asks.

"No, Manon, we always paid whatever we owed, so no problem there."

"Do you owe any money to banks or anyone else that can sue and try to seize the money?"

"I may owe a few hundred dollars to Visa but nothing more than that. Lana doesn't owe any money either."

"Then I don't see you having any problem leaving it in the accounts. The money is safe."

"Okay, like I said, let me think about it, and I'll get back to you, or I'll have my daughter reach out to you. Manon, great job, thanks for everything," I tell her.

"Thank you. I'm happy I could help. I'll prepare a bill and send it to your daughter. You will have to arrange for me to get paid as soon as the accounts are released," she says.

"Of course. I'm happy to pay that. Thank you. We'll talk soon."

Once I get off the phone with Manon I wait the required thirty minutes permitted between calls and relay the information to Stephanie. She promises to pay attention to her inbox. For the first time since this whole thing happened, I feel good about something. Now we'll be able to help our kids while we're in prison.

But my happiness is short-lived. About a week later, I'm told to go downstairs and directed to legal. After the standard metal detector screening and physical pat down, the CO points me down the hallway to one of the meeting rooms. Through the glass door I see Marty, Stewart, Lana and who's that?...wait a minute, I know him, that's the AUSA who works with Anna Garbo, Peter Demore. He was in court when I pleaded guilty. Why is he here?

I open the door and greet everyone except Peter Demore. I give Lana a quick hug and kiss and tell her I love her. She holds on to me and doesn't let go.

"Lana, you need to sit down," Stewart tells her. "We don't want to get into trouble."

I give her another kiss on the cheek, and we sit.

She looks at me, and I get the sense she's trying to tell me something with her eyes, but I don't know what.

Marty says:

"Warren, Peter has something to talk to you about. It's quite serious...."

"Mr. Stelman, I won't mince words. We know you have an attorney representing you and your wife in the Dominican Republic.

279

We also know that she's in the process of having the government there release the funds you have in bank accounts that were seized when you were arrested. The US government wants that money. You are to instruct her to cease and desist immediately."

I'm so stupid! I should never have called Manon from here. I can't believe it. What's amazing is how fast they work when they want to. It can take two weeks for an inmate to get some underwear and socks or access to the telephone to call his family, but, in barely a week, they're all over this. Damn!

I look at Marty. "That money has nothing to do with our case. It was earned legitimately. It should never have been seized in the first place. The attorney has demonstrated that to the Dominican authorities. That's why they've agreed to release the money," I explain.

"It doesn't matter, Warren," Marty says. "Listen to him."

"Mr. Stelman, if you don't instruct her to cease and desist, we will tear up the plea agreement. Then we will enhance your wife with a leadership role in the conspiracy. We will also add back three points to both of your sentencing guideline calculations for non-acceptance of responsibility. You, Mr. Stelman, will be looking at no less than ten years and your wife at least thirteen." He pauses. "I suggest you do as I say."

I can't believe what I'm hearing. This prick just threatened us unless we comply with his demands. It's unbelievable that he's threatening us with more prison time. It's outright extortion!

I look at Marty in disbelief, and before I can utter a word he says:

"They'll do it, Warren. Don't play around. You need to do what he says."

"I don't understand how they can do this to people. The government can commit any type of flagrant abuse and get away with it. We're going to prison for stealing money while they steal our money. Make no mistake about it, that's what this is. And to ensure we do nothing about it, they threaten us with more prison time. What the fuck is this, the Soviet Union?" I ask peering straight at Peter Demore.

"We can do it, and we will," he says to me.

"They will," Stewart says to drive the point home. Then he looks at Lana. "You guys need to do what he says."

Lana has her eyes to the floor. She's shaking, and I know she's scared to death. She's been through so much, and I know they've broken her resolve. She's tough, and she's a fighter, but I need her to use the strength she has left to fight for her life, her health, and to get home safely to the kids. That's what's important. Money is ultimately just money. Her well-being and the well-being of our children is what has to be the priority. I know I can't take the chance that this disgusting prick is bluffing. Marty and Stewart don't think he is. I'm so angry though. I don't want to be bullied. On the other hand, I've seen what they do to anyone who doesn't play ball with them. They're heartless. After a year in MCC, I've seen guys decimated because they didn't take what the government offered or refused to cooperate with them. I need to accept this as another part of this miserable experience. We'll make money again when we get out. Let this go…I have to.

"Alright." I tell her. "But I want the government to put in writing that any money seized has to be applied against the outstanding restitution. Otherwise, I won't drop it, and you, Mr. Demore, can do whatever the hell you want. If you don't agree, I won't agree."

"Well, Mr. Stelman, that's not something we do," he says. It sounds like "nobody tells us what to do."

"Okay, then, I guess we're done here. Marty please call the CO. I want to go back upstairs. Lana, I love you, but we're not going to let them steal from us, send us to prison and make us pay twice for something we never received in the first place," I say.

"Hold on a minute, Warren," Stewart says. "Peter, can I have a word with you outside for a minute?"

"Yes, okay."

The two of them leave the room, which gives Lana and me the chance to talk. "If we don't get them to agree to this now, we'll never get another chance. We'll never have any leverage again."

"Warren, please, don't mess with them. I want us all to be together again."

"So do I, Lana. It's about this double-dipping. It's ridiculous. Let's see what happens. Stewart may get somewhere. How have you been Lana? How are you feeling?"

"Not so good. My stomach is a mess, and I'm having problems with one of the girls on the unit. My bunky has my back though. She's a big Russian woman. I want to get out of this hell-hole. I can't take it anymore."

"Lana, I know it's not easy, but you've survived the worst. In a few months, you'll get sentenced, and with any luck, you'll get a short sentence or maybe even time served. Stay strong, keep it together, and stay away from the girl that's bothering you. But, if she won't stop, then you may have no choice. Go crazy on her. After you spend a few weeks in the hole, no one will bother you when you get back to the unit. But that's the very last resort. Only if there's no other option.

"She gets me so mad. She thinks I'm scared of her, and I was at first, but now I just want to punch her in her face. I just don't want to get into trouble. She never bothers me when my bunky's around though."

"I know exactly what you mean. There are a lot of predators in here that like to pick on people they think won't fight back. Let her think you're scared, and when the time comes and you have no choice, go nuts. It won't last long. I know you, she doesn't. She's in for a surprise."

"It may happen any day if she doesn't leave me alone," Lana says.

"Try to avoid it. These things have a way of working themselves out. She'll probably end up in the box for something else she's doing."

"I will. Warren, will we be okay?" she asks again.

"Yes, Lana, for sure."

Just then, Stewart and Peter come back into the room, and Stewart says: "Warren, Lana, we've discussed it, and the government will not give any assurance because that's up to the judge, but they agree to put in writing that they don't object to the forfeiture amount being applied against the outstanding restitution. Peter...."

"Yes, Mr. Stelman. We'll do that. I'll draft a letter to that effect and both your attorneys will receive it today," Peter says.

"Alright then, fair enough. How do I handle this? Do I just call her?" I ask.

"No, Marty will draft a letter that you'll sign," Stewart says.

"Okay, that's fine, but there is one more thing. I'm on some type of email watch list. It takes three to four days to send and receive emails. Between Lana and me, it takes five. It's ridiculous. I can write a letter, mail it out, and she can receive it faster than she receives an email. This has to change. Everybody else has a two-hour delay. I want the same," I say and look towards Peter.

"That has nothing to do with us, Mr. Stelman. That is entirely BOP jurisdiction. I can make a request, and I will, but I can't guarantee anything."

"When I complained about it, they told me the government requested it. You guys make a mountain out of a mole-hill. We aren't going to mount a cyber-attack from these computers. We won't do anything improper, ever. I think you know that. There's way too much unnecessary drama attached to our case. I'm sure if you request it, they'll do it," I say.

"I'll see what I can do."

With that, the meeting, as well as our chance to have some money to help our kids is over. If I ever wondered how closely they monitor phone calls and email I definitely know now. It's possible that the Dominican Government advised the FBI that they were releasing the money, and that's how the AUSA found out, but I doubt it. It all happened too fast. No, this is my fault. I should have done it another way.

Chapter 50

He Delivers

"SO, HOW WAS IT?" Aram asks.

I just got back from my Pre-Sentence Report interview with the probation office. It took place downstairs in legal. Marty was there with me. The report goes to the judge before I'm sentenced. This report is supposed to give the judge insight into who the defendant is, what he did and why.

He asked me questions about my upbringing, my relationship with my parents and brother, my education, my work history, my children, my relationship with my wife, and then there was a whole section on any assets I may have. In any event, it's over and I think it may have gone well.

I've really been thinking hard about firing Marty and asking the court to appoint another CJA attorney to defend me. There are guys on my unit who have done this, and it is within my rights and discretion to do so. I'm convinced Stolberg doesn't like Marty, and it's becoming obvious to me that Marty doesn't really care about me or my family. Still, I'm reluctant to fire him for fear that it will irritate Stolberg who will take it out on me at sentencing. I keep delaying my decision, hoping he will do something to change my mind or inspire some confidence. Today he delivered.

"The truth, Aram, I have nothing to compare to, but my sense is it went very well."

"Really? In what way?"

"I think I came across as sincere and likeable, which was good, but Marty was amazing. I'm very happy. He finally did something to make me feel comfortable with him and upbeat about my chances. He steered the whole interview and knew exactly what to say and when to say it. I could tell the probation officer was hanging on his every word and writing notes verbatim on what he was saying. I'm not sure it could have gone any better, considering the reason for having it was to send me to prison. Maybe Marty's claim that he's a good lawyer is true after all."

"That's great. I told you to give him a chance."

"Yeah, you did. If he can handle my sentencing the way he handled the interview, I'll be satisfied. So, now I wait on the draft before it goes to the judge. I get some time to review it, right?"

"Yes. They'll send the draft first. If there's anything in it that's incorrect or objectionable, you'll be able to present those objections for modification. The parole board may or may not agree to the modifications, but I'm sure from what you're saying, Marty will know how to manage that. Remember though, they also get input from the AUSA's office and the FBI when they prepare the report. Neither of them will paint you as anything less than a degenerate criminal."

"Nice. Well, I hope the draft is somewhat favorable. I know the interview went well. Marty was smooth, so we'll see. The probation officer said it would be ready by next week."

"Next week? I'd be surprised if you get it that quickly. It usually takes a month."

"Apparently, Stolberg is pushing for the sentencing. Let's see what happens."

It was ready in a week.

I was called down to legal, and Marty was there, draft in hand. He sat silently while I read it, and when I finished, he said: "So what do you think?"

"I have no experience, Marty, but aside from the fact that I committed the crime, it seems pretty positive. Am I right?"

"Yes. You're right. It's positive. In fact, in all my years practicing law, I don't think I've ever read a more positive PSR.

Alright, so let's tally this. In all his years practicing law, he's never had a worse prosecutor, a worse judge, and now a better PSR. I wonder if the score's tied, or if I'm still down a field goal.

"How do you like that line where he says once you're released, he believes you'll be a successful businessman again. I told him that, and he wrote it," Marty says proudly.

"I mean…I think that's good. If they have confidence in my future success, it suggests that the probation office believes my criminal deviance was an anomaly and out of character. I think that's good," I say.

"It is good. Most PSRs are negative and don't paint a very bright picture. In fact, most are pretty damning. I'm starting to believe you have a chance at a low end of the guideline sentence," he says, with a big smile on his face.

"Marty, we talked about this already. I'm hoping for much better than that. You need to set your sights higher or maybe lower, depending on how you look at it. With such a great PSR, the fact that I'm a first-time offender, no violence, and considering my age, I should be looking at thirty-six to forty-eight months. If I get thirty-six months, with good time reduction, it'll net out at about thirty-one months. Deduct the twelve I already have in, and I'll have twenty-one remaining. That, Marty, would be a successful outcome."

"I don't disagree. The only problem is your judge. It's hard to say with him."

"Marty, you received all the letters my family and friends wrote in my support to send to Stolberg. You also received my letter. What did you think of them?"

"I think they're all great. I like the one from Stephanie and the one from your parents. They were very moving. Your letter is excellent. I had some of the lawyers in my office read it, and they thought it very sincere and very heartfelt. It really explains what you were going through. It's very emotional. You write very well," he says.

"Thank you, Marty. Over the years in school and in business I developed some writing skills. It also helps when you're writing about something you feel passionate about."

I don't know if he's playing me, telling me what he thinks I want to hear, or if he's being truthful. I want to believe the latter. If everyone agrees that the letters will have some effect, then maybe they will. Anyway, they can't hurt.

"Yes, well it shows. So other than the small changes we've listed, is everything else in the report acceptable?"

"I guess so. I mean, I don't really know. Is there anything else we can do to improve it?" I ask.

"No, not really. As I said, it's one of the most positive PSRs I've ever seen. Let me send them the changes and hopefully they'll amend the report without any objections."

"Alright, Marty, I'll leave it in your hands. Marty, I have a question. Do you think it will help to have my children and my parents in court for the sentencing?"

"No. I don't think it matters."

"Why would you say that? You don't think it will impact the judge seeing my four children and my elderly parents? How so?" I ask.

"I just don't think it will impact the judge's decision."

"Well, I guess it depends on when he makes his decision. Does he come into the sentencing with his mind already made up? If he does, then what's the point of the hearing altogether? He can just sentence me in writing. Don't I get a chance to address the court? What's all that about then? Is it just a charade? Everything I've read and heard suggests judges like to see strong familial relationships. I would think my whole family being there to show support for me would be a strong indicator of that. Don't you?"

"Yes. Yes, of course. Yes, definitely. You should have them come," he says.

Shit, here we go again. There's the old Marty, flip flopping all over himself. He just deflated my recent bullishness about him. This guy is about as trustworthy as a hooker on crack. I guess I'll have to figure this out on my own, but I'm inclined to have them there. I don't see how it could possibly hurt. The only real consideration is the cost. It's too difficult for my parents to make the long drive, especially because my father is on dialysis. The alternative is flights from Montreal to New York the day of the sentencing. Each return flight is about 700 dollars, so that's 4200 dollars for all of them. That's a lot of money. Then they'll have to come back for Lana's sentencing.

"Marty, your position changed very quickly. Are you just trying to appease me? If it won't help at all, I need to know. It will cost about four thousand dollars for them to come here, which is a lot of money they can't afford. Should they come or not?"

"Yes, they should. I agree that it can only help. I just wish Stolberg wasn't your judge," he says.

"Yeah, I know, I know, me too...."

Chapter 51

The Night Before

THE PAROLE BOARD MADE the changes to the PSR without any objections from the government. Good sign? I don't know, but you clutch at straws when you have an 800-pound gorilla standing on your neck.

After further contemplation and in-depth consultation with experts on the unit, I concluded my family has to be in the courtroom. This way, Stolberg will see a close, loving and unified family, and he'll put real faces to the letters. He'll also see four well-adjusted and supportive children and two loving parents.

With years of experience sentencing criminals with and from dysfunctional and broken families, he'll be able to understand that Lana and I must have done something right to have such great kids.

So, along with my parents, the four of them are flying here for my sentencing. They were able to find a slightly better deal on tickets, 600 dollars return, per person, taxes extra. So, still a chunk of change. I hope it'll be worth it. The flight leaves at six in the morning, and it's fifty minutes to LaGuardia gate to gate. The sentencing is at one o'clock, so they have plenty of time to make it downtown.

"You read it?" I ask Ricardo Alvarez, a Puerto Rican drug dealer with a history of violence who has spent most of his adult years in and out of State and now Federal prison. He's here at MCC on a drug conspiracy case with his older brother, Paco. They're both looking at serious time.

"Yeah, it's mad good. It choked me up," he says.

289

We're referring to my letter to Stolberg. I was with Ricardo the other day helping him with his GED, when he told me he has his sentencing date. I asked if he wrote a letter to his judge, and he said he hadn't because he doesn't know what to write. I told him I'd help him if he wants, and then told him about my letter. He asked if he could read it.

Okay, choked him up. If I can get to a hard guy like Ricardo, then maybe it will have an effect on Stolberg. I'm encouraged by Ricardo's review, as devoid of detail as it may be. Clutching at straws again.

"So, based on your experience, you think it might help me with the judge?" I ask. This is jail-house market research.

At this point, I've convinced myself and everyone around me, after Stolberg reads my letter, he will give me a downward variance. I explained concisely what led me to the crime and described my alcohol induced weakened state. Surely, he'll recognize someone can make a mistake and show some mercy. I even have Aram believing there might be a chance. In my last meeting with Marty to review the government's sentencing memorandum and to prepare our response to it, I prepped him to ask for a twenty-seven to thirty-one-month sentence. He's ready to go and do his very best.

"Yeah, bro. It's one of the best letters I been read. You gonna write one like that for me?" Ricardo asks.

"Sure, Ricky, as long as I'm still here, I'll be happy to help you write your letter."

"My brother read it too. He thinks it's great. He don't think a letter will help him though. He been pled out to twenty years, and he's sure that's what the judge gonna give 'im. He's gonna career him."

"I'm sorry to hear that. I guess there's only so much a letter can do. At some point, the judge won't ignore a long pattern of the same behavior. Hey, how old is Paco?" I ask.

"He's forty-nine. When he gets out he'll be turning seventy. I'll be fifty-seven if I don't catch a break. I pled to fifteen. I can't fucken believe I'm back in this shit again. I was killing it out there," he tells me.

All the majority of these guys know is the street life. They grew up in it. Sell some dope, get some money, live big for a while, shoot someone or get shot, and eventually go back to prison. By the time they realize none of it was worth it, it's too late. Sad.

That night, I call Stephanie to make sure everything is okay.

"Hi, sweety."

"Hi, Daddy, how are you?" she asks, concerned.

"I'm okay, a bit nervous, but otherwise good. How are you, baby?"

"I'm okay, Dad, just really stressed out. I'm so worried about tomorrow," she says.

"I know, Roo, me too. Are you guys all set?"

"Yeah. We're sleeping at Bubby's house, and we'll be at the airport for four thirty. You think that's enough time?"

"Yes, sweety, that's fine. You'll get through check-in quickly because you have no bags, and then customs will be fast. Did you speak to Marty to confirm there are no last-minute changes?"

"Yeah, I called him this morning. He's going to meet us in the court house at ten thirty. Dad, I'm so nervous, my stomach's been bothering me. I haven't been sleeping well. I'm also worried about Zadie, he's been feeling really tired. It's hard at his age to go to dialysis three times a week and still get up every morning and go to work until two thirty. I told him to stop working, but he won't listen."

"Steph, your grandfather is the toughest guy on earth. Working is what keeps him alive. Most of his friends are gone. I disagree with you. He would die of boredom if he didn't work. He worked all his life, since he was a little boy. He needs it. He'll be okay, I guarantee it. He'll be there when I get out, whenever that will be, you'll see. As for you, I don't even know where to begin. I'm sick with guilt for the situation we put your brother, sisters and you in. I'm so sorry. But I want you to remember something: Nothing is as bad as it seems, and nothing is as good as it seems. Ever. I know you didn't ask to be put in this situation, but it will make you stronger and a better person. It will make you all stronger. It will also be over before you know it, and we'll all be together again. You have to learn to take things slowly and understand that everything will pass. Even though I'm in jail, I'm your father, and I love you more than life itself. I'm always here to talk, and any way I can help you cope, I will. Tomorrow you get on a plane, fly to New York, come to my sentencing, and whatever happens, happens. We will do the best we can, and we'll all survive it. Okay, honey?" I ask.

"Okay, Dad. Thank you, I love you so much," she tells me, but I'm dying inside.

"Dad, I don't know what to do. Jace is doing great in school, like always. He's on high honor roll, but Andie is struggling with math. She needs a tutor, and I can't afford it on my salary. I went to a Jewish agency that helps families having financial hardship, and they said they may be able to help, but I still haven't heard anything. I don't think the tutoring can wait because she needs to catch up."

"Stephanie, what are you thinking about? You have the money I gave you. That's what it's for. I'm okay here. I don't need anything. They feed me and give me what I need. Use that money for Andie and for any other expenses that have to be dealt with. Use it to help Mom when she needs money. This should not be keeping you up at night. With any luck, you'll hear back from them soon, and they'll help you deal with it. Okay?"

"Okay, Dad. I just worry that you'll need money in there, and I won't have any to send you. Daddy, are you okay there? Is it dangerous? Are you safe? You never tell me anything." She starts to sob on the telephone.

"Stephanie, you know me. I can take care of myself. I mind my own business, and I stay away from trouble. No one bothers you if you don't bother them. I promise you I'm safe, and nothing will happen to me or your mother. Now please stop worrying.

"It was bad in the Dominican Republic, and I survived that. Stop worrying, honey. I promise.

"As for your mother, she's the second toughest person I've ever known. She may act like a baby, but believe me, that's the last thing she is. I've seen her deal with things that most people would die from. She once had major bowel surgery and got out of bed and started walking the same day. I'll never forget it. She'll be around to drive us all crazy for a long time, Roo, I guarantee it."

"Steph, you need to get your stomach checked. Unfortunately, Crohn's disease is hereditary, and Mom was about your age when she

292

was diagnosed. Call Mom's doctor at the hospital. He's head of gastroenterology now, and tell him who you are. I'm sure he'll see you right away. Don't play with this. You need to be on top of it. They know a lot more today, and they have much better drugs to manage it, if it's that. Okay?"

"Alright, Daddy. I'll call him next week after the sentencing is behind us. I promise."

"Good girl. Steph, listen, I need to save my minutes. I'm sure we'll have to talk after the sentencing, and I only have fifty minutes left. We need to get off now. I'll see you tomorrow, baby. I can't wait to see all you guys. Maybe we'll be allowed to hug each other, but don't be disappointed if we're not, okay?"

"Okay, Daddy. Dad, thanks. I love you."

"And I love you, Roo," I say and hang up the telephone. I want to cry.

Chapter 52

Disaster

SHOW TIME...

I am up when the CO pops the cell door at five forty-five. I didn't sleep much.

"Stelman, get ready, you're going to court," he tells me.

"I need a shower. Give me thirty minutes," I tell him.

"You got it, but I need to send you down by six forty-five, so hurry up."

I've heard that before.

After the sickening process of stripping down, being body searched, changing into blues and being escorted through the tunnel in cuffs and shackles by two Marshals, I'm placed in one of the big holding cells adjacent to the court house. There are eight other guys in there waiting on court appearances. It's the same old: bad lawyers, worse judges, prosecutors they're going to kill, baby mamas cheating on them, homeboys dying or getting long bids, at least one wanna-be-rapper, someone else doing pushups. I try to tune it all out. I can't wake up from this bad dream.

"Yo, white boy...whatup?" a black guy, sleeve of tattoos, asks me.

"All good, man. Just waiting to be sentenced. Don't feel much like talking though. You understand," I say.

"Got ya, brother, good luck," he says.

"Thanks, brother," I reply.

He turns and starts talking up someone else.

About twenty minutes later, I hear my name being called, and a few seconds later, a Marshal appears at the barred door. I stand up and approach.

"You Stelman?"

"Yes."

"Let's go," he says.

We do the handcuff jig, and off we go. He brings me to one of those little interview rooms with the thick tempered glass and leaves me there. I know it's not time to go into court yet, so I assume Marty wants to meet to go over some last-minute details. Very thorough.

A few minutes later, he appears at the window.

"How are you, Warren?" he asks.

"I'm okay, Marty, you?"

"Not so good. There's been a terrible mix-up. The sentencing was postponed by the judge, and I just found out a couple of hours ago," he tells me nervously.

What did he just say? Did he say the sentencing was postponed? Is that what he said? I feel the bile rising and the anger mounting.

"Say that again, Marty. Did you say the sentencing was postponed?" I ask, praying he'll say he didn't say that.

"Yes, I'm sorry," he says, looking down.

"You're sorry? Sorry? Marty, my whole family flew here. You knew that. It cost them over four grand. They're probably here already. What do you mean postponed? Stephanie told me she spoke to you yesterday morning, and you confirmed it was on. When was it postponed?" I'm starting to get loud.

"The judge's office sent it on the web. I never got it. It's not my fault. They sent it last week," he says, pleading innocence.

"What the fuck are you talking about? The web? You mean he sent an email! It's called email! Email! You incompetent idiot! I can't believe you're representing me! I knew I should have fired you when I had the chance! Shame on me! What are they supposed to do now? Turn around and go home, then come back again for another four thousand dollars? Are you going to pay for their flights? I can't believe this. Have you seen them?"

"Yes. I saw them just before I came to see you, and I told them. Your father was very upset. He started yelling at me and called me a liar. I told him I'm sorry, that it wasn't my fault. I didn't get the email."

"It is your fault! You didn't get it because you don't know how to use email!... STILL! I thought your secretary opens them and prints them for you. That's what you told me!"

"She does, but she's been out of the office for the last week with a throat infection. I'm going crazy trying to manage everything."

"Marty, you're selfish, irresponsible and unprofessional. You probably could care less that my family wasted all that money and time. You're lucky I'm in handcuffs and behind this glass!" I say. I really want to kill him. They can add one more count, manslaughter.

"I'm sorry, it wasn't my fault. They should have called or sent a letter."

"Who would have answered the phone? Who would have opened the letter? You're full of shit! Did the AUSA know the sentencing was cancelled? I bet she got the email! Everyone uses email! I can't believe this is happening! Did she know? Tell me!"

"Yes, I spoke to Peter Demore. He's the one who told me the judge rescheduled the sentencing. It's next Friday at one o'clock," he says, meekly.

"So, he got the email. Marty, I don't know who's going to pay for this, but I'm holding you responsible. Where's my family right now?" I ask.

"They already left. They're on their way to the airport."

"Did you tell them about the new date?"

"Yes! Of course, I did," he says, as if I've insulted his intelligence. What a scumbag.

"Marty, I'm not sure if they can, but if they do come back, will this happen again?"

"No! Of course not! I guarantee it. It won't happen again."

"Why? because you're a professional? You're a clown! I have nothing more to say to you. Get out of my sight!"

"I said I'm sorry, Warren."

"So did I, Marty, but so far the government hasn't seemed to care."

Chapter 53

Broken

"GRANT ME THE SERENITY to accept the things I cannot change."

A keystone principal and prayer of alcoholics anonymous. It teaches that the alcoholic mind wants to control everything. The Big Book (the AA Bible) says the alcoholic is like the director of a play; as long as all the actors show up and read their lines on script, his world is a perfect place. If they go off script, his world comes crashing down. For me, hearing this was powerful. I know I can't control everything.

Take that lack of control and magnify it one-hundred-fold when you're incarcerated. I can't control what the prison guards do, right or wrong. I can't control other inmates. I can't control what's happening outside "on the street." I can't control what my kids are going through, my parents, my wife. I can try, but it won't work. I'm helpless.

The whole pre-trial system is a scam. It's set up to impede a defendant's ability to defend himself. It sounds nice that everyone receives legal representation, but it's only done for appearance. Stimulation of the legal economic system is the real purpose. Prosecutors, lawyers, judges, court clerks, police, probation officers, prison guards, medical staff and all the other support and auxiliary jobs it takes to fuel a corrupt, broken, justice system. Pre-trial detention is the feeder system for the economic machine: the farm team.

Lawyers, appointed free of charge, push their clients to cooperate with the government that pays them and distorted and abusive applications of conspiracy laws are used to trap, convict and imprison people and place them in institutions that employ thousands in communities all over America. Political careers are built on the promise and delivery of prisons and economic stimulus to their constituents.

Hard to believe? I didn't believe it at first, but now I do. Seeing and experiencing is believing. This fact has been validated, confirmed and argued by many professionals close to the situation, including Sydney Powell, a former Federal Prosecutor in her book "Licensed to Lie" and in "The Tyranny of Good Intentions" by Paul Craig Roberts and Lawrence M. Stratton. Fascinating reads.

Young men charged with drug trafficking in quantities of as little as an ounce, who in many cases did it to feed their own depraved habit, sentenced to years in prison. Most civilized Western countries put these people in treatment and rehabilitation programs, not prison. Businessmen indicted and all of their assets seized by a government whose true motivation is to get their money.

I don't have adequate access to law materials, modern technology to craft a legal brief if I needed to, time with my lawyer, telephone time, internet access, even library time to defend myself. The brief meetings I get with my lawyer are so rushed and incomplete, there's always something that goes unresolved. The only real advantage to pre-trial detention is you get to see what happens to people who really believe in their innocence and take the government to trial. The outcome is always bad.

"Can you believe that son of a bitch? He knew my family was flying from Canada, but he didn't feel it important enough to check that everything was okay before he told them to come," I say to Frank and Aram after our workout.

"No, man, that shit's crazy. He's a real prick," Frank says.

"I know. All my life when my instincts told me something I was well served listening to them. I knew I should have fired him. Now if I do, it'll just piss Stolberg off because it's so last-minute. He'll think I'm stalling or playing around."

"No, he won't like it. He'll get pissed, and he'll make it worse for you. He'll go home after, eat supper, read a book, and go to bed without even giving a second thought to the extra time he gave you, just because he didn't like you," Frank says.

"I'm so upset with myself for not doing what I knew was right," I say.

"Warren, believe me, it's impossible to know what would have happened if you fired him. Based on what I've seen over the years, I'd say a new lawyer would have been the same or worse. Careful what you wish for. He was good with the probation office, maybe he'll be good at the sentencing," Aram says.

"I can hope, and I do, but my gut tells me the sentencing won't go the same way, not with Stolberg. Anyway, whatever happens, happens. I can't control it at this point. One thing I know for sure, worst case scenario will be the sixty-three months the probation office recommended. In the back of my mind, I'm prepared for that."

"Like I said all along, you should be. To the Feds, five years is a free pass. When a judge gives you five years, he feels like he's doing you a favor," Aram says.

"Yeah, somewhere, someone is doing sentencing projections to ensure economic stimulus is met," I say.

"Shit, they offered me ten, and the prosecutor made it sound like it was my lucky day. My guidelines are ten to twenty. I'll end up doing eight and a half. Judge will feel like I got off scot-free, I sold marijuana for fuck's sake. By the time I get out, it'll be legal all across the country. It's really fucked up," Frank says angrily.

"Yeah, Frank, that's actually ridiculous," I say.

"Then, when we're released, we're so vilified by this government, it's almost impossible to pick up the pieces. I'm educated. Imagine what it's like for most of these guys?" Frank says to us.

"They have almost no chance. They don't even have vocational training to prepare them for life after prison. At least if guys could learn a trade...instead they're set up to fail again and again," Aram says.

I just nod my head, thinking what a crying shame because a lot of the guys in here would be productive in society if they were given a chance.

I call Stephanie later that evening when I know she'll be back in Montreal.

"Zadie was so pissed, Dad. I thought he was going to kill Marty right there in the courthouse. He started screaming at him, and he called him a liar. He was yelling so loud that security came over."

"Yeah, sounds like your Zadie. Marty said something about it. I'm so sorry for the wasted time and money, Roo. If I wasn't in here, I would do something about it. I don't know what, but something. The bigger problem is how we're going to deal with next Friday. I need you guys in the courtroom."

"We know, Dad. We already discussed it, and we're coming. We can't afford flights, so we'll drive or take the train and stay at my friend Cindy's apartment. She'll be in Montreal visiting her parents. Zadie can't come because he needs to be at dialysis, but Bubby will.

"Okay, that's great. I wish Zadie could be there too, but I understand. You and Paige will be able to get off work again?"

"Yes, we have no choice. We have to."

"Hey, Steph, does your boss know about Mom and me?"

"Dad, everyone knows. It was in the newspaper. Most people are very understanding and sympathetic. People who know you always ask how you're doing. It doesn't seem like they judge that much either. Anyway, it doesn't matter what anyone thinks."

"Steph, I have no illusions about what people must think of us, and frankly, I don't blame them. It was a shameful, disgusting thing we did. Unfortunately, no one will remember the good things we did over the years, they'll only remember this. I'll probably be treated like a pariah by some people when I get out.

"Of course, no one will ever say anything to my face. The funny part is, as soon as I start making money again and have success, half of them will want to do business with me or be my partner. They'll say, "He's a good guy. He just made a mistake. Shit happens.""

"That's so true, Dad. That's exactly how people are."

"You know, Steph, if a guy's dead broke and walks around talking to himself, people say "that guy's crazy, he needs to be in a mental institution." If the same guy's rich, people say "he's so eccentric.""

"Ha, ha...that's so funny. You're right though, amazing what money does."

"I love to hear you laugh, Roo. It makes me happy."

"You always make me laugh. I love you, Dad."

"But you know what, Stephanie, money is the reason I'm here. I was so misguided by money and material things. I want my children to know that they shouldn't live their lives consumed with the pursuit of money. It's not living. It's not happiness. We need to be happy with who we are and what we have. We need to live within our means, large or small, with what we can afford. We especially should never worry about what others have. But most of all, we have to cherish our lives, our time here on earth with the people we love and who love us. It goes by fast, Stephanie. I really do understand this now. Too bad it took this nightmare to make me understand. I hope you guys can learn this from our mistakes.

For the next fifteen seconds neither of us says a word as we take it all in, and then I ask:

"How are Paige, Andie and Jace doing?"

"They're okay. Paige was very upset at first. She had a lot of anxiety coming in the first place, but she's okay now. Andie started crying mainly because Paige was, but she's fine. Jace is Jace. He's fine. They'll be okay, Dad, don't worry."

"I wish it were that easy Roo...I worry constantly about you guys. It's the worst part of the punishment."

"Don't worry, Dad, we're fine... I love you, Daddy," she says.

"I love you too, baby. Hey, Roo, we better get off. We must have used close to ten minutes. We're gonna need these minutes after Friday. Tell everyone I'm sorry about what happened, and tell your sisters and brother and Bubby I'm so happy they're coming back next week."

"Okay, Daddy, I will. I love you...I love you so much, bye Dad."

"Bye Stephanie."

Chapter 54

Sentencing

I LOOK AROUND THE courtroom. Like last time, there are spectators in the bleachers here to witness the blood sport. My mother and children are sitting right behind me. We're separated by a wooden guard-rail.

Anna Garbo and Peter Demore are at the table to my right with their game faces on. Next to me, Marty is writing some last-minute notes. The emperor is on his throne, preparing to start the games and readying himself for today's sacrifice. The coliseum is called to order, and the emperor looks towards the government's table. They introduce themselves and tell the court they have the FBI case agent with them, just in case.

The judge reads off a list of documents he's received pertaining to the matter at hand, and then asks counsel if there is anything missing.

Marty stands up and says, "Your honor, I'm sure that one of the letters you mentioned that I sent to the Court contained a letter written by my client addressed to your Honor, Mr. Stelman's own submission, so to speak."

Stolberg: Yes. Well, if you sent it to me, it's there.

Marty: Okay.

Stolberg: And I believe I remember reading it. Let me make sure. You sent so much. Which letter did you send it with, do you know?

Marty: You know, off the top of my head judge I...don't right now.

Peter Demore: It's with the April 25th letter, your Honor.

Shit! What a great start. I should have had the sentencing postponed until Peter Demore went into private practice. Then I could have hired him to defend me.

And that's how it goes for the next thirty minutes. Marty stumbles all over himself while the government delivers a damning and concise condemnation and testament to the heinous crime I committed. It's like showing up to compete at the Olympics without having trained. I have no chance. Marty's presentation to the court is limited to reading excerpts of the letters sent by my family and friends.

Stolberg is listening impatiently, until at some point, he interrupts to say reading the letters is redundant and, in not so many words, a waste of time. Marty loses his bravado. I lose my mind.

Listening to Marty try to convince the emperor that I am worth saving is like offering a drowning man more water. Of course, it didn't help that I robbed seniors. Stolberg can't wait for him to shut up so he can proceed to point his thumb-down. Any hope I hold out that he will be as good in court as he was with the probation office vanishes.

I understand, if I hadn't already, that the game is won or lost long before the sentencing hearing. This isn't about guilt. We all know I am guilty. This is about trying to get the emperor to show mercy. The government has a slam dunk. There is never any doubt. Anna and Peter will be celebrating their latest conquest tonight while Marty will probably be checking the web for more murder cases.

"It is the judgment of this Court that you be committed to the custody of the Attorney General of the United States or his designee for a term of imprisonment of sixty-three months on Count One, plus an additional twelve months to be served consecutively, pursuant to 18 United States Code Section 2326(2) for an aggregate term of imprisonment of seventy-five months."

I look back at my family and whisper sixty-three months, but they look confused. I tell them I love them, and just like that, the marshals whisk me out of the courtroom.

Wait a minute. Did he say consecutive? Fuck! Consecutive, not concurrent! No wonder my family looked confused when I said sixty-three months. They heard what he said. I was so prepared for the low end of the guideline range like the probation office recommended that I just assumed the twelve months was concurrent. Damn! He tacked on an extra twelve months. That's more than six years!

More than six years...

Chapter 55

Abuser

SIX OF US SIT waiting in the bullpen for the last guy to finish his hearing. Once he does, we are taken back to MCC through the tunnel. After we are stripped out and dressed in browns, we're directed to a food cart where a CO named Russell is handing out cold, eight-hour-old, lunch trays. The last time we ate was when they gave out the bag at seven thirty this morning. We are famished. I am third in line.

The first guy in line takes his tray and says, "Yo, Russell, lemme get another one. I'm starvin'."

"No," Russell answers.

Someone in line behind me says: "Why not? There's eight of us, and you got a full cart. There must be thirty trays in there. Let us get two each. We're hungry man. We ain't eaten all day. The COs always gives two if there's enough."

"I don't," Russell says.

"Why not?" I ask. "What are you going to do with the extra trays?"

"Throw 'em in the garbage," he answers.

"So, you'd rather throw the food in the garbage than give us some cold, shitty seconds. What's that about, Russell?"

But, before he can answer, a mean-looking black guy from another unit, who's behind me in line, says:

"We ain't tryin' to hear that shit. Give us another tray, Russell."

"Nope. Be happy with one, or you won't get that."

"You's some shit. You's an asshole!"

"Asshole? You calling me an asshole? Come here!" Russell says to him.

The guy walks to the front of the line and stands there staring straight at him. Russell counts eight trays, places them on the counter and says: "Make sure everyone gets one. Then go over there and get that garbage can. "You and…" He scans the line, looks at me and says, "You…the two of you dump the rest of them, and stack 'em back in the cart!"

This guy is unbelievable.

"Fuck that! I ain't doin' shit! Dump 'em yourself!" the black guy says.

Congratulations, Russell! You got what you wanted, I think to myself.

"Oh, yeah?" Russell asks. You ain't doin' shit? Are you refusing a direct order?"

"Fuck you and your order!" he says and knocks all the trays to the floor.

Russell reacts quickly. He hits his body alarm, grabs the guy by the neck in a choke hold almost breaking it, and twists him around violently, taking him to the ground. Seconds later three other COs crash through the door and start screaming….

"Get down on the floor! Get on the fucking floor! Now! Get down! Everyone down!"

I hit the floor stomach first, like they expect, and place my arms on my head. More COs come running in while the first three are trying to cuff the guy. He's resisting, and I know this will end badly.

One of the COs kicks him in the ribs, another presses a knee into his back, and the third takes out a pepper spray canister and sprays him in the face. Everyone's yelling. The COs are screaming at him to stop moving, he's screaming and cursing at them, and we're all yelling "leave him alone!"

The pepper got to him, so he stops moving. His eyes are closed shut. The other COs wheel in a restraint chair, forcefully lift him off the floor, and slam him into the chair. Then they tighten the straps around him and place a black spit hood over his head even though he hasn't spit at anyone. I think to myself, he probably can't breathe because of the pepper.

He begins to yell....

"Take this motherfuckin' thing off my face, you motherfuckers. My eyes is burning...fuck you...you motherfuckers. I swear I'm gonna kill you...I'm gonna kill you...you dirty motherfuckers... Russell, you filthy motherfucker...I swear I'm gonna kill your punk ass...you and your whole family... you fuckin' pig..."

From the corner of my eye, I see Russell approach the chair. He winds up and slaps the guy across the head with an open hand. "Oh, yeah, tough guy? You gonna kill me and my family? How the fuck you gonna do that?"

Another CO steps between them and says: "Okay Russell, enough...he isn't killin' anyone...move back!"

"He threatened me and my family. Fuckin' punk. You guys heard what he said...he threatened to kill me and my family...."

Just then a Lieutenant walks in.

"What's going on here?" he asks.

"Lieutenant, this guy was getting violent, so we had to restrain him," one of the COs says.

I can't take the injustice anymore, so from my position on the floor I say:

"You started the whole thing, Russell. All we wanted was an extra tray...all we had was the shitty bag lunch they gave us at seven o'clock this morning. We're hungry...instead, you pushed everyone's buttons for no reason. If you weren't here, nothing would have happened. All you had to do was give us a second tray, like every other CO always does. We're supposed to get three meals a day and all we had was one. It was completely unnecessary. None of us had a good day, and then we come back to your abuse. It's your fault everything happened."

"Okay! That's enough!" the Lieutenant says, looking directly at me. He then turns to Russell and asks:

"Why does he have that spit hood over his head? Was he spitting?"

The CO who sprayed the pepper says: "We were afraid he would. He wouldn't lie still so we used pepper."

"Yeah, Lieutenant, and he was threatening to kill me!...Punk!" says Russell.

"Take that thing off his head, let him out of the chair, and take him to medical to wash his eyes. Then bring him to the SHU," he orders. Looking at us on the ground he says:

"The rest of you, get up and move into that holding cell over there."

Thirty minutes later, they unlock the cell and tell us to leave. As we're heading to the door, a CO says:

"Hey, guys, grab two trays each and go upstairs."

Russell wasn't there, and I kept thinking how that bastard instigated the whole thing. None of this had to happen. In jail, you never know what type of bad news someone received on a visit, on a phone call, by mail, in court, or worse, delivered by the Chaplin. Who knows what kind of news that guy got today? Obviously, Russell's bullshit was more than he could take.

It's a stressful environment, and anyone can snap at any time. That's why you learn to mind your business and "stay out of the way." If you bump into someone by mistake, say "excuse me." Keep out of other people's conversations, even if you have something positive to offer.

When I first got here, two guys were sitting next to me at a table on the tier and talking. I added something useful, and their reaction was "mind your business!" I only had to hear it once to learn. Some guys just wait for anyone to give them the slightest reason.

Russell knows this, and he purposely tried to get a rise out of us. He's a bastard. A miserable son of a bitch. I don't understand why so many of these COs are so miserable. They have good jobs with good benefits. A lot of people would love to be in their place. Harder to understand is why some are so abusive. Power in the wrong hands and all that....

Chapter 56

Hazardous Work

"SEVENTY-FIVE MONTHS? DAMN!...that's the high end," says Aram.

"Yep...high end," I say, sick to my stomach.

"But it doesn't surprise me," Aram says.

"The probation office recommended the low end, didn't they?" Frank asks.

"Yeah. I never saw this coming. I was hoping for thirty-one months. I thought the worst case would be sixty three," I say.

"I mean he did give me the low end, sixty-three months. Then he tacked on another twelve months for the second part of the statute. The statute had zero to twenty with an additional zero to ten. I never really understood why, and every time I asked, I was told not to worry about it. So, I figured it didn't really matter. Man, was I wrong."

"Shit," Frank says.

"At first, I thought he said concurrent, which was what I was expecting. Then I realized he said consecutive. The whole thing was a nightmare. It was obvious to me that Stolberg can't stand Marty. He talked to him in a sarcastic and condescending tone the whole time. Add to that how he feels about me, and it was the perfect storm. I never had a chance. He had his mind made up before I got there. He didn't give a shit about my family or the letters. I don't even know if he read them."

"Yeah, you knew going in he was tough," Aram says. "Look, it's longer than you were hoping for, but it's not so bad. With good time you have about sixty-five months to do. Deduct the thirteen you already have in, and that leaves fifty-two. By the time you get designated and packed out, another month or two will go by so you'll have fifty-one left. Basically, four years and change."

"Four more years of this shit? Fuck!"

'It's not as bad as this. Once you get to a real spot it'll be different. You're not stuck in one place all day. You get to move around, go to the yard. You'll be able to play handball all day if you want, not just for an hour every three days. You'll get into great shape. There's all kinds of programming. You said you like to play the drums. You can do that too. All the prisons have music programs, and they have these rooms where you can jam with other guys. In Victorville, there's always guys performing for different occasions. I guarantee, before you know it, your bid will be over. Time goes fast if you do it right. I got eight in and the truth is, it flew by. When you get to where you're going, the first three months will be the slowest, always is. Once you get a routine, the time flies," Aram tells me.

"Wow, you make it sound so enticing, like an all-inclusive resort. I almost feel like I should be paying to go to prison," I say jokingly. "What about the down side, the violence, the gangs, all that shit? Is that included in the package?"

"Yeah, well there's that too, but you know how to move. Mind your business, and you'll be okay. Your paper work's good so you shouldn't have any problems," Aram assures me.

"It's owing money that leads to problems. Stay away from drugs and gambling. And always keep your business to yourself," Frank adds.

"Well, I don't do either. Anyway, gentlemen, I have to go and pass out the toilet paper now. I'll talk to you guys after. Thanks for the motivational talk."

I go upstairs to the counselor's office to get the box of toilet paper and start going tier to tier passing it out. I've been doing this for a couple of months now, and I place two rolls on the floor of each cell. Most guys leave their cell doors open, but when they don't, I open them, place two rolls on the floor and close the door. If someone's inside with the door closed, I knock first, wait for a nod, then enter. Respect.

I cross over to 1 Tier, where a group of guys are throwing home-made dice against the back wall. One cell door is closed, so I open it, place the toilet paper on the floor, and close the door.

"Yo! My man...why you goin' in my cell?" I hear someone say.

I look toward the voice. It's one of the guys playing dice, a New York Puerto Rican who got here about ten days ago. I haven't met him, but I've watched him. He's late twenties, loud and obnoxious. I'm not in the mood for his grandstanding bullshit.

"I'm passing out toilet paper. You want some, don't you?"

"Yeah, my nigga, I do. But you don't just walk up in my room!"

Oh boy here we go, I think to myself.

"Listen, my man. I'm just doing my job. If I leave it outside the door, someone will take it, and then you won't have any toilet paper. This is how it's done. It was done like this before I started doing it, and it'll be done the same way after I stop," I say digging deep for patience that's in short supply, while trying to sound non-confrontational yet firm.

"I ain't tryin' to hear that shit! Nobody walks up in my room who I don't know, cabron!" he says.

"Yo, Martinez, let it go, Pappy. He cool...he just giving out the paper," one of the other Puerto Ricans says.

"I don't give a fuck. You aks next time you go in my room, motherfucker!" he says to me in a threatening tone of voice while looking around to see who's watching.

I don't know what came over me. Maybe it was the pent-up frustration from my sentencing, or maybe it was just dealing with this type of ignorance for the past thirteen months, but before I could think about what I was doing, I just lost my cool and said:

"Hey, my man! Fuck you! I won't ask you shit! Fuck you! Next time you won't get any!"

"Who the fuck you think you talkin' to, cabron?" he says to me.

"I'm talking to you! All I'm doing is passing out toilet paper, motherfucker! Fuck you!"

311

I throw the two rolls of paper I'm holding back in the box, and I get ready for whatever's coming. I'm so mad I want to kill this punk. I'm just so tired of this ignorance, and he pushed me to my limit. I know what I'm doing is stupid, but I don't care.

He moves away from the table and in my direction. One of his homies, a guy I've known since I've been here, says: "Pappy, he's cool. Canada don't bother no one. Cut this shit, my nigga! He just doin' his job!"

But he can't, and he won't, back down now. His homies can't do anymore to stop him either. They certainly can't take my side, right or wrong…prison politics.

I decide to get him before he gets me and, in one swift motion, I move quickly, kicking downward with a straight leg to his knee, and connect perfectly. He tries to move back, but I continue forward yelling:

"Fuck you! You think I'm scared of you, motherfucker? Fuck you! I don't give a fuck!

I don't want to be alone here. The Dominicans live downstairs, so I'm hoping they'll hear the commotion and come fast.

I swing at his head a few times, and I get one good shot in. He's swinging back, and he lands one on the side of my head just behind my ear and another to my chest. It hurts, and I'm momentarily stunned. My ear's ringing, but I know not to stop. I continue swinging, and I get another one in that glances off his shoulder. He hits me in the ribs, hard. Shit! This kid is tough. I need to stop him before he kills me. I throw a side kick at the same knee. His leg collapses, and he falls down. I'm getting ready to kick him again when I feel someone grabbing me from behind.

"Get off of me! Take your fuckin' hands off me!" I'm yelling loud because I think I'm getting jumped by his homies. Then I hear someone say in Spanish: Tranquilo, Canada! Tranquilo! Parate! La policía viene…! Sal de aquí rapido! He's telling me to stop. The police are coming, leave now!

I turn around, and I'm happy to see Palito, a Dominican. He's with two other Dominicans, and he's telling me to leave fast, so I do. I grab the box of toilet paper, drag it down the stairs and start walking across the unit when a bunch of COs crash through the main door. As I walk, I feel a trickle of blood behind my ear. I'm struggling to catch my breath from the shot he gave me in the ribs. Behind me, I see the COs running to 1 Tier, paying me no mind. I'm climbing the stairs to 2 Tier when I hear it:

"Lock it down! Lock it down! Everyone in your cells!"

Minutes later, we're all in our cells. My bunky's lying on his rack reading.

"What happened, Canada?"

"I don't know, Toke, must have been a fight."

"Oh yeah? You're bleeding behind your ear. Was it you?"

"No. I slipped going up the stairs to 2 Tier with the box of toilet paper and banged into the handrail. I'm fine."

He gives me a funny look. He knows I'm lying to him but respects the fact that I won't talk about it. I know not to. I get on my rack and wait. I'm hoping for the best, but I know I may have a problem this time.

Fifteen minutes later, a CO comes down to our tier and shouts:

"Body search! Everyone stand up! Shirts off!"

Another CO joins him along with a Lieutenant, and they go cell to cell inspecting everyone's bodies and hands for signs of violence. I'm not bleeding anymore, and it's just a small cut, but it's impossible to hide if someone checks closely.

When it's my turn I try to stand on an angle with the cut hidden from view, but as I put my hands out I notice my knuckles are scraped. Unfortunately, I wasn't the only one who noticed, and the Lieutenant tells me to turn around. I do so quickly, and he says: "Turn around again, slowly." He knows his business.

"What's that near your ear?"

"Oh, I was passing out toilet paper and when I was lugging the box up the stairs to 2 Tier, I slipped and banged my head on the railing. I'm okay Lieutenant, it's nothing. I was about to report it when all this happened."

"I'm sure you were. Turn around, and put your hands behind your back," he says.

"Why, Lieutenant? I didn't do anything wrong."

"Turn around!" he says again, a bit louder.

I know there's no point arguing or trying to change his mind, so I do as he says, and he cuffs me.

"Alvarez, take him," he says to one of the COs.

Fuck! I'm going to jail!

As we walk towards the unit door, I don't see them taking the other guy, so that may be a good thing. There are no cameras on the tiers, so they won't see what happened. I know the CO working the unit didn't see anything.

If no one talks, they won't be able to prove anything. I'll stick to my story and deny I was in a fight. SIS will sweat me to get me to confess and give up the other guy, but I won't. Hopefully everyone who knows what happened will keep their mouths shut. I'm not worried about the guy I fought with because, like me, he has too much to lose. It's the rats who think telling will somehow help them that I'm concerned about. On the other hand, the Puerto Ricans don't normally talk, and I think they were the only ones there.

What an idiot! So close to getting out of MCC, and I go and do this. What was I thinking? I wasn't. Now I'll be in the hole for a while, and if they find out I was in a fight, it'll be worse. I'll have to see the Disciplinary Hearing Officer (DHO).

The DHO is a judge for inmates who get into trouble. If found guilty, I'll receive a 200-series shot. They'll take my telephone or email, or both. For sure I'll lose commissary. Worse, they'll probably take some "good time." All because of my stupid ego. I should have let it go. I should have told him I was sorry. No, doing that would have driven me crazy in another way. I just couldn't listen to that asshole. What am I doing though? What am I becoming? This place is changing me. How can it not. This is my reality, this is where I live. To survive here I do what I have to do.

My transfer to prison may also be held up until SIS investigates what happened. My family will be so upset with me. They'll never understand and, frankly, I can't blame them. Damn! Stupid, stupid, stupid....

Just as Control cracks the door open, I hear voices behind me, so I look back. Oh shit, they've got him. He failed the test too. He must be marked up a bit. Either that or someone told, but I doubt it. They won't do it in front of everyone. No, that's the kind of thing they do by "dropping a slip"—a written note to SIS. Whatever the case, we're both going to the hole. I hope he keeps his mouth shut.

Chapter 57

The Hole

I'VE BEEN IN THE hole for ten days, so has the other guy. He's three cells over. His name is Ramon Martinez. They call him Pappy. We sent messages through the orderly who wheels the library book cart around. He's not supposed to deliver books unescorted, but the COs don't like to wait while inmates choose books, preferring instead to stay at their station. This makes the library book orderly the de facto communication medium. We've agreed not to say a word about what happened, no matter what.

The first two days I was grilled by SIS twice for close to an hour each time. They take you out of your cell and bring you to an interrogation room, which was nice because I got a change of scenery and a break from the boredom. On the third day, they took another stab at me but gave up after thirty minutes.

"Stelman, this is your last chance to tell the truth," an SIS officer named Brenner tells me. "We already know everything, so we just want to hear it from you."

"Brenner, I don't know what to tell you that I haven't already told you. I don't know what happened. I didn't see anything, and I wasn't there," I say.

"So, explain how you got that mark behind your ear."

"Really? Again? Okay. I'm an orderly on the unit. I've had the job for the past six months. Every Friday I pass out toilet paper. Usually, I have someone else helping me because the box is big and awkward, but he was on a visit that day, and I decided to do it alone. I was lugging the box up the stairs to 2 Tier when I dropped the front corner, and it jammed against the stairs. I lost my balance momentarily, fell sideways and smacked my head on the wood railing. That's how…" I explain for the fifteenth time.

"We looked at the tapes, and we didn't see that. C'mon Stelman! Stop jerking around! You're lying! DHO will go easier on you if you tell the truth."

These guys want to be real police. They even talk like TV cops.

"I don't know why you didn't see it. You should have—because it happened," I say.

I know the cameras could never have picked it up because the view to 2 Tier is out of camera cover. He doesn't think I know, but I do. The counselor mentioned it to me once when something else happened.

"Brenner, you're wasting your time. Personally, I don't care because it's nice to be out of that filthy stinking cell for a while, but I'm sure you must be busy with real cases that need your attention. I don't know what you saw on tape, if anything, but what I told you is what happened," I say with conviction.

I'm hoping that by telling him how busy and important he is, he'll feel good and decide to drop this. I doubt he has much to do, ever.

Years of watching cop shows on television helped me in my role as tight-lipped suspect. I'm pretty sure they won't make me take a polygraph or send any skin or clothing samples for DNA testing; apparently Horatio has a full case-load at the moment.

"Okay, Stelman, I tried to help you. Just so you know, Martinez already told us what happened," he says, trying to get me off balance. Interrogation Tactic 101.

"Brenner, I also told your colleague the other day that I don't know who Martinez is. There are so many guys on the unit, and it changes so often that I hardly remember anyone's name. Besides, no one uses their real name, you know that."

"Alright, Stelman, it's too bad. You're supposed to be shipped, and you will be, but now you'll go as a SHU inmate. Pretty uncomfortable way to travel," he says.

"Hey, Brenner, what can I do? That's your call, not mine. I don't like being in the SHU, but at the end of the day I have time to do, and it goes by just the same. On the bright side, I'm losing weight, and I can do ten sets of fifty push-ups in an hour. Don't get me wrong, I hope you let me out, but if not, I'll survive. Do what you've got to do," I say politely.

He just looks at me and says: "Okay, Stelman," and walks away.

On the twelfth day, my counselor shows up with good news. She spoke to SIS. They can't prove we were involved in a fight, so we're being released on Friday. I'm happy to hear that.

"The bad news is you're going to 11 South until you leave," she tells me.

"Aw, c'mon, Miss Larson, why? That unit's a nightmare. They say it's like living in the projects."

"It was the unit manager's decision. Martinez's going to 7 North. Just be happy you didn't end up with a shot. Anyway, they're going to pack you out soon, so you won't be there long. It's the best you're going to get, Stelman. I tried to convince him to let you come back, but he won't do it."

"Can't I go to 5 North?"

"No. He won't change his mind, and I'm not going to ask him again."

"Shit. Well I guess I'll be there until I leave. I'll have to manage. Thanks for trying, Miss Larson. Hey, can I call my family? I only spoke to them once since last week, and I know they're worried about me."

"I'll tell the CO to make sure you get a telephone call today."

"Thanks, I appreciate it. Will I see you again?"

"I go to the south side a couple times a week. I'm sure we'll see each other."

Chapter 58

Finally

A MONTH LATER, I'M woken up at five fifteen in the morning and told to pack my shit. I only fell asleep two hours ago. I'm leaving in an hour for Allenwood Prison in Pennsylvania.

The past four weeks have been terrible on 11 South. The tiers are dorm-style with twenty double bunk beds separated by three feet of space. The noise is intolerable. A lot of guys sleep by day and stay up all night talking and shouting, with the TV blaring, without any consideration for those who want to sleep.

I don't want any more trouble, so I keep my mouth shut and deal with the noise. I'm really sleep deprived at this point. Another problem is the complete lack of privacy. In a cell, you can get away from people, not here.

Then there's the hygiene issue. The place is filthy. Forty men living on top of each other. The stink of body odor from guys who either don't shower enough, or don't use deodorant. The garbage cans overflow with rotten, discarded food. There's one common mold-infested bathroom with two disgusting toilets and a rust-crusted wash sink. I feel like I'll contract scabies every time I go in there. The only shower is in the bathroom and guys use it to smoke dope at all hours of the day and night. If you need to use the toilet or shower, you'll likely walk in on someone smoking, and you'll get a "not right now" look. Try and argue.

There's a spray bottle with some natural non-chemical disinfectant for cleaning, but it's always empty. I doubt the stuff works anyway. The BOP won't allow bleach because an inmate can use it to poison someone, or himself. The orderlies try to keep the place clean, but the overcrowding makes it impossible. At least on 11 North I had a sink and toilet in my cell, and I could keep it clean.

Using the telephone is hard. There's a high-profile Jamaican gang here on a murder, kidnapping, and drug conspiracy case, and they run the telephones. After count, they have the first twenty spots in line, and if you have an important phone call to make, you have to pay to get anywhere near the front of the line. I wait until much later, after everyone's used the phone, to make my call home.

This place is a jungle. I doubt the projects are this bad. On top of it, such unnatural living conditions make everyone testy, so there are fights all the time. I've only been here a month and we're locked down more than not. What's crazy is there are guys who have been on this unit for years.

As expected, my kids were very upset that I went to the SHU. I told them how sorry I was and that it was collateral damage. They should work for SIS because I don't think they believed me. It's hard to explain to people outside what life is like in here. In the case of my family, I don't want them to know. I want them to believe that their mother and I are both safe. They have enough to worry about.

Chapter 59

The Bus

I'M HAVING A BITTERSWEET experience. I'm out of this dump, headed to Allenwood, which is good, but I'm cuffed and shackled again, not as good. It's six thirty in the morning, and I'm in a holding cell in R&D. I've been waiting thirty minutes.

"Let's go, Stelman! Your ride's here!" a CO barks as he unlocks the door.

"You sure it's mine, the blue town car?" I ask.

"They upgraded you. It's bigger," he answers.

"I don't need bigger. I'm a simple man. Send it back and get the town car," I say.

"Very funny, Stelman. You're a barrel of laughs."

I follow him and, after some security procedures at the Control window, I'm asked to sign a piece of paper, which I do with great difficulty. Handcuffs impede my free-flowing cursive artistry. The door to enter the garage pops open and he says:

"Walk straight outside, Stelman. They're waiting for you. Have a good trip. Don't come back."

"I won't...promise!"

"I heard that before," he says.

It's mid-October and freezing. There's an unseasonable cold front that has come down from the country of my birth, blanketing the entire north-eastern United States. It can't be more than thirty-five degrees Fahrenheit, and I'm only wearing the standard BOP travel attire: T-shirt, socks, matching blue pants and top, and blue canvas shoes.

The bus is parked and running in the middle of the street. As I exit the garage, I see a CO with a shotgun at the ready in case anyone tries to make a run for it. He's standing twenty yards from the entrance to the bus, and he's watching me approach.

There are two COs smoking cigarettes at the front of the bus and two more sitting inside a van next to the bus. It's the chase car, and it follows behind the bus the whole way. I awkwardly climb the stairs but only after one of the COs tugs on my cuffs and shackles to ensure they're secure.

I'm relieved to feel the warm air and look down the aisle to see about sixteen more prisoners. As I take a seat towards the back I notice a hard link enclosure with a chair for an armed guard. It's not being used, so I assume that no one here warrants the extra oomph, or maybe they changed protocol.

There's also an exposed toilet so they can watch the handcuffed and shackled prisoners relieve themselves on a moving bus. Probably no point lifting the toilet seat. Besides, there isn't one.

It's a touring bus, but the seats have been refitted with school bus style bench seats. Someone thought to make sure the scumbags aren't too comfortable.

All of these guys came from Metropolitan Detention Center (MDC) Brooklyn. I'm the only one representing my alma-mater, MCC, today. It's a big burden to carry. The white guy in the adjacent seat looks at me and says:

"Just you?"

"As far as I know. I was alone in a holding cell, and I haven't seen anyone else, so yeah, I think so," I tell him.

"I'm LB. I'm from Houston, but I got jammed up here in New York. I'm headed home to Texas."

I don't really care, and I don't want to talk, but I don't want to be rude, so I answer.

"I'm Canada, and I think I'm going to Allenwood Low in Pennsylvania. At least I hope I am, the Low, I mean."

"You got a lot of time?" he asks.

"Not much, another four and change."

"I got nine. Already gave them two sitting in that shit hole," he says.

"Yeah, I did fourteen months here," I say.

The bus starts moving, and I tell LB I'm going to try and catch a few. I close my eyes and lay my head against the cold window. Although I wake up a few times and look around over the next couple of hours, I must be really tired, because I sleep. I keep switching my head from the window to the seat back. It's terribly uncomfortable, but we're resilient creatures, and we adapt to our environment.

I wake up for good after my head bangs against the window for the fiftieth time. A few minutes later, we pull into a huge parking lot right near an airport. I can see the main terminal and traffic control tower in the distance. I wonder where we are, so I turn to LB.

"Where are we? "

"Harrisburg Airport, Pennsylvania. We wait here for the Conair flight to land. Guys coming from other regions. Everyone meets their buses here."

I scan the parking lot and see at least ten other BOP buses parked and waiting. There's also a whole caravan of chase vans and BOP cars. There seems to be as many COs as inmates—a serious operation. The bus driver parks next to the last bus in line, and leaves the engine running so that we have heat. We wait.

Two hours later, there's activity outside as COs start heading to their respective stations. My neck and shoulders are throbbing from sitting so uncomfortably for so long, and the handcuffs are driving me crazy. I take advantage of the bus being parked and used the toilet, but now I feel like I have to go again. I better go now before the bus starts moving.

Twenty minutes later, a bus enters the parking lot. It's packed full of prisoners and, shortly after, they get off and head to their assigned buses. Just then, a CO, clipboard in hand announces: "When I call your name come to the front of the bus and give me your number."

This operation reminds me of the airport in Punta Cana where tourists arriving on different flights are organized to go to their respective hotels via tour bus. Of course, the difference is that when we arrive at our destinations we won't be greeted by a group of sexy hotel animators handing out Piña Coladas.

A few minutes later: "Stelman."

I walk to the front and say "91903054."

"Bus number five," he says.

I'm attacked by the piercing cold and wind as I walk off the bus. I feel like I've been punched in the face. My eyes tear up, and I begin the uncomfortable trek to bus number five. The leg irons are cutting into the skin on my ankles. I climb the stairs to the bus under the watchful eye of a rifle-toting CO and find a seat. There are about twenty guys already seated and a few more board after me.

With my trained eye I can see there is a mix of security classifications on the bus. I pay particular attention to four heavily tattooed and muscled guys across from me who look like they would cut your eyes out and eat them. I'm assuming they're headed to a USP. Some guys are reunited with inmates they know from other prisons, and it makes me think of the high school reunion I missed. They catch up along the way.

About three miserable hours later, the bus turns off the two-lane highway we've been traveling on and enters a huge complex with a sign that reads USP Canaan. It's a massive building with thirty-foot-high walls surrounded by an electrified fence on the perimeter and topped off with barbed wire. There are guard towers on each corner that look similar to the air traffic control tower at the airport we came from. Once inside the fence, we approach a garage door that opens up to swallow our bus. What are we doing here? I wonder.

"Listen up!" a CO announces. "When you exit the bus, give me your name and number and follow the painted red line on the floor in single file."

Check, double check, triple check. These guys are thorough....

I turn to the guy next to me and ask: "What are we doing here?"

"There's a hold over unit here in the pen. We stay here for a bit until we get routed to our final destination. My co-d stayed here for two weeks on his way to Oklahoma. You aren't doing your bid here."

"I hope not, too stressful."

We exit the bus where two COs are removing our travel gear. I'm so happy when it's my turn. We follow the red painted line down a wide corridor with very high ceilings. We're told to stay on the right side of the red line.

The place is very industrial and very institutional. It's the culmination of best practices in the warehousing of human beings. Tension bleeds off the walls in an eerie sort of way. There's a heaviness in the air that I am acutely aware of.

We pass a few large areas with double doors; inmates are at work inside. I look at them curiously and a few stare back at me like I've just invaded their homes. They are hard men, some of them older. I know a lot of them are lifers. They'll never leave until they die. I think again what it must be like to live in this environment with no hope of ever seeing the outside world again. If these guys had a chance to earn their freedom, would penitentiaries be as violent as they are? I wonder.

We finally arrive at the hold-over unit. The place is packed with inmates. Everyone is waiting to go somewhere. It's an enormous odd shaped triangular configuration with two levels of cells built around a common area. There are TVs hanging from the ceiling and tables with built in stools bolted to the floor.

Three enormous COs are getting us settled. One must be six feet eight and 300 pounds of solid muscle, the second a smaller man only six five and 275 pounds and the third, six four and as wide as the double doors I saw earlier. Their demeanor is different from the COs I've been around up until now. They are deadly serious and equally mean-looking.

"Make a straight line and fall off in twos into a cell down the range. Grab a bed roll from the stack as you do," the giant orders. "We lock down at three until six tomorrow morning. Make sure you're in your cells!"

I learn after that Canaan has been in a state of lockdown for over a year because an inmate stabbed a guard to death. He used two home-made shanks to stab the CO over 200 times. Apparently, he was facing life in a state prison in Arizona for another murder, and he wanted to do life in the Feds instead. He got what he wanted.

Everyone follows the CO's instructions, and I end up in a cell towards the back of the unit with another white guy in his early sixties. I grab the bottom rack before he does, and he doesn't seem to mind. If he does, he doesn't say anything. We make some small talk and, after a few minutes, he asks me:

"How much time do you have?"

"Seventy-five months," I answer.

"You?" I ask.

"Ninety-four months," he answers.

"Oh, yeah? Long time, what for?"

"Fraud," he tells me.

"Really....me too, how much was your fraud?" I ask.

"Fifty thousand," he answers.

"Fifty thousand? That's impossible. No one gets ninety-four months for fifty thousand," I say.

"No, ah…I meant 500 thousand…." he says, sounding nervous.

I begin to understand. He's lying about his charge, but he hasn't rehearsed his story. This guy's a sex offender, a pedophile. Great.

"Listen man, no one gets ninety-four months for a 500-thousand-dollar fraud either. I don't know where you're heading or what it'll be like when you get there, but you better get your story straight in case the environment isn't friendly. Are you a sex offender? Yes or no, I won't bother you either way," I say. "I just don't want you lying to me."

Being so direct must have caught him off guard because he answered truthfully.

"I was charged with trying to procure an under-age boy for sex. He told me he was nineteen, but he was only fourteen. It was a mistake," he says.

"What was a mistake? The charge or the young boy?" I ask.

"I didn't know how old he was…."

"Hey, listen. I'm not a judge. You don't need to explain. We're in the same cell for a short time, and you won't have any problems with me...let's leave it at that," I tell him in a tone that means I don't want to hear it.

Chapter 60

Allenwood

MY STAY IN CANAAN lasts two weeks. Just like when I was waiting to leave Najayo, I wake up each day hoping this will be the day the bus leaves for Allenwood. It's terribly boring. With no telephone, email, library or recreation and, being locked down every day at three o'clock, time moves slowly. These two weeks feel like two months. It reinforces how important staying busy is when you're doing a bid, so I'll dive right in when I get to Allenwood. I do manage to hook up with four other guys to work out every day after lunch. We do burpees and use the under-frame of a staircase to do pullups. This helps a bit.

I meet a lot of guys during the two weeks that have been in other spots and a few who have been in Allenwood at some point in their bid or past bids. From what I'm able to ascertain, Allenwood is a pretty decent spot. One guy I spoke with was there in 2002, and he called it "sweet." I can't imagine calling any place that imprisons you and robs you of your freedom "sweet," but I guess it depends on your point of reference.

I've spoken to my bunky again since the first day, and I've learned he's sixty-one and married with three grown children. Since his arrest no one in the family talks to him except his oldest daughter. In fairness, he did say his wife may take him back "once I get better," whatever that means. There's obviously a lot more to his story. I still can't believe I'm in a cell with a sex offender. If there were any in MCC, I couldn't spot them. These are people you hear about on the news. Over the next few years, I realize they're everywhere and from

327

all walks of life. It's downright disturbing. Turns out he's also going to Allenwood.

On Thursday of the second week, a CO wakes us up and tells us to get ready. Finally. Two hours later, I'm back on the bus. Allenwood is a huge prison complex with a pen, a medium, and a correctional low. A correctional low is where they send inmates who have gotten into trouble in regular lows. Even though it's called a low, it's run as strict as a medium. I think the low is where I'm going, but I'm still not sure. Some guys have said I could start out in the medium.

Along the way, the bus stops at Lewisburg Penitentiary, "The Big House," which is about a twenty-minute drive from Allenwood, to drop off a few of its newest residents. As we enter the Allenwood complex, the bus makes a stop at the pen to drop off one inmate: a white kid who looks no more than twenty to me. The medium is next and six guys get off there. I'm relieved my name wasn't called. It's mid-afternoon when we pull in to the low.

The scenery is beautiful. So far, so good. The entire complex is built in a valley offering panoramic views of the mountain range. For the first time in almost a year and a half I'm awakened by the sight and smell of nature. The buildings are brown brick with aluminum green roofing, typical of that nineties commercial architecture. Entering the parking lot, I think how easily the main building could pass for the lobby and reception area of a Best Western Hotel.

When we get off the bus, we're directed through a door to R&D and herded into a holding cell to wait. I'm sitting with seven other guys when a CO comes in and removes our cuffs and shackles. Over the next two hours we're processed. Our pictures are taken, we're fingerprinted, and handed IDs. We're instructed to wear them at all times.

We're given temporary clothing and told to go to laundry at six tomorrow morning to pick up our clothing. Once dressed, we're led back to the holding cell until we're called one at a time. When it's my turn, I follow a CO to a small office. Another CO is sitting in front of a computer screen. He tells me to take a seat.

"My name is Krieger, SIS," he tells me. "Name and number."

"Stelman, 91903054."

"Any tattoos on your body?"

"No."

"Any other identifying marks, like scars?"

I show him the barely visible scar on my arm from a surgery I had as a teenager.

"Nothing else?" he asks.

"No."

"Do you have, or have you ever had any gang affiliations?" he asks.

"No."

"Are you sure?"

"Quite."

"We'll find out if you're lying," he warns.

"I know you will."

"Did you testify against anyone on your case?" he asks.

"No."

"Do you have any reason to fear walking on the compound?" he asks.

"Are there poisonous snakes?" I ask.

"What?"

"No, I have no reason to fear walking the compound."

"Have you ever been in the US military?"

"No, sir. I'm Canadian, and I've never lived in the US."

He must know I'm a foreign national, and I've been extradited. I guess he's testing me to see if I'll slip up somehow. Real tricky these SIS people.

"It says in your file that you got into trouble for fighting in your last institution. Are you going to fight here?" he asks.

"I have no plans, sir, and I didn't fight. They thought it was me at first, but it was a big misunderstanding. I cleared it up."

He appears to ignore what I'm saying and writes something in a file. A minute later, he lifts his head, peers right at me and says:

"There are sex offenders on this compound. Are you going to make any trouble for them?"

"Trouble? Why? I won't bother anyone. I just want to do my time and go home," I say.

"Okay, because if you do, we'll find out."

"I know you will, sir."

"Okay, Stelman. Keep your nose clean, and you'll be fine. Make trouble here, and you won't be so fine. Got that?"

"Yes, sir. Loud and clear. Promise."

"Okay, grab a bed roll and head through that door towards the first building on the left. You're in Brady Unit."

"Okay, officer, thank you."

As I grab the bed roll, I turn to the CO who uncuffed me and ask:

"Hey, CO, it's really cold outside. Is there a jacket I can wear over this T-shirt to keep me warm?"

"You'll get a jacket at laundry tomorrow."

"Oh, okay, CO. Thanks anyway."

I walk out the door onto the compound and stop dead in my tracks. It's even colder now as the sun is setting, but the discomfort pales in comparison to the excitement I feel when I look out at the vast green landscape. I see four separate buildings that I assume are housing units. Straight ahead of me, about a football field away, is a long building that anywhere else would be a strip shopping center. I learn the next day that it houses laundry, commissary, the massive kitchen, the chapel, library, leisure center and the Unicor factory where inmates are used as labor to make furniture. They're paid pennies an hour.

In a self-contained building at the top of the compound is a huge building with a gymnasium and dedicated rooms for free weights and cardio machines. Behind the gymnasium building is a massive yard that has a regulation-size running track, soccer field, football field, baseball field, handball and racket ball courts, sand volleyball court, bocce courts, horse shoe pit and outside picnic tables that are used for playing chess, cards, or just gathering and talking.

It's beautiful—if you can somehow ignore the eighteen-foot-high electrified fence and balls of razor wire on the outside perimeter with patrol cars that circle twenty-four hours a day. Attached to the building I just came out of are the administrative offices which includes the

Captain's office and, to the right, medical services, and finally, the SHU.

I start the walk towards Brady Unit, my new home, but I feel hesitant. I realize that I haven't been free to walk on my own, uncuffed and unescorted outside, for a long time. Part of me feels like I'm doing something wrong, something I'll get into trouble for. I check myself and think: No, it's okay. This is what he told me to do.

When I realize that this may be the new normal here, I am overcome with emotion. I feel such a sense of joy that tears come to my eyes. This is the closest I've been to feeling free in a long time. I've been existing in such a harsh environment for so long that this easing of the reins is almost impossible to rationalize. I understand for the first time that I've become institutionalized. Just fifteen months of living as a prisoner…they've changed me—probably forever.

Chapter 61

Lay of the Land

SO THAT'S HOW I ended up here, where I've been living for the past three-plus years. Our housing facility is a two-winged unit joined in the middle by a large day/TV room. Each wing has sixty-two cubes constructed of cinder block walls. When the prison was built in the nineties, they designed the cubes for two men. With the success of the United States Government's tough-on-crime policies, they began locking people up faster than they could provide for, so overcrowding is the norm. There are three of us living in this shoe-box-sized-cube, on three bunks, or what we refer to as racks: hard steel frames with thin mats that are our beds. Most guys have back, hip or shoulder problems from the hard surface, and no one knows a good night's sleep.

There's no real rest here. What there is, in abundance, is noise. You either get used to it, or you don't. Talking, shouting, rapping, farting, coughing, sneezing, burping, all day, all night. Three hundred and sixty-four men living on top of each other. It doesn't matter who you were or where you came from, we all live the same way. To the right of me is a guy convicted of second degree murder. To my left is a drug cartel pilot, and across from me is an addict who robbed a bank. Next to him a gang-banger.

Line-ups. Always line-ups. For the bathrooms, the showers, the ice machine, the telephones, the computers, to get your mail, to use a microwave, to see the unit counselor. It's maddening, but there's nothing you can do about it except shut up and wait. You develop patience; you have to. Or maybe it's acceptance of a situation you can't do anything about. Either way, you wait. Oh yeah, don't complain.

What I have to be concerned about is who lives in my cube. The wrong bunky can make your bid a nightmare. You want people you can live with amicably.

The unit counselors understand this, so they try to accommodate, but they'll also use it as a tool to punish. Make their jobs harder than they have to be and they'll move someone in who will make living intolerable. I've been doing this long enough that I have some strict prerequisites. No chomos, no rats, and I won't live with someone who isn't clean, or someone who won't leave the cube.

A lot of sex offenders are held at low custody institutions for their own safety—not that they have it so easy here. The really bad ones, the violent ones, go to mediums and even pens where some feel they get what they deserve.

There are a lot of them here. They take up almost one quarter of the tables in the chow hall, which seats 1300 men. They are usually easy to spot, and they stick together by choice and out of necessity. On the surface, they seem like normal people. Most of them are educated, and I guarantee you there are some living in your community right now. You just don't know it. I will never walk through a mall again and look at people the same way.

For me, the real problem begins when I find out what they did to end up here. Things like trying to lure a twelve-year-old girl or boy to a rendezvous for sex so they can violate and film them, or trying to buy a six-year-old boy from the boy's uncle or father. Some real sick shit. Many of them are here for downloading, possessing, or trafficking in pictures and or videos of children in sexually explicit situations. In my mind, they're as much a part of the problem for contributing to the market that supports and promotes these abuses. I understand that many of them were probably victims themselves. I get that.

I'm not one of these guys who tries to make their lives miserable, but I won't deal with them. I won't buy anything from them or sell anything to them, and I won't socialize with any of them. I have four children, and although they're older now, they were young at one time. Plus, I hope to have grandchildren in the near future. The thought of something like this happening to any child makes me sick to my stomach. I definitely won't live with them.

Now what about a rat, a snitch, an informant. There are a lot of rules in prison. Many of the rules are enforced, but many more aren't. A lot of the petty rules can be used against you if the cops want to make your life miserable but, most of the time, they ignore the small stuff.

I'm talking about real stupid shit, like how many books or magazines you're allowed to have in your personal property or keeping kitchen food in your cube. Maybe you added a home-made unauthorized shelf to your locker to store your things. All of these are against the rules and can get you a 300-series "shot." These shots affect your "good time," the 13.87 percent reduction of your sentence you receive if you've stayed out of trouble. If you have two or more 300-series shots, you can lose good time, and they keep you in prison longer than you have to be.

I know a lot of guys who have lost all their good time. I don't want to lose mine. The crazy part is some cops try hard to take it from you. They like when the prisons are full; job security and such, or what I refer to as the customer retention program.

What reason could I possibly give my children, after all they've been through, for not coming home when I'm supposed to. Well, there might be some. They would understand if I got into trouble defending myself, but certainly not because I got caught with apples from the kitchen.

Back to the rats. I know, sounds cliché, but look where I am. They're predisposed to "telling." They did it to get time off their sentence, and the cops know that. They use them and their predisposition to find out who's doing what and to target guys they want to get. Now, if you have an argument or dispute with a stand-up guy, it gets settled quietly. It may mean going into the back of the block or the showers, away from the cameras, to settle it by force, but it will remain between you.

A rat, on the other hand, will rat. He'll "drop a slip" a "cop out," a written form he'll put under the counselor's door, or send to SIS anonymously, but he will do it. It's in his DNA. At some point, you'll have a disagreement with that guy if he lives with you, and he'll retaliate by doing what he does: rat.

To further complicate things, you can't leave that unchecked because everyone will think of you as a bitch, and you'll get abused in every way imaginable. So, you have to step up and smash him for ratting on you. If you think this way of thinking is savage, irrational, barbaric, and ignorant, you're right. It's all of those things, but you have to do it anyway, or your life will become very hard. Oh, and by the way, the rats get nothing for telling. They don't get extra food or extra telephone time or more time off their sentences. They get nothing, and they do it anyway. It's some sort of sick pathology.

As for my third prerequisite, there are guys who, in the heat of summer, will go up to the yard and work out until their clothes are soaked with sweat. Then they come back to the block and fall asleep on their rack. They may even stay in those same filthy, stinking clothes for days. That bad. Eventually someone "checks" them, but I don't want to be in that situation to begin with.

There are guys who go to the bathroom and don't wash their hands. Every time I see it I shake my head in disgust knowing soon they'll be using the computer, the telephone, or the microwave ovens. It doesn't matter if you say something either, they just walk away pretending not to hear. A few weeks back, a new guy got beaten down for not washing his hands after he was told to repeatedly. He is in PC (protective custody) right now. He was working in the kitchen serving our food.

Finally, I won't live with someone who never leaves the cube. There are plenty of guys like that. They stay in bed all day, reading or sleeping. It's long-standing prison etiquette to leave the cube for fifteen minutes when your bunky returns from taking a shower or if he has religious devotions and wants to pray. Yet there are guys who disregard etiquette and won't leave. This inevitably leads to conflict. Conflict in prison usually turns ugly, so, best to avoid it. To avoid it, I live with people who spend their time outside the cube, like I do.

When you first arrive it's not so easy to pick who you'll live with, but as time goes by and you gain seniority, you can move someone in by going to the counselor and making a bed change request. Most of the time, provided you're cool with the counselor, these requests are granted.

Sometimes more drastic measures are required. It happened to me when my bunky was taken to the hole one day. I was up at the yard and when I got back to the block one of the Dominicans stopped me at the front door to tell me a new inmate that just arrived was designated to my cube by R&D because they saw an open bed. He warned me that the guy is a chomo. I was furious and went straight to my cube to find him sitting on the bed with three other chomos, talking. I lost my mind and told the three of them to get the fuck out. Then I told him he had twenty-four hours to go to the counselor and arrange to move out or we'd both be going to the hole after I kicked the shit out of him.

Rarely will the counselors deny a request like this because they don't like child molesters either and don't expect us to live with them. He was gone the same day, having arranged to move in with other chomos, and I was happy it didn't take losing good time to make a lasting point. Word of my threat spread quickly through the block, ensuring, if for any reason something like this might happen again in the future, the chomos in the unit would arrange to have the guy moved as quickly as he arrived.

Chapter 62

Chairs

INMATES WATCH A LOT of television. At night in the housing units, there isn't much else to do. Like all things here, there's a system in place. When I first got here I went out to the TV room and sat down in one of the beige plastic chairs they set up in front of the televisions. A few minutes later, someone tapped me on the shoulder and said, "This is my chair." I wasn't sure what he meant, but, having already spent fifteen months in a few rough spots before being transferred here, I knew if I had any questions, best to ask them once I got up. I did, and he explained how things work.

The room is about 1500 square feet with nine televisions suspended from the ceiling along the front and side walls. The chairs are laid out in rows. Each chair is designated for someone; it's his chair. New guys don't just get a chair. They need to acquire one. The common way to acquire one is to be given it by someone who is leaving. A transfer of ownership, if you will.

Once you have a chair, you want to make sure to use it consistently for the first few weeks so that people get used to seeing you in it, kind of like a dog marking his territory. If not, someone else will try and claim it through intimidation. They may try anyway, and you'll need to make a stand or else you'll lose it. Some bullies stack two chairs for added height; some form of statement. There are guys with no chair, but they have two. Try and take one…let me know how that works out.

Sex offenders don't get chairs. They're forced to stand at the back of the room, or in the adjoining room looking through the glass. That's the way it is. As long as this protocol is followed, there are no problems. When someone tries to buck and someone always does, there are serious problems. I've seen a lot of fights and stabbings in the last five years over chairs. Most recently, someone was stabbed in the face for repeatedly sitting in someone else's chair after being warned.

I've also had fights over chairs.

There's a white guy from Cali they call Motor who's been here for about a year. He's here for cooking crystal meth. He's had a lot of issues on the pound.

We've never really talked, but one night I go out to watch TV, and he's in my chair. I tap him on the shoulder, as is customary, and say, politely:

"Motor, can I get my chair please? "

"This isn't your chair. It's the BOP's chair. I'm watching a movie right now," he answers disrespectfully.

"Listen Motor, you know how shit works here. This is my chair. I want to watch TV, so please get up," I say again with a bit more eagerness.

"I'm watching a movie. I'll get up when it's finished."

By now everyone's looking at what's unfolding. Ball's in my court. I need to do something or else. I can't let this asshole "punk me" in front of everyone or my time here will get hard, so I say:

"Look, Motor, I don't want any trouble, so I'm gonna ask you again, please give me my chair."

He looks up at me, takes his headphones off and says: "I already told you, I ain't moving!"

I nod my head as if I understand and start to walk away. Then I turn around fast and say: "Oh, you're moving, motherfucker!"

Before he can react, I grab him in a choke hold from behind and fall backwards like a UFC fighter. He squirms, trying to break my grip, but I'm not letting go for nothing.

Several inmates move in front of the inner window to block the CO's view. If they see the fight, they'll hit "the deuces"—their body alarm—and then the unit will be overrun with cops. In prison, we refer to the COs and anyone who works in the security apparatus as cops or police, in addition to correctional officers. Motor and I will be hauled off to the hole, and the rest of the unit will be locked down. If they don't see, none of that will happen.

"I can't breathe!" Motor says, barely getting it out.

"Fuck you! I'm gonna kill you, motherfucker!! I said that's my chair. Stay the fuck out of it! Do you understand, asshole?" I say.

"Yeah! Yeah! Let me go! I can't breathe!" he says again.

I'm not ready to let him go yet, mostly because I don't trust him.

A few guys urge me to let him go before I kill him. A Latino shot-caller for a Central American gang walks over and tells me to stop. Because I speak Spanish from living in the Dominican Republic, I get along with the Latinos on the compound. They like the "gringo" who speaks their language. He tells Motor if there's any more trouble he's going to be sorry. He also tells him never to sit in my chair again even if I'm not there because I'm "with them." News to me.

Before I let him go I say:

"Is this over, asshole? "

"It's over, let me go! I'm sorry, bro."

Even though he's been told I need to make sure he understands I'm not worth the trouble. I don't need him jumping me when I'm in the shower or on the toilet or sleeping in my rack, so I say:

"If you even think about coming near me, I'll kill you! Don't fuck with me! You hear me? I'll kill you. I'm not playing," I say in my most menacing voice.

I'm not about to kill anyone but neither he or anyone else knows that.

"Okay, okay, we're cool! It's over! I got some bad news from the street! I'm sorry, bro. We're cool."

I release my grip, jump up fast and back away from him.

The whole exchange took less than a minute and a half and the cops never heard or saw a thing. They were sitting in their office, talking. A few guys move towards the CO's office to warn off anyone who may want to tell them there was a fight. This sends a clear message.

Now the politics begin.

I'm not in a prison gang, and I have no affiliations but I need to make sure I won't have any trouble with Motor's people, the "White Boys," so I speak with Flaco, the "shot-caller" for the Puerto Ricans and the de facto shot-caller for all Latino gangs on the pound. The CEO of sorts.

Flaco is forty-three years old, and he's been in prison since he was eighteen. He was sentenced to thirty years for murder, started out in the pen and worked his way down. He's humble, tight lipped, and deadly serious. He and I play a lot of handball together, a game I discovered in prison. He's a great player. He's had a lot of practice.

He lives on my block, which is good for me. He wasn't in the room when it happened, but the news already reached him. He tells me not to worry. He'll speak to the shot-caller for the White Boys on the yard. Once they know Flaco is looking out for me, everything will die quickly. They are severely outnumbered.

Having his backing is also good if anyone is thinking of "telling." Everyone knows if Flaco finds out someone talked, they'll have a serious problem. The cops need guys like Flaco to make sure the pound runs smoothly, and if he wants to find out who told, he will. I don't owe Flaco anything. This isn't the movies. I'm a stand-up guy, and I did what I had to do. Or, as they say here, "put the work in" when I had to. I've earned his respect.

A few days pass, and everything's quiet. It wasn't my first fight, but hopefully it will be my last. Most guys already knew I would "go" if I had to. Those that didn't, know now. Usually an effective deterrent.

Chapter 63

Cinnamon Buns

CONTROL SHUTS THE TVS off at a quarter to four in the afternoon, our signal to go to our cubes for stand-up count. No matter where you are or what you're doing, you stop and return to your cube. All across the country this process is unfolding. There's nothing more serious than stand-up head count.

At exactly four o'clock, two COs walk through the B side door of the unit and yell:

"B side count. Rows one to thirty-one, stand up!"

One of the officers begins his descent down the range while his partner remains at the top, making sure nobody runs from one cube to another covering for someone who may be missing. Half way down range, he stops. I know this even though I can't see him because I no longer hear the clanging and jingling of the huge key-ring he wears on his security belt.

"Shut the fuck up! I'm counting! I'll tear this fucking place apart!"

Some idiot's talking...It's Garcia, and it's not the first time.

"Rows one to thirty-one, RECOUNT!"

Now they're going to drag this thing out just to show us who's boss.

When they finish, instead of clearing count and letting us return to whatever we were doing, they keep us in our cubes for an extra thirty minutes. Everyone's screaming obscenities at the culprit.

"Just shut your mouth during count, Garcia. It's not that hard, my nigga. I'm missing Judge Judy now. Cabron, do it again, and we're gonna fuck you up!"

It's coming from everywhere.

This will keep Garcia quiet for the next few months, until he feels comfortable again. Along with Lucky and Bebo, Garcia's three-man cube has a combined IQ of ninety-seven.

I need to get out of this place! Every day for more than three years, I've been dealing with this. I'm at my wit's end. These assholes will never learn. Most of the cops don't fuck with us, so just let them count!

I say nothing. There's no point. Eight more months.

From the back of the range where I live, over the noise that has steadily built to a deafening crescendo, the result of 186 frustrated men confined to too small an area for too long, I hear Kessman the CO yell:

"Next time shut your mouths when I'm counting, or I'll lock you motherfuckers down all night! B side clear!"

"Go fuck yourself!" someone yells as Kessman shuts his door.

Everyone starts laughing and jeering.

As COs go, Kessman's not a bad guy. He's been here for sixteen years doing the same crap every day just like us, except at some point, we get to go home. Kessman, on the other hand, will still be here counting, doing routine shakedowns and sitting in the office until he can retire. What an existence. Kessman knows it and, other than count, he doesn't take his job too seriously. He's one of those COs who doesn't bother anyone. As long as you aren't causing him any problems, he leaves you alone. He just wants his shift to go by uneventfully and go home to his wife and kids.

Every quarter, the COs get new job assignments. I remember the last time Kessman was working "compound," the grounds outside the housing blocks.

I was leaving the chow hall after breakfast with ten cinnamon rolls individually wrapped in plastic and tucked into every spot on my body I could find, to hide them. You're not allowed to take food out of the chow hall.

I knew Kessman was at the exit door, and I also knew he wouldn't bother me. He doesn't care, but hiding them is necessary because I don't want to put him in a difficult situation. It's about respecting him and not doing it in his face.

When I reached the door I was surprised to see two Lieutenants outside shaking guys down. They must have just arrived because they definitely weren't there when I went in. Every once in a while, to keep the inmates off balance, the Lieutenants decide to buckle things down and enforce rules that are rarely enforced.

Guys take cartons of milk, fruit, bread, artificial sweetener, and anything else they can eat or sell from the chow hall. Breakfast is especially popular for food misappropriation because milk is served, and it provides much needed protein for weight training.

The cinnamon rolls have no protein, but I love them. They only make them once every two weeks, so when they do, I come up at six in the morning and grab as many as I can. I hit the line two or three times asking the line servers to double me up. They aren't supposed to, but if the cops standing guard aren't looking, some will. The cops are on the look-out for guys going through the line more than once, but they know me by now, so they pretend not to notice.

There are usually a few guys I'm friendly with who won't eat their cinnamon rolls because they're watching caloric intake, so I may score a couple this way too. I eat the spoils of the hunt for breakfast with a mug of coffee every morning for as long as they last. Screw the calories, a man has to live.

By the time I saw the Lieutenants, it was too late to turn back. Three guys in front of me made it through unscathed. They got lucky. Me, not so much.

"Kessman, check him," one of the Lieutenants says. This Lieutenant just came over from the pen where he would never bother an inmate for such a petty thing. Here he can because most guys want to go home. He knows that, so he abuses his power.

I'm hit. Fuck! I'm going to the hole for sure. I won't be there long, only a couple of weeks, but I can kiss my commissary, telephone and email good-bye for thirty to sixty days. Just my luck. I may even lose my rack which would be terrible because for the last six months,

I've been living in one of only three two-man cubes in the unit with my bunky, Panama.

"Come here, Stelman. What do you have?" Kessman asks me.

I don't answer and instead assume the position: legs spread, arms out. Almost five years in, I've got it down pat.

He pats me down and feels every piece of contraband baked product on my body.

Wait a second… He's not telling me to take them out.

Instead, he says:

"He's clean, Lieutenant."

The Lieutenant looks at me and says, "Okay, get out a here."

"I nod to Kessman. As they say here, I'm happy as a motherfucker. Kessman doesn't sweat the small stuff. He knows this whole shake-down is bullshit, and they won't do it again for another three months when a Lieutenant wakes up feeling ambitious.

Chapter 64

İnmate Classification

LIKE MILLIONS OF PEOPLE everywhere, Kessman hates his job, but because he works for the Federal government, he's locked in. The pay, benefits, and the retirement pension...

Many COs are ex-military and would have liked a better job in law enforcement, but for one reason or another, couldn't make the cut. Many Federal prisons are located in rural areas and are the largest employer in those communities. Candidate qualifications often rank second to local relationships.

Most COs want to survive the day with as little trouble as possible. They're easy to deal with if you stay out of their way, respect the way they like things done, don't bother them, don't draw the attention of their superiors, and don't ask stupid questions.

Stupid questions is a big one.

"Excuse me, CO," says a new guy who came off the bus. When he got to the unit last night he was greeted by a welcoming party of chomos so I assume he's one. Right now, he's taken the liberty of walking into the office to ask a CO named Goetzer a question. Goetzer is an enormous man with the disposition of a junkyard dog. He's on the phone, and he doesn't like or care to multi-task, so he ignores the inmate.

I'm watching this from a chair at the computer stations just outside the office. It's seven forty-five in the morning, and I'm waiting to go into the microwave room to heat up my coffee. The orderly who cleans the microwave room is still working, so I'm waiting until he is done. Respect.

The new guy realizes Goetzer's on the phone, so he waits while standing in the office.

A minute later, Goetzer hangs up the phone and starts writing in his log book with his head down, ignoring the guy. I'm smiling, thinking, this should be interesting.

"CO, can you tell me what time I need to go to laundry to pick up my clothes? I just got here last night."

Goetzer lifts his head and says:

"Does this look like an information desk to you? I mean do you see a sign that says "information" anywhere on my desk or on my door? Or maybe you think this is the front desk at Motel 8. You think you're in a fucking hotel? Why are you in my office? Did I say you can come in? Get the fuck out of my office now!!"

The guy turns completely white. He's scared to death and tries to patch the damage. "I apologize but..."

Goetzer, all six foot five inches of him, stands up, leans over his desk and shouts: "Shut your fucken mouth, asshole! I said get out of my office!! Give me your ID!"

He removes his ID from around his neck and hands it to Goetzer who grabs it less than delicately and throws it on the desk.

"I don't want to hear a word out of you! Get the fuck out of my office! Now!"

Scared and confused, the new guy leaves not understanding how or why everything just went so badly. Without his ID, he can't leave the unit. He has to have it around his neck at all times on the compound. He definitely can't get his laundry pick-up without it. His plans are ruined.

First rule: Never, ever, speak to the cops. There is hardly a good reason to speak to them. They are not our friends. They aren't here to help us. Stay out of their way.

He just learned a valuable lesson, or at the very least, he's acquired the raw data necessary to deduce the lesson to be learned. If you need to know something, ask another inmate. Hardly here a day, and already Goetzer has him on his shit list. He's got a bumpy road ahead. Now every chance he gets, Goetzer will shake him down and point him out to other like-minded colleagues on the pound. What's more, Goetzer doesn't like sex offenders.

This shit is hilarious. Welcome to the Feds asshole. You just made your first mistake. The cops aren't here to help you, especially when they don't know you. I've come to understand they have an informal system they use to classify us.

To them we're "scumbags." Therefore, we all start off in the "scumbag pile." After some time, and I mean at least two years, you may move to the "maybe not a scumbag pile." But that's a weak maybe. When you're "maybe not a scumbag," they go a little easier on you. They may even give you a pass once in a while when they catch you doing something wrong. Stay the course, do your time like a man, don't whine, don't cause problems, stay out of their way long enough, and depending on what you're here for, you may make the "definitely not a scumbag" pile. That's where I am now with most of the cops, but it took time to get here. And it wasn't always easy.

Chapter 65

Just Doing His Job

IT'S MY FIRST YEAR when I bump heads with one of the super-cops that works here. Pezzone has about twenty years in, and he's miserable. Inmates call him "Tightass" because his pants look like they are two sizes too small. He runs around all day yelling at inmates from a distance and quoting regulations by statute number from the BOP handbook. Personally, I think he's a lunatic.

He hates being called Tightass and, if he hears you calling him that, he'll send you to the hole. The guards don't like him either and when talking with inmates they refer to him by his nickname which really adds fuel to the fire. Anyway, he's a notorious abuser, always looking to jam somebody up over the pettiest of things. He has a tireless ability to make a mountain out of a mole-hill.

One night, he was working our block, and he had already sent two inmates to the hole for cutting hair at the back of the range. The government issues disposable razor blades for shaving, but prison "barbers" open them up and embed the blade in a comb to make a make-shift, knife-like razor for cutting hair and trimming beards.

Most cops couldn't care less about this, but Pezzone isn't one of them. He caught them, so, after sending them to the hole for possessing shanks, he spent the next two hours dismantling their cubes, packing their property into green military issue duffel bags and throwing out as much of their personal belongings as he could get away with. Pezzone knows exactly how many of each item an inmate is allowed to have at any given time.

They'll both be back in a couple of weeks but only after losing a fair amount of their property, their racks, telephone and email privileges, and the right to shop at commissary. All they were doing was trying to make a couple of fish. Cutting hair is their hustle.

You would think this "bust" would have satisfied Pezzone, but even after all that damage he decides to make me his next target.

I'm at the computer station sending my kids an email at eleven thirty at night, just before I hit my rack. I have my plastic bowl and mug that I washed and dried earlier. I placed them on the computer table while I write the email.

Pezzone just finished his shift, and he's leaving the unit through the B side doors to go home for the night when he stops behind me.

"Nice sign there above your head. Can you read English?"

I turn around to confirm what I suspect. It's Tightass, and he's talking to me. Shit, this idiot now.

I look up and see the sign he's referring to. It reads "No Food or Drink." Okay, that's pretty straightforward.

"Yes, officer, I read English very well. I can also read and speak Spanish and French," I say, offering a little bit of unnecessary attitude to further antagonize him. "Thank you for asking." Not smart on my part, but I can't stand this asshole.

I continue: "It says no food or drink, and I have neither. What I have are two plastic containers that are both clean and dry, without contents."

"Same difference. Put that shit on the floor!"

"I am not putting my clean bowl and mug on the floor, officer. They contain neither food nor drink and, as such, I am not breaking any rules or regulations. Your request is unreasonable." I love sounding intelligent with these guys, so I always try to use big words. They're not used to it, and it throws them off their game, out of their comfort zone, so to speak.

"Listen, I'm not gonna argue with you. I said put that shit on the floor, now!"

"Officer, I object to your unreasonable order, and I insist on seeing the acting Lieutenant to review this situation. If I am wrong, then I will accept whatever consequences result. Please call him. I need clarification, and it will probably be good for you as well, in case a similar situation arises in the future." I'm such a linguist, I think, amusing myself.

He looks sick to his stomach at this point. He probably assumed I would be an easy lay-down because most are, but he was wrong. He knows that if he calls the Lieutenant for this stupidity, he'll piss him off because he's probably sleeping or watching TV. To add to this, he isn't sure what I mean when I say it will be good for him as well. I can see by the look on his face that he is starting to lose conviction.

I also know that total victory is not the outcome because he'll make it his business to try and get back at me in the future. No, I need to let him off the hook and make him feel like he has a win, while at the same time, send him away knowing that picking on me isn't worth it, especially when he has such a large victim pool to choose from. So, I say:

"Look officer, I know you're just doing your job, and I respect that. Why don't I put my bowl and mug right here on this empty chair next to me, instead of leaving it on the computer table. Does that make sense?"

"That will be fine, and that's right; I'm just doing my job, nothing more."

I place the stuff on the chair, and Pezzone turns and leaves through the side doors.

I underestimated his ambitious nature, however. A couple of weeks later, he's working our block again, and I'm watching the news. The room is pretty empty, and I have the back of my right leg resting on a chair in front of me. Suddenly, I hear a rapping noise on the window. I look up and see Pezzone, flashlight in hand, signaling me to take my leg off the chair. I can't believe it. It's not like I have my feet on the chair. It's only the hamstring part of my right leg, the same body part that would touch the chair if someone else was sitting on it. I raise my hands in the air and mouth: "What?"

He immediately barges into the room and shouts: "Come with me!"

I follow him into the office, and he orders me to close the door. Then he begins to berate me about abuse of government property. I let him talk and, when I think he is satisfied with his demonstration of authority and power, I say:

"Mr. Pezzone, may I speak?"

"What is it? Speak!"

"Mr. Pezzone, I didn't abuse government property. You're talking about a cheap plastic chair that's designed for people to sit on. When they do, their asses and the backs of their upper legs make contact with the chair. Guys take these chairs into the showers and use them as clothes hangers because there aren't enough hooks on the wall for clothing. They sit naked on them in the shower, and I'm sure some even piss on them. They use them as table surfaces to eat their food. They use them to hang wet and dirty laundry. Pezzone, unfortunately we live here. You need to stop being so unreasonable. I don't make trouble. I don't do anything wrong. I just want to do my time and get back to my family. Stop trying to jam me up! I will never disrespect you, so please have some respect for me!"

"I'm just doing my job," he says.

"I know, Pezzone, I know. That's what you always say. We all know you have power and control, but that doesn't mean you have to abuse it. Just stop, please!"

With that I turned and left the office without waiting for his permission.

That was three years ago, and Pezzone has never said a single word to me since. He's never once patted me down during shake-downs anywhere on the pound, and when he works the block, he leaves me alone. Even when he has to do a routine cube shake-down, he barely touches my locker or any of my stuff. Man, have I arrived.

Chapter 66

By the Book

THERE'S ANOTHER TYPE OF cop: the rookie. New COs are hired regularly, and they always start out in housing blocks.

Still young and idealistic when they start their fulfilling careers with the Bureau of Prisons, they show up with a gleam in their eye believing their jobs have profound meaning and purpose, and they will somehow make a difference in the rehabilitation of felons, while maintaining public safety.

They've been formally trained in all the correctional sciences which include counting, walky-talky radio communication, mail distribution, cube and cell searching, body searching, hand cuff deployment, and the most important of the sciences, locking and unlocking of doors. They have all the tools of their trade and the skill to go with it. Now what's left is to put theory to practice in the field. Exciting.

When they begin, they are in a probationary period, where their every action will be reviewed by the prison Lieutenants and Captain, similar to the debriefing process run by senior Special Operations Command at the Pentagon when Seal Team Six returns from a covert mission. The rookies, therefore, are careful to do everything by the book.

"CO, can I get a roll of toilet paper please?" I ask. They store them in the office.

"They gave them out on Friday night. It's only Wednesday today. You should have one," he replies.

"Yeah, I know, CO, but I have a sinus infection, so I went to medical, and they put me on an antibiotic which is giving me diarrhea. I keep running to the bathroom, so I finished the roll they gave me on Friday. I need to go again right now. Can I get one please?" I explain.

"We give toilet paper out on Friday night," he tells me, emotionless.

"I know, CO, but I have to take a shit now. I can't hold it in until Friday night."

"They sell toilet paper at commissary," he says, probably thinking this will somehow be helpful.

"Yes, CO, they do, but our unit goes to commissary on Monday, and it's Wednesday today," I say.

"So, then, you just went two days ago. Why didn't you buy some then?" he asks as if I'm crazy.

"CO, I went to medical early Monday morning, but I only picked up the antibiotic at pill line on Monday afternoon at three. I didn't know the antibiotic would give me diarrhea so when I went to commissary late Monday morning, I didn't think to buy toilet paper. I never took this antibiotic before, and I certainly didn't know it would upset my stomach. I'll be better prepared in the future, should this happen again. Anyway, my stomach only started acting up on Tuesday afternoon. CO, can I get a roll please? I really need to go right now!" I say, expecting he'll understand.

"We give out toilet paper on Friday night," he says again.

"Okay, thanks, CO, for your understanding. I'll get one some other way," I tell him.

By the book. The book says one roll per inmate every week on Friday night. Like a cop once said to me, "You don't like it, don't come to prison."

Chapter 67

Politics

I NEVER LIVED IN America, so I didn't understand how pronounced racism is in day-to-day life. In prison, racial divisions run deep. It's a segregated environment and one need only experience a housing block TV room to understand how.

With nine TVs and close to 400 men in each unit, it's impossible for everyone to watch what they want. A race-based system exists that extends to TV management.

The first four TVs are Black. No, not the color of the TV monitors; they're all Black. I'm referring to who controls them. There are black cars in each unit that are geographically based. There's the Philadelphia car, the New York car, the DC car, and the Carolina car. These cars have their chairs in front of the TV they control. The shot-caller for each car will run the TV, but in his absence, others are authorized to change the channels.

Now even though the rules are clear, the controller from one car may decide, on his own, or through some form of consensus, to change the channel on another car's TV. This is rare, but when it happens there may be a battle for control of the Kingdom.

A Black from the New York car gets up and changes the channel on the Philadelphia car's TV.

"Yo, my nigga, I was watchin' that! What is you doin'?"

"We gonna watch the Nicks game on this TV."

"Watch it on your TV, my nigga...I'm watchin' a movie on this TV. That's disrespectful. You don't just change the channel I'm watchin'. That's fuckin' disrespectful, nigga!"

"Hey, my nigga, we already been talked about it yesterday. Everyone wants to watch the BET Music Awards on our TV. We ain't missin' the Nicks game for some punkass movie they gonna show twenty times this month. Nobody tryin' to hear that, my nigga."

"Yo, my nigga, I ain't decided shit. Nobody aksed me shit. Fuck that! Put my movie back on my nigga, or we gonna take this somewhere else!"

"What dat mean, my nigga? You disrespectin' me, my nigga! Who the fucks is you talkin' to, my nigga? I's a grownass man! Some games I don't play, nigga!"

Chairs are pushed out of harm's way, guys stand up, and a wave of tension fills the room. This can only go one of three ways:

The two TV controllers will fight for their respect, after which, they will be handcuffed and marched off to the hole for at least ninety days. Both won't be allowed back on the pound for security reasons, and by then, the one that does will have ceded control of the TV to someone else by default. Because he was strong enough to control the TV in the first place, he will likely regain control of at least his chair, ousting whoever bet that he wouldn't be the one returning.

Over time he will reassert his control of the TV. It will start by being very friendly and, occasionally, with group consensus, he will change the channel. This will be repeated daily until it happens with frequency. By now, the community will be used to him changing channels and offer no interference. This prompts him to become more determined, forceful and committed, until he has regained total control. Of course, this requires sufficient effort on his part, obliging him to spend a great deal of time in the TV room, so that his position be known.

The second way it could go is both will square off until one of the two backs down, usually claiming his desire not to get into trouble, when really, it's his fear of losing as the reason to avoid the fight.

"Fuck this shit, my nigga. I ain't jackin' my bid for this stupidass shit. Niggas got me fucked up. Anybody try this shit again I'm gonna go, you hear? Word...nobody disrespects me! Stupid punkass niggas, nobody told me shit! I'm gonna leave up out of here, but tomorrow I'm watchin' my shit!"

The battle for control of the Kingdom is settled without a shot being fired or anyone harmed, save for the ego of the surrendering party. He will now do a lot of behind the scenes lobbying to explain why he decided not to fight, trying to convince his constituents that it just wasn't worth it, in order to ensure their continued support. Most will nod their heads in agreement to avoid any conflict, but a few will say:

"He disrespected you, nigga! You laid down like a bitch. No man disrespects me like that and gets away with it! He punked you like a bitch, nigga! You is a punkass nigga!"

This loss of status will eat away at him, and he may decide, for the sake of his remaining time and wounded reputation, to do something to prove that he is not a bitch. Fear aside, he will go back into the arena and call out his adversary, inviting him to the back of the block, or the showers, to settle it.

He has a second option, however. He can do nothing and stay in his cube for a couple of weeks out of the public eye, to avoid embarrassment, gradually coming out but nowhere near as loud as before. Over time, as guys leave and new guys come, his vigor will be renewed, and he may once again take a shot at the Kingdom.

The third thing that can happen is the community enters the fray, talking both guys down, until it appears that calmer heads settled the matter, leaving both egos intact even though one of the two had to capitulate. This may be the most civilized solution, but it will only manifest in a future blowup due to the perceived increase in power of the winning party. One day, his unchecked confidence will lead him to try this with "the wrong nigga," one who will bypass the customary and traditional system of conflict resolution and just "knock him the fuck out" right there and then, without saying a word.

The fifth TV is controlled through a joint venture agreement. This is a white TV, and the only white TV, which reflects the demographic makeup of the unit and the prison population in this region as a whole. The reason the joint venture is required is simple to understand. When a program, big enough, inspiring enough, and socially relevant enough is broadcast, such as Empire, the Hip-Hop Awards, March Madness, or any number of shows during Black History Month, control is temporarily ceded to all the Black cars to ensure everyone sees the important broadcast. This arrangement is peaceful, requiring nothing more than a few days' notice between cars. It is important to note, however, that it is a one-way non-reciprocal arrangement.

The sixth TV is exclusively for sports and is controlled by another group of Blacks. Anyone can watch it, but only a few of the Blacks can touch it. There can be an exception to this rule, and a like-minded White or Latino inmate can touch the TV with consent, when, for example, the controller has a broken arm or broken fingers. Gambling on sports is a big pastime in prison and a full-fledged book making industry exists to service the needs of inmates. This TV serves as the de facto source of sport score information and is constantly switched from sports channel to sports channel to check the scores on the scrolling tickers.

The seventh TV is controlled by the Latinos, specifically, Flaco, the Puerto Rican shot-caller and the informal shot-caller of all the Latinos including the Dominicans, Columbians, Mexicans, Mexican-Americans, and a spattering of others. He's fluent in English, so it's not unusual to see this TV tuned to English programming, such as Life Network, for its romantic movie content, the closest thing to soft porn available to us, or the other extreme, UFC and boxing matches.

Being the confident and all-supreme leader that he is, he does not oppose anyone else changing the channels as long as there is Latino community consensus.

The last two TVs are also Latino and always tuned to either Telemundo or Univision, Spanish language networks. The Latino community is a tight knit group and rarely is there any infighting. Different guys change the channels and I have never seen any problems occur between them. Whether or not this is the result of unity, good organization or the fact that there are only two channel choices, remains to be seen.

Chapter 68

Tension

THE ONLY PROBLEM I ever saw involving the Latino TVs came from outside interference. A DC Black named Cutty is watching one of the Spanish TVs. They're broadcasting a re-run of "Bellaza Latina," a talent and beauty show featuring hot, scantily clad, gorgeous women. If you've ever had a chance to watch Spanish television or even the Spanish news, you know that they pull out all the stops to find the sexiest, most beautiful creatures possible. Bellaza Latina is like a feeder system to the "big leagues," and each year's winner usually ends up with a broadcasting job.

In prison, you're obviously starved of women, so to watch this is a treat.

It's late in the afternoon before count and Cutty is sitting in one of the many empty Latino's chairs, watching the swimsuit segment of the competition. I'm sitting in the back of the room watching CNN when I notice several of the Mexicans enter, head right to the TV Cutty is watching, and to his chagrin, switch the channel to a soccer match. Needless to say, Cutty is not happy.

"What the fuck, man. I was watchin' that! How you gonna come up in here and just change the channel when I'm watchin' something?" He asks.

The Mexican who changed the channel, and at whom this outburst was directed, doesn't understand a word of English and doesn't realize a) Cutty was watching the show, b) that he offended him or c) that Cutty is even talking to him.

"Hey, nigga…I was watchin' that…turn it back! What the fuck is wrong with you?"

At this point, the Mexican realizes that Cutty may be talking to him and may be upset about something, but he doesn't know what. With a puzzled expression he shrugs it off and sits down to enjoy the soccer game. Cutty interprets this as a sign of total disrespect. In what seems like an over-the-top, unwarranted demonstration of emotion, he stands up, grabs the chair he's sitting on, and hurls it towards the Spanish TVs where it crashes into a protective metal barrier designed for this very sort of thing.

Silence descends on the room. The few people present, myself included, jump up and stand at the ready. Cutty, satisfied that he made his point, storms out, muttering profanities under his breath.

The Mexicans are stunned. They can't believe what just happened, nor do they even understand why, but this is serious shit. It's an affront to the Mexican community that will not be tolerated. This incident transverses racial divides and has offended the entire Latino race. It will be avenged.

There is an immediate call to arms. The shot-callers for the Paisas and Sureños lead the charge, and they reach out to their counterparts with the Trinitarios, Ñetas, MS-13 and Latin Kings. This is very real. Nervous tension fills the recirculated air on the block as a meeting takes place at the back. Men are stationed at focal points along the range to warn if the COs are coming.

-El pinche negro va a pagar por esto! ¡Nos faltó el respeto! A la verga!

That fuckin' Black will pay for this! He disrespected us! That fucker! says Chicharo the shot-caller for the Paisas and whose men are the target of the insult and disrespect.

- ¡Tenemos que matar a ese hijo de la chingada! ¡Tienen que saber quiénes somos! ¡Dejemos de hablar y actuémos ya!

We need to kill that son of a bitch! They need to know who we are! Enough talk! Let's do it now! says Mando, the shot-caller for the Sureños.

-Claro, no tenemos opcion. Nadie puede hacer esa mierda. Pero antes de hacer algo, alguien debería hablar con Mook, el jefe de los morenos de D.C., para ver qué hará.

We have no choice. No one can do that shit. But before we do anything, someone should talk to Mook, the boss of the DC Blacks to see what he'll do about it, says Loco, the shot-caller for the Dominican Trinitarios.

-Sí, esa es la forma de manejarlo ... déjame hablar con Mook más tarde.

Yeah, that's the way to handle it...let me speak to Mook later, says Flaco.

-Ese negrito es un cabron. No estoy seguro de que hagan nada, pero estoy dispuesto a darle una oportunidad.

That Black is an asshole. I'm not sure he'll do anything, but I am ready to give him a chance, says Muñeca, the shot-caller for the Latin Kings.

-¡Chicharo, espera entonces! ¿Oyes? Necesitamos darles la oportunidad de arreglarlo. Si no lo hacen, ¡entonces vamos!

Chicharo, wait! You hear? We need to give them a chance to fix it. If they don't, then we go! says Flaco.

Chicharo is out-voted by the other shot-callers, and he won't challenge Flaco's authority, so he concedes, and will wait to see what happens.

Chapter 69

Meet and Greet

LATER IN THE EVENING after mainline, surrounded by a large group of Ñetas and Latin Kings, Flaco enters the yard. Word has spread in whispers through the chow hall, and everyone knows something may pop off.

Every night, there are regularly scheduled baseball, basketball and soccer games, but tonight no one is taking the field. This in itself is a hint to the guards who work recreation that something is out of the ordinary. They don't know specifically what's going on, but they know something is amiss. They notify the Lieutenant's office, and minutes later, there's an increased presence of nervous compound guards both in and outside the fence.

All the players are here. The Blacks are united on one end of the basketball courts, and the Latinos are on the soccer field. There are shanks, locks placed in socks, and razor blades tucked in mouths, all at the ready.

This isn't a White, Italian, Russian or Albanian problem, so they stay in the background waiting to see what happens.

Cutty, in the meantime, is presenting his position and pleading his case to Mook, who is growing increasingly concerned. Mook knows the Paisas don't play games with these sorts of things, and he will have to find a way to resolve this or things will turn ugly. He knows Cutty was wrong.

Two Ñetas approach. Flaco sent them to tell Mook he wants to meet.

"Mook, he's on the handball courts," one of them says. Juan Carlos Figueroa, El Gallo, (the rooster) is a stone-cold killer who's been down twenty years for a gang-related, double-homicide and has four years left on his sentence. He doesn't want to be involved in anything that can ruin his bid or make him lose any more good time. He lost most of it years ago when he was in the pen, but he'll do whatever he has to. That's the way it is in here.

"Tell him I'm coming. I just wanna finish talkin' to my man," Mook tells El Gallo.

El Gallo nods and walks away.

Ten minutes later, Mook approaches. Flaco is standing with El Gallo, Chicharo and Loco. They give Mook a nod and walk away so he can talk to Flaco. Flaco asks Mook to take a walk with him to the back of the handball courts out of camera view.

"Mook, these motherfuckers is mad angry. They wanna know whatsup. That fucker disrespected them, and they ain't gonna let it go. So, what you gonna do? You gonna fix it?"

"Flaco, they disrespected him! He was watchin' the TV, and they just come up and change it without even asking...you know how that shit go...he felt disrespected. He wasn't wrong, Flaco," Mook argues.

"Mook, that shit he did was bad. They're tight Mook. He can watch our TV, but he don't tell us what to watch. They watch soccer at that time every week. Anyway, it don't matter. He has no say in those TVs. Who the fuck he thinks he is? We don't tell you what to watch on your TVs. Fuck his stupid ass. I need to tell the Paisas somethin', Mook," Flaco says.

Mook knows that Cutty screwed up. He did his best to support his man, but he knows, and everyone knows, Cutty was wrong.

"No...that nigga went overboard, I know. I been talked to him about it. What if he humble himself and apologize?" Mook asks.

"Mook, you know these Paisas, what you think? Mook, I need to tell them whatsup...you gonna do the right thing here?" Flaco says, cold as ice.

"Yeah Flaco...we got it. I'll run him up the hill," Mook says.

That means he will force Cutty to ask to be placed in protective custody until he can be transferred to another prison.

"Nah Mook. Ain't gonna be that way. You need to do the right thing here, Mook."

"Alright, Flaco. I'm tired of that nigga anyway. He always doin' stupid ass shit. We gonna fix it, and then run him up. Gimme a day, too many po-lice around right now," Mook says.

"Okay, Mook, I'll tell 'em. Best way Mook. No one wants trouble," Flaco says.

With that they fist bump and walk off to their respective minions.

The next day after four o'clock count when the COs are busy calling in the count numbers, distributing mail and getting ready for rec and mainline moves, it happens.

The DC Blacks are meeting at the back of the B side with Cutty. They've posted lookouts at the top of the ranges, but they know it's unlikely any CO will be patrolling the block at this time of the day.

Suddenly, a scuffling sound, and Cutty begins to shout: "C'mon, this is bullshit! You gonna disrespect me like this? Fuck this! You's a buncha motherfuckers! Fuck you all!"

Minutes later, it's all over.

Mook green-lighted Cutty (gave the order to have him smashed), and the DC Blacks in our unit carried out the order.

Someone runs to tell the COs that somebody's hurt at the back of the unit.

They get there to find Cutty lying on the floor, his face bloody, and he's doubled over in pain. He's holding his arm and breathing heavy. There's blood pouring out the top of his forehead from a nasty cut. The COs hit their body alarms and start screaming to lock the unit down.

The building is overrun by thirty COs. They come from everywhere. We're ordered back to our cubes and, forty five minutes later, the body inspection begins. Cutty claims he slipped and fell while working out, but they know he got attacked. He's carried out of the unit on a stretcher and placed in the back of the compound ambulance, a large, modified, golf-cart-type vehicle. They take him to medical and then to an outside hospital.

The body inspection yields two guys who were involved in the melee and three more that had nothing to do with it. They are all handcuffed and lugged off to the hole. The Lieutenants, Captain and SIS will spend the next few days getting to the bottom of it, and eventually the innocent parties may be released. The ones they think are guilty will spend three months in the hole under investigation and get transferred to another facility.

The compound stays on lockdown for forty-eight hours, while our block endures ninety-six. They feed us our food in Styrofoam trays.

Odds are Cutty won't tell SIS what happened because wherever they send him, it will just be a matter of time before inmates there learn he's a rat, and he'll be subjected to additional prison justice. A week later, someone else being released from the SHU reports that Cutty is back, and in the hole. He suffered severe breaks to his nose and arm, and a fractured cheekbone. He also received forty stitches to repair the cut on his head. Apparently, it was the result of a sharp object.

Life in the TV room is back to normal with everyone being particularly mindful of the rules. Everyone agrees that the current management and dispute resolution systems are efficient and require no modifications.

Chapter 70

The Bookie

IT'S A HOT SEPTEMBER day, and I'm in the yard. I have approximately four months to the door. A lot of guys who are about to leave can cite how many days and hours they have left, but I never cared to do the calculation.

"Hey, Canada. Let's go. Best of three fo' twenty-five fish. Gonna slay you're ass!"

That's big Shaq a black guy from North Carolina who lives on my block. He's very popular on the compound, and we're friends. He has a great attitude, always smiling and laughing. He's not a very good handball player, which is what he's challenging me at, but he'll bet on anything.

He can afford it. He has lots of money. He runs the poker table in our block and the biggest gambling ticket on the pound. Shaq is a prison bookmaker. He receives the Vegas betting lines via email, which oddly enough isn't against prison rules. Using them to take bets is.

Once he has the lines, he makes them slightly more favorable for himself and then has a few of his North Carolina homies create little pieces of paper called "tickets," offering the games and the spreads. They photocopy them in bulk at the library. They need to be careful because anyone caught with gambling tickets can go straight to the SHU, although it rarely happens. Gambling is so widespread and common, the cops just ignore it. Some things can't be controlled. Besides, with things like prison rape, violence, drugs, alcohol, and cell phone smuggling, they've got their hands full.

Anyway, the homies hand the tickets off to other inmates in each unit, and they distribute them to betting customers. The majority of inmates gamble, so there are a lot of customers. It's a lucrative business, especially with the less-than-fair point spreads. The same guys handle collections. Shaq's picky about who he hires because every once in a while someone loses more than they can pay, and when that happens it can get ugly. So, he hires guys who will "put in the work." Oh, and Shaq doesn't own the only ticket on the pound. The Italians and Chinese have their own versions.

"Motherfuckin' Giants blew my ticket. Had a three pick and those motherfuckas didn't cover. Bumass Robbie Gould missed two point afters. Motherfucka!" Tunes, one of the chow hall cooks complains as he works the grill.

"Bengals blew ma motherfuckin' ticket. I'm done. Can't git a win," answers Bryant Hicks, a white boy from Arkansas.

"You always sayin' the same shit, Hicks. Stop fakin', motherfucka. You been bettin' tickets since you come on the pound and every motherfuckin' day you say the same dumbass shit. You's a fakin' motherfucka."

That's the sound every day all over the pound. First thing in the morning, guys run to the sports TV to check scores. Moments later, torn tickets litter the TV room floor. Later, the same guys huddle in groups to try and determine the right picks for the next ticket. They analyze stats, injuries, and weather conditions and find out who other guys "like" and why.

"Rock, lemme get the NBA book. I'll bring it back in ten minutes," says Chad, a white guy from the mid-west doing twenty years for crystal meth.

"It's on top of my locker. Take it. I did my picks. Tell me who you like for the under/over with San Antonio and Minnesota." Rock's a drug dealer from Northern California who lives and breathes basketball, college, and pro.

Some guys do win, which keeps everyone coming back. It's common to see laundry bags full of fish being delivered to someone's cube by one of Shaq's homies. It's far more common, however, to see losers delivering their fish to pay Shaq.

"Hey, Shaq. I would but I'm on restriction. I'm not allowed to play singles, only doubles. I just finished playing with Mike, Red, and Tio."

Handball is a passion of mine and a big sport here. I learned to play in prison, and I'm pretty decent. Shaq takes a seat next to me on the bench, behind the first court where I've been watching two New York Puerto Ricans, the best players on the pound, play an intense grudge match for ten fish.

"What that mean? You can play doubles but not singles? Don't make no sense."

"Yeah, I know. It's ridiculous. For some reason, which he can't explain to me, my PA will only let me play doubles. I'm not restricted from indoor ball hockey, football or basketball, all gladiator sports in here, but I'm not allowed to play singles. Go figure."

"That shit's crazy! That cause of your back?"

"Yeah. You have no idea how hard it was to get him to let me play doubles. They're all the same. It really is crazy."

"C'mon, Canada, forget that shit. Nothin' gonna happen if we play. The po-lice don't care. You just scared to death to lose to me, nigga."

"Shaq, trust me, if they catch me, I'm going to the hole. That new rec cop, Kurby? That prick has my picture on the wall over his desk. Every time he walks the yard, he looks my way. I'm not fucking with these people. You know how they are."

"Fuck outa here. For real, for real?"

"Yeah, for real. Anyway, better for you I can't play. You get to keep your twenty-five fish. I know you need them."

"Ha, ha, ha,…you a crazy motherfucka, Canada."

Ever since that beating I took in Santo Domingo, something wasn't right with my back. It wasn't bad enough to stop me from playing handball every day, but after playing, I was always in pain.

In April of 2016, I was in the gym playing when suddenly the left side of my body locked up, and I was in excruciating agony. I couldn't walk so a few guys carried me to medical. The nurse on call evaluated me and told me I shouldn't go to work for the next three days. That was the extent of her professional intervention.

That night the pain was so intense and unbearable, I couldn't stand up for count. The CO took one look at me and knew I was in real distress, so he called medical. I'm grateful to him because not too many COs would have cared. I'm also grateful the nurse I saw earlier wasn't working. Medical showed up, as did the compound Lieutenant. This particular Lieutenant was known for being a ball-breaking pain in the ass. She was never nice to anyone.

God was watching over me though, because the same CO convinced them to call an ambulance. Because non-prison vehicles can't enter the prison grounds, we had to meet them at R&D, a 200-yard walk. I begged them to take me there in the compound golf-cart ambulance, but the battery wasn't charged.

They put me in a wheel chair, and I held myself up by the arms of the chair in a contorted position the whole way because my left side wouldn't bend and I couldn't sit. The ride and the pain were so horrible that I remember asking them to shoot me.

To make matters worse, the Lieutenant was pissed off that she had to deal with this. She would have to assign two COs to escort me and approve the trip to the hospital. It required a lot of paperwork. When the ambulance technicians were examining me and taking my vital signs, she asked them if I could wait until morning and see my PA. The technician looked at her like she was crazy and told her my blood pressure was dangerously high, and I could have a stroke any moment. She had no choice. There's even more paperwork to do when an inmate dies.

Two days later, they operated. I had a bad disk herniation at L3 and L4. The surgeon said the reason I was in such intense pain was because the nerves were so compressed that the IT band, the band of tendon that starts from the hip and runs down the leg to the knee, had rolled up. Imagine those Charlie horses you get in your legs from time to time when you're sleeping. You know the ones. You wake up in agony and crawl on the floor. Now multiply the pain ten-fold, but unlike those Charlie horses it never stopped. Even after the surgery, the pain was so bad that they kept me in the hospital for six more days. Of course, they never gave me enough pain medication to make me comfortable, and I was under twenty-four-hour guard by two COs who kept me handcuffed and shackled to the bed.

When I got back to prison I thanked the CO who helped me. I got lucky because more often than not guys will suffer for weeks and months before they're given adequate medical attention and care.

"So, you're out of here soon," Shaq says.

"Yeah, I'm short."

"You goin' back to Canada?"

"Yeah. I get deported, but that's okay. I was never in the United States. I was extradited from the Dominican Republic. My family is in Montreal."

"How come you never got the extradition transfer?"

"You mean the treaty transfer? I tried."

There's a treaty between countries that allows prisoners to serve their sentence in their home country. Both the United States and Canada are parties to it, so when I got here I applied knowing that once in Canada I would do far less time and maybe even get released. I was extremely confident I would be approved. It was also the opinion of a treaty transfer consultant I hired. Based on the non-violent nature of my crime, my age, and the fact that it was my first offense, she saw no reason I wouldn't be. The United States had to agree to transfer me first and then Canadian acceptance would have been almost automatic.

Three months after applying, I received a letter from the US International Prisoner Transfer Program office in Washington DC. They denied me because of "the seriousness of my crime." Unbelievable. Isn't any crime that sends you to prison serious? I could only re-apply in two years. Because I had forty-four months remaining on my sentence when I was denied, I would only be able to apply again when I had twenty-four months left. Deduct from that the ten months it takes to be approved plus at least two months to be transferred to Canada and at least two more months to have a Canadian hearing, and that would bring me to ten months remaining and what I could save. The problem was I would have a foreign conviction on my Canadian record and to me that wasn't worth saving ten months.

"Damn! These motherfuckers is vicious!" Shaq says.

"Just a few more months, Shaq..."

Chapter 71

Down to a Wake-up

IT'S MONDAY, JANUARY 15, 2018—a crisp winter day. I'm walking the track with Panama, my bunky. We just finished working out. The sun is shining, and the usual northern wind has taken a break, so it's pleasant. The track is the only place to talk that offers any semblance of privacy; not alone but out of earshot. A lot of meetings take place on walks around the track. The New York families use it as an office.

So, this is it. I'm out of here early tomorrow morning, but I'm not going home. As my luck would have it, today is Martin Luther King Day, a federal holiday which delays everything by one day. Just like I predicted, ICE decided to take me to the closest border crossing, the Rainbow Bridge at Niagara Falls. Two officers from Syracuse, here for a meeting tomorrow, have been tasked with driving me to the border but only on their return trip the following day. So, I'll only be freed on the seventeenth.

Here's the rub though. The BOP wants me out of here on my release date, tomorrow. For the last four and a half years, they've done everything to keep me here, and now they won't let me stay one extra night. I assume potential exposure for unlawful imprisonment is their concern.

When I first got here I played pool with a black guy named Rudy. He was sixty-four years old and had been locked up for thirty-five years. He spent years in the pen and medium and finished his last twelve here. He had no family or friends or anywhere to go. He didn't take the half-way house time they offered him either. Prison is all he

371

knew, and the thought of being in the outside world terrified him. If you've seen Shawshank Redemption, you'll understand.

The morning of his release, he refused to leave. A bear of a man, it took eight COs to drag him, kicking and screaming off the compound. They left him at a bus stop.

So, yeah, when your time is up, you go. The local ICE office will take me to a county jail, and my ride will pick me up from there in the morning.

As far as Allenwood goes, I'm down to a "wake-up," what we refer to as our last night in prison. Guys I'm close to know I'm leaving, but many don't. It's not the kind of thing you want people to know for a very important reason. Some inmates have so much time left and are so jealous you're getting out, they'll do anything to "jack your bid."

A fight, for example, can delay my release because I still have all my good time. So, best not to talk about it. Of course, it's hard to keep a secret in prison, and guys have stopped me as we walk to say good-bye and wish me luck.

As my time got shorter, crazy things happened with other inmates and the cops. Things that easily could have interfered with my release date.

A couple of months ago, I talked to Flaco about some of the things that were happening.

-Cuidate es el diablo.

Be careful, it's the devil.

-¿De Verdad?

Really?

"When I'm down to four months, I'm checking in, Canada. No one will know my release date," he says.

"Why?" I ask.

"Because the devil tries to keep you in prison, Canada. I've seen it so many times over the years. Be careful, brother. I know what I'm talking about."

I thought he was being overly dramatic, but now I understand. I'm convinced there's something to what he said. Guys I've never had problems with before start arguments with me over the dumbest shit. I came close to a fight with someone who's been living in the cube next to mine for the past four years. We've always gotten along and never had bad feelings towards one another.

Some of the cops are even harassing me for nothing. A few weeks ago, I was heading to rec, and I was the last guy on the compound. The move wasn't closed yet, so it didn't matter. As I approached the gate from twenty-five yards away, the rec cop, a real asshole named Walters, got up and locked it.

"C'mon, Walters, the move isn't closed. Why would you lock me out?"

"Why are you the last one to get here, Stelman?"

"What difference does that make? I'm not late, just last. Someone's always last."

At that moment, they announced the end of the move over the PA.

"Now you're late," he says with a smirk.

"Are you serious, Walters? Why are you doing this? Let me in, man."

"No. I'm not letting you in. Go to the Lieutenant's office, and complain to him."

"You're a piece of work, Walters."

"Hey, Stelman, this is my house," he said, laughing, and walked away.

I walked in the direction of the Lieutenant's office, but I stopped outside medical. A nurse was leaving so when she unlocked the door, I went inside and sat down like I had a call-out. She didn't say a word. I waited there until they called the next move and went back to the block.

Walters was just trying to bait me into an argument so he could send me to the hole.

Even Pezzone bothered me a few days ago because I had my ID in my hand instead of around my neck. I got so frustrated, I said: "C'mon, Pezzone, leave me alone with this stupid shit." He said: "Say one more word, Stelman, and I'll walk you to the hole."

So, yeah, the devil. Maybe. Or is it the customer retention program?

Panama and I walked and talked until recall at three fifteen and then returned to the block for the second to last stand-up count of my life.

At seven thirty, a few guys I kick it with brought over a couple of pizzas to celebrate my release. They sell pizza kits at commissary, and we cook them in the microwaves. We had some laughs, and they all wished me good luck.

It's nine fifteen. Panama's lying on his rack, and I'm cleaning out the last of my property. It's customary to give things of value away to other inmates when you leave. Things like leather workout gloves, bowls, utensils, books, extra food, anything someone can use. I've given pretty much everything away already, but guys keep coming.

"Hey, Canada, can I get that pillow? I don't have one."

"Sorry AJ, already spoken for. I promised it to Slice. He's coming by to get it."

"What about them shoes? Can I get 'em?"

"Sorry, dude, everything's gone. All I have left is this nail clipper and this old coffee mug."

"Shit, I'll take those, thanks."

I turn to Panama and shrug my shoulders.

"Nervous?" he asks.

"No. I mean I have some concerns about how easy it will be to settle in after living this dog's life for so long, but I'm so excited to get back home to my family."

"They're the most important thing. Enjoy them."

"I just want to be with my kids again and build a great future with my wife. I can't wait to walk Stephanie down the aisle in June."

Stephanie has been living with her fiancé Adam for the past several years. They got engaged about ten months ago, and they're waiting for me to get out so they can get married. Having their wedding to look forward to has made this last year a little easier. It represents a real turning point in my life, in all our lives. It'll be the first great milestone event since all this shit happened. It's-symbolic.

"Don't forget to send me pictures," he says.

"I got you, Panama."

"You know, I've learned a lot. Most of all gratitude for the things I have: four great children and a wife that love me very much. That's something that can't be taken for granted. I've also learned to live in the moment and enjoy life instead of living for the future and worrying about things I don't have and how to get them. Yeah, I'm going to live my life with more passion, appreciation, and gratitude, that's for sure. You're almost there too, Panama."

"Four more, Canada. Only four more years. I'm real short now."

"Crazy. Your short is a sentence for a lot of guys. I can't believe how long you've been locked up for."

"Eighteen fucking years. How stupid I was. What a waste."

We just look at each other and nod. We both know.

"It's actually hard to believe it's really happening. It's only been five and a half years, a fraction of what you've done, but it's enough. It's scary that this life is all too normal now. It's time to get out of here and get my life back."

"That's a long time, Canada. Go slow. Give yourself time to adjust. You're institutionalized."

"Institutionalized? Why do you say that?" I say with a smirk.

He just smiles and says: "When you're out there, don't overreact. Remind yourself you're not in prison anymore. People will do stupid shit. You've been living like this for so long you may have a hard time for a while. Take a deep breath and think. I've seen so many guys come back on violations because they had trouble adjusting. So, go slow."

"I appreciate that, Panama, but I promise, if you ever see me again, it won't be in prison."

"I know."

"Are you worried about what people will think of you?"

"To be blatantly honest, for the most part I don't care what the majority of people think. But there are some, and I wonder how they will act towards me. I mean, you know how I feel about my crime. I'm so ashamed and feel so sorry for the victims. What a terrible mistake."

"Canada, you paid your dues. You did your time. You need to let that go, otherwise you'll never find peace."

"Yeah, I know. I rationalize all the time that I can't allow it to be my legacy. I need to earn back my children's respect. I love them so much, and I know they love me, but there's no way what I put them through didn't diminish their respect for me.

"I took advantage of the weak, the needy, and for the next five and a half years, the legal system devoured me, piece by piece. I became the needy, the destitute. I did my best to survive an 800-pound Gorilla doing the tango on my chest, and, at times, I almost lost my breath. But here I am, humbled, and bowing to fate, but alive. I have survived this horrible tango, and I'm going to do things right. I'm going to work hard to make up for lost time and do what I can to make my children's lives better.

"I don't think I could ever explain to anyone how profoundly this affected me. None of us can. But you know, I've grown a lot from this experience. I've caused and seen so much misery and suffering and, man, I suffered so much myself. I have a different perspective on life now and on what's important. I'll take things slow and easy, but I'll always move forward in a straight line with my head down. I just want to be a great father, husband and son. I want to be a good person and do positive things. I know it won't be easy at the beginning, and I'm prepared for the worst, but hey, I've already survived the worst of the worst, so bring it on, motherfucker!" I say with a smile.

He laughs and says: "Yeah, Canada, we suffer, that's for sure."

"Hey, I got something for you, Panama. I read a quote from Ghandi at the library last week that says it all. It inspired me so much I wrote it down.

"'Strength does not come from winning. Your struggles develop your strengths. When you go through hardship and decide not to surrender, that is strength.'"

We look at each other. Neither of us says a word.

Chapter 72

Going Home

I'VE HARDLY SLEPT. I tried, but it wasn't there. The CO comes for me at six in the morning.

"You need to be at R&D by seven, Stelman."

"Okay, Gardner, thanks."

"Hey, Stelman, good luck to you."

"Thanks, Gardner."

I go to breakfast to eat my last piece of coffee cake for the rest of my life. Practically every day for five and a half years I've had coffee cake for breakfast, and I swore to myself I'll never eat it again after I'm released.

I'm at R&D by seven.

"You have clothes here sent by your family, or do you need some?" Miss Barns, the CO, asks.

"No, my family sent me clothes."

"Okay, what's your number, Stelman?"

"For the last time, ever, Miss Barns, it's 91903054."

She smiles and says: "Okay wait in that holding cell while I find them."

I never celebrated Christmas, but I understand now how a five-year-old child must feel when he wakes up in the morning and opens his presents.

I open the box carefully, and for the first time in almost six years, I touch real clothes. I know they're mine, but I'm having trouble processing the fact. Black jeans with a brown belt, black Adidas sneakers, burgundy sweater, underwear, socks, and a black bomber jacket. All brand new and all mine.

I've been dressed in the same institutional prison khakis for so long, I'm overcome with excitement. For a second, I hesitate before putting them on. Part of me wants to keep them brand new. Part of me feels like wearing them isn't right. I dress and use the reflection of a window outside the holding cell to look at myself.

I smile. I was 200 pounds when I was arrested, and now I weigh a whopping hundred and fifty-two. The last time I was close to this weight I was sixteen years old. I used to wear an extra-large shirt. Now the medium sweater is a bit baggy. I love it.

At eight thirty, the local ICE cop shows up. He has me sign a few documents, hands me a bank debit card with the balance of my commissary account funds and says: "I have to cuff you. Give me your hands."

"Cuff me? Why? I'm done my time. I'm not going anywhere. I don't want to stay in the United States. I want to go home to Canada. I'm not running away. Cuffs aren't necessary."

"Sorry, that's the way it is. Hands."

Of course, I think to myself. That's the way it is.

He puts me in the back of his SUV, and we make the one-hour drive to Clinton Correctional Center, a county jail and ICE designated facility. At intake they ask me to remove my clothes and place them in a locker bag.

"Can't I wear them? I'm only here tonight. I'm leaving in the morning."

"No, you have to wear orange. You're staying in the SHU tonight. Here's a locker bag."

I don't want to give up my clothes. I'm terrified I won't get them back, that they'll get lost or stolen.

"I'm not giving you my clothes. I'll wear the overalls, but I want to keep the locker bag with me. Please!"

"You can't. Listen, I give you my word they'll be fine. No one will touch them. We keep them right here in R&D. Come here. I'll show you where they'll be."

I walk with him around a corner, and he points to a hanging rack with a bunch of named and numbered locker bags.

I turn to him. "Are you sure they'll be okay? Will you be here tomorrow morning when I leave?" I'm panicking at the thought of something going wrong.

"I promise you they'll be fine, and yes, I'll be here. Stop worrying, okay?"

"Okay," I say, but I can't stop worrying.

I'm taken to the SHU. It's actually a range of two-man cells with barred doors. It's nothing like the SHU I'm accustomed to, thank God. There's a television suspended from the ceiling outside the cells that everyone can watch.

I'm placed in an empty cell, and the first thing I do is take the awful mattress from the top rack and put it on top of the awful mattress on the bottom rack. I'm hoping I'll be able to sleep away the hours I'll be spending here.

Next door to me, another inmate keeps yelling for the guard. I try to tune it out, but I can't.

"Yo, my man! I'm trying to sleep here. Can you stop making so much noise please? Besides, they don't come when you yell," I say.

"Motherfuckers said I can get a shower. I've been waiting since yesterday. I need a fucking shower!"

"I understand, but the more you yell, the less attention they'll give you. That's what they do. Trust me, I know."

"Fuck! CO! Can I get my shower! CO! I want my shower!"

"Hey, I asked you to stop yelling! Try it, and you'll see."

"Okay fuck."

An hour later my neighbor gets his shower, and I finally fall asleep. At five o'clock they bring my supper tray. I eat everything.

A CO comes to my door at seven and tells me I'm getting a cellmate, the kid next door. I ask him to let me stay alone, but he says there's no choice; place is full.

He escorts the kid in, and I see he is young, early twenties. He's white with a few tattoos on his arms. I look at him with my best hardened convict face and say:

"Kid, listen to me. I don't want any noise in here, and I don't want any trouble. I'm leaving tomorrow morning, and I want a nice quiet night. Understand?"

"Yeah, but can I watch television?"

"I don't care what you do as long as you don't bother me."

"What do you mean you're leaving tomorrow? You're getting out?"

"I'm on my way home to Canada. I just got released from prison. I'm only here for the night."

"Oh. How long were you in prison for?"

"Five and a half years."

"Wow. That's a long time."

"You have no idea."

"I'm doing four months, and it's too long. I'm going out of my mind."

"Okay, I'm going to try and fall back asleep now. I don't want to talk anymore."

"Okay."

In the morning after breakfast a CO unlocks the door and tells me ICE will be here in a half an hour, so I need to get ready. I walk with him to R&D, pick up my clothes that are exactly where I left them and change. Then I sign some paperwork.

They arrive soon afterward. A middle-aged white guy with a female partner of about the same age. They introduce themselves and tell me to follow them to their SUV.

"We're not going to cuff you, Mr. Stelman. We don't think you will cause any problems."

I look at him expecting him to say he's pulling my leg, but he doesn't. It's becoming real. Up until now I knew I was going home, but it was still hard to believe, new clothes notwithstanding. No cuffs…hmm…

"Thank you," I say.

Halfway through the drive, he stops to fill up his tank at a gas station that has a Tim Hortons donut store. Tim Hortons is a Canadian chain, and I didn't know they were in the United States. I really want a coffee.

"Excuse me," I say to the female officer. "I need to use the bathroom, and I'd love to get a coffee. May I?"

"Sure, bathroom is inside the Tim's."

"Okay, thanks," but I don't move because I'm expecting to be escorted.

After a few seconds, she turns around and says: "Are you going?"

"You mean I can go on my own?"

"Yes, you can go on your own. Try and hurry though, we want to get back on the road."

"Okay, I will."

I use the bathroom, and when I come out, the male officer is ordering coffee. I take out my debit card and ask him:

"Can I pay with this or do I need to get cash from the ATM? I want to buy a coffee."

"No, don't worry about it, Mr. Stelman. I'll buy you a coffee. Are you hungry? Why don't you get something to eat, also?"

I look at him in shock. He must see it because he laughs and says:

"Been a long time since someone in law enforcement offered to do something nice for you, huh?"

"Yes, it has. Thank you."

"You seem like a nice man. It's my pleasure. Go ahead and get something."

"Thank you. Can I get a bagel with cream cheese?" I say cautiously.

"Sure. Do you like it toasted?"

"Man, I'll eat it frozen. I love bagels. I haven't had a bagel or cream cheese in close to six years. Toasted is fine, thank you."

"Well, let me get that."

As we're about to pull out of the gas station the woman agent turns to me and says: "Mr. Stelman, we're going to let you call your daughter now. We spoke with Stephanie yesterday and told her we would be bringing you sometime today. We'll be at the Rainbow Bridge crossing in two hours, so why don't you let her know?"

Stephanie told them we live seven hours from the border, and she has to leave well ahead of time to be there. They were nice enough to tell her approximately when I would arrive, so she and Andie drove to Toronto yesterday afternoon and slept there. The border crossing is a ninety-minute drive from Toronto.

"Hi, Steph."

"Dad! Is everything okay?"

"Everything is fine, honey. They let me use the phone to call you. We're two hours from the border. Where are you?"

"We're still in Toronto. They told me they would let you call at some point. We were waiting. We'll leave now and meet you at the border."

"Okay, drive carefully. I can't wait to see you guys!"

"I know, Dad. I can't believe this day has come."

"I love you, Roo. See you soon."

I hand the agent her phone and take my bagel out of the bag. I want to eat it slowly and savor the taste but that doesn't happen. I practically inhale it.

When we arrive at the Rainbow Bridge border crossing, the male agent walks me in to Canadian Customs and Immigration and hands a customs agent my file. I'm asked to take a seat while they complete their business, and five minutes later the agent bids me goodbye and leaves.

A few minutes later, someone in plain clothes comes out of a back office and asks me to follow him.

We go into the office, and he says:

"Mr. Stelman, please take a seat. I'm with the Canadian Security Intelligence Service. I would like to ask you some questions."

"CSIS. What do you want with me?"

"I have some questions."

"Questions? About what? What can you possibly ask me that would be relevant to your work? Aren't you a spy agency like the CIA?"

"Yes. Mr. Stelman you were just released from prison. I would like to ask you about any relationships you may have developed with persons that may be of interest to CSIS."

"I have no relationships with anyone that would be of interest to CSIS. Sir, I'm uncomfortable being here, and I have nothing to say. Am I obligated to answer your questions?"

"No. It's voluntary."

"I see. Well then, I would like to leave. Sir, as I understand it, I have no criminal record in Canada. Is that correct?"

"Yes, Mr. Stelman, that's correct."

"Good. Do I walk myself out?"

"Yes, thank you for your time."

I ask the customs agent if I can use a phone to call my daughters. Stephanie tells me to go outside and look for a parking hut across from the building. They're waiting there.

Once outside, I walk quickly. I see her and Andie running towards me. We're separated by a guard rail, so they jump it and run to me. I wrap my arms around Andie, hug her tight and kiss her cheeks a thousand times. Then I hug Stephanie so hard she says she can't breathe.

The three of us are crying tears of joy and relief.

"I'm home, guys. I'm home. The nightmare is over. It's over."

"It's really over, Dad. It's really over," Andie says, crying.

I just look at her and smile. I place my arms around both their shoulders and say:

"C'mon let's get the hell out of here."

As we're walking, I look up at the open sky and close my eyes for a second. Thank you, God.

Acknowledgments

I would like to extend a heartfelt thanks to the following people. To my editor, book publishing coach, and advisor, Maggie Pagratis, for whom I am eternally grateful. Your hard work, professionalism, dedication, and support helped me see this to the end. Thanks for putting up with me. To my wife Lana, whose strength, love, and devotion never wavered and carried us through and beyond. To my children, the loves of my life, Stephanie, Paige, Andie, and Jace, who kept me determined and steadfast to overcome all the adversity so that we can be a family again. To my amazing parents, Jackie and Sam, who always loved us. Without you, I don't know how the children would have survived. To my brother, Ian. To my dear friends, Tom and Laurence, who helped me so much and never judged. I could always count on you. To Artur, my friend, who I am so grateful to have met, and for all your help in those tough early days. To Panama, my brother in the trenches, who had my back in Allenwood. To Dov and Matt, dear friends that made the time easier. To that one ex-navy CO who cared about my pain when I couldn't stand up and did what few in his shoes would. To Rabbi Spritzer at Reaching Out and to the Aleph Institute for supporting and helping me and so many others who can't help themselves. Finally, to Ometz for making my children's lives easier.

Made in United States
North Haven, CT
24 November 2021